VEGAN
COOKBOOK

VEGAN
COOKBOOK

A comprehensive guide to vegan food and
eating, with advice on ingredients, nutrition, and
over 140 deliciously healthy recipes

**TONY AND YVONNE
BISHOP-WESTON**

LORENZ BOOKS

CONTENTS

Introduction

Veganism is much more than simply a particular diet to be followed. There is a wide and varied philosophy and lifestyle behind it that incorporates many of the issues which are becoming growing concerns in the modern world. For example, animal welfare and environmental issues have long been vital components of veganism and these are reflected in today's headlines, dominated by the quest to reduce our carbon emissions, both on a personal level and within industries such as livestock farming.

People are now increasingly looking for a way of life to counteract many of the global issues and problems that face us. One of the most appropriate of those lifestyles is veganism.

WHAT IS VEGANISM?

In the most basic terms a vegan is someone who avoids consuming or utilizing any product that is, or was once, part of an animal or is sourced from an animal.

Humans are one of the most complex and adaptable species on the planet and can survive in many extremes and on a vast range of diets. Vegans believe that a varied plant-based diet produces the optimal state of physical and mental being, and that the principles of veganism are kinder to people, animals and the environment. The vegan line

is drawn somewhere between algae being from the plant kingdom, which is acceptable on the diet, and plankton from the animal kingdom, which is not acceptable.

The Vegan Society, the first-ever vegan organization, which was founded in the UK in 1944, defines a vegan as a person who, "excludes all forms of exploitation of, and cruelty to, animals for food, clothing or any other purpose". Therefore, vegans seek to lead a lifestyle, where practically possible, that is completely free from animal products for the benefit of all people, animals and the environment.

Fundamentally, it is the risk of the exploitation and harm of a living creature and causing it suffering that is an important part of veganism – not just avoiding the direct responsibility of causing an animal's death, as is the case with vegetarianism.

Vegetarian philosophy permits the use of products where there is at least a theoretical possibility to produce a product (milk, eggs, honey, silk, shellac) without killing the exploited host creature. The problem is that in a commercial, profit-driven environment male dairy calves, male chicks, bees and silkworms nearly always get killed as surplus to the processor's requirements. Vegans find it easier and more consistent to just avoid all animal products rather than get tied up in knots with what is an acceptable level of exploitation and cruelty. For example, The Vegetarian Society approves the use of free-range chicken eggs, that are not fed fish and are not caged, but with no stipulation on how male chicks are killed. Vegans use plant-based alternatives to milk, cheese and eggs, such as soya, and agave or maple syrup instead of honey. Vegans also use cotton, linen, hemp and synthetic fibres instead of silk, leather, wool and other items that are made from animals.

The minute details of how a product is made will have a big impact on whether it is acceptable to vegans. For example, beers and wines are often made with isinglass (made from the bladder of a fish) or gelatine, so vegans choose filtered alternatives or products fined with bentonite (a mineral) or seaweed extracts. Vegan wines and beers are now widely available thanks to an interest in natural produce and a growing trend to avoid unnecessary additives.

Products that have been tested on animals are also avoided by vegans because of the harm they cause. Vegans prefer to use cosmetics and toiletries that are tested on humans or cells in a dish rather than allow suffering to animals.

Left: Gone are the days when vegan food was considered dull – today there is an incredible range of tasty vegan dishes available in local cafés and restaurants.

Donald Watson, who founded the Vegan Society, was a conscientious objector who believed that humans would struggle to be kinder to fellow human beings if they failed to show compassion to helpless animals. He argued that true civilization depended on accepting the responsibilities that come with our human advantages of choice.

Rather than constantly having to make decisions about an acceptable level of animal cruelty or discomfort, Watson insisted that vegans should opt out of exploitation of another sentient being's life and use the many ethical, practical and sustainable alternatives that nature provides us with.

Above: Vegans believe that a varied plant-based diet is the key to physical and mental well-being.

USING THIS BOOK

The biggest hurdle that many people have to overcome when following a vegan diet is to have plenty of exciting, healthy and delicious recipes to cook. The following chapters will help to answer the question that many vegans get asked: 'What do you eat?' Even to those people who are contemplating a vegan lifestyle, the prospect of a wholly plant-based diet can be daunting. The recipe section in this book is brimming with ideas demonstrating the options that are available to vegans.

However, this is more than just a guide to cooking. Veganism is a complex philosophy that impacts on every aspect of life, from the shoes we wear to the shampoo we use and the medications we take. The first chapter, The Vegan Life, examines and answers many of the issues affecting vegans, from the reasons for choosing the lifestyle and the essential nutrients needed, to shopping, medicine and advice for pregnancy

The main section of the book offers 140 recipes that demonstrate that being vegan today is to eat well and healthily with no compromise on taste.

The Vegan Society definition of Veganism

"The word 'veganism' denotes a philosophy and way of living which seeks to exclude – as far as is possible and practical – all forms of exploitation of, and cruelty to, animals for food, clothing or any other purpose; and by extension, promotes the development and use of animal-free alternatives for the benefit of humans, animals and the environment. In dietary terms it denotes the practice of dispensing with all products derived wholly or partly from animals."

THE VEGAN LIFE

Although becoming a vegan can be an intimidating prospect, it can also be an exciting and fulfilling adventure. This chapter looks at the many issues around veganism, such as the history of the movement and reasons for choosing the lifestyle. There is also a wealth of essential information on nutrition, health and pregnancy, as well as a guide to ethical shopping.

History of veganism

Veganism is a logical progression from vegetarianism – the exclusion of meat and some other animal-derived products from the diet – which has a long and varied history around the world. As a concept and practice, vegetarianism has been recorded as early as the 6th century BCE in communities in ancient India and the classical Greek world. The reasons for abstaining from meat were mainly religious and concerned the idea of non-violence toward animals, which was termed *ahimsa* in Sanskrit, the ancient Indian language. Pythagoras (c.582–507BCE), the Greek philosopher and mathematician, abstained from eggs and the flesh of animals, as part of an ascetic and philosophical way of life. In fact, until the formation of the Vegetarian Society in the UK in 1847, which popularized the term 'vegetarian', those who did not consume meat or fish were known as 'Pythagoreans'. The formation of the Vegetarian Society reflected the growing popularity of an animal-free diet.

THE BIRTH OF VEGANISM

Over time, vegetarians became concerned about the practices of the dairy industry and its relationship to the meat industry. At a meeting in London in November 1944, a

Below: Local markets offer a huge choice of fresh vegetables and fruits suitable for those following a vegan diet. Produce is likely to be from nearby farmers, thereby reducing carbon emissions.

handful of members of the Vegetarian Society, led by Donald Watson (1910–2005), a teacher who largely practised a non-dairy vegetarianism, decided to form a new society that would address their beliefs. They needed a new term to call themselves, and Watson coined the word 'vegan' to describe the new philosophy, using the first and last letters from 'vegetarian'. He described the new concept as 'the beginning and end of vegetarian'.

Another leading pioneer in the very early days of the movement was Arthur Ling, who founded the company Plamil (whose name came about by contracting 'plant milk'). His dedication to the vegan cause helped bring soya milk to the UK and he went on to perfect other vegan products, like chocolate and mayonnaise.

VEGANISM IN THE USA

American veganism owes thanks to a man called H. Jay Dinshah, a lifelong vegetarian born in Malaga, New Jersey. His father was a Parsi from Bombay in India and his mother was an American of German descent. He founded the American Vegan Society in 1960. There had been a regional vegan society in California for just over 10 years, but it was Jay Dinshah, with his wife Freya, who carried the vegan flag nationwide in a series of lectures across the USA and into Canada. They wrote books, published a regular magazine called *Ahimsa* and hosted conventions around the USA which

The Vegan News, 1944

Below is the introduction to the first Vegan Society newsletter:

"The use of dairy produce has revealed very strong evidence to show that the production of these foods involves much cruel exploitation and slaughter of highly sentient life. The excuse that it is not necessary to kill in order to obtain dairy produce is untenable for those with a knowledge of livestock farming methods.

For years many of us accepted that the flesh-food industry and the dairy produce industry were related, and that in some ways they subsidised one another. We accepted, therefore, that the case on ethical grounds for the disuse of these foods was exceptionally strong, and we hoped that sooner or later a crisis in our conscience would set us free.

That freedom has now come to us. The cruelty associated with the production of dairy produce has made it clear that lacto-vegetarianism is but a halfway house between flesh-eating and a truly humane, civilised diet, and we think, therefore, that during our life on earth we should try to evolve sufficiently to make the 'full journey'."

Right: Donald Watson, who coined the word 'vegan' and founded the Vegan Society in November 1944.

spawned and inspired other groups, in particular a group of doctors calling themselves PCRM (Physicians Committee for Responsible Medicine), who advocate a vegan diet.

Members of the Seventh-day Adventist Church were also very influential in the spread of veganism in the USA. They achieved this partly by practical example in proving how healthy the vegan diet can be, but mainly by inspiring and supporting a network of health-food stores and restaurants. The Farm (a community in Tennessee) has also supported veganism, publishing books on vegan cooking and nutrition. These enterprises have allowed people to sample veganism and have made vegan foods more accessible.

GROWING POPULARITY

Although veganism really started to come to the attention of the general public during the 1960s, it has since moved into the mainstream. Vegan societies and organizations spread across the world, and a vegan diet was promoted by many other groups and societies during the latter half of the 20th century. Now into the 21st century, the movement towards meat-free living continues apace.

In recent years multinational big brand companies have released an avalanche of new vegan products and menus. Vegan sandwiches, cheeses, ice cream, beer and pizzas, as well as a choice of plant milk at coffee shops, has become routine. The number of vegan festivals has more than doubled in the UK and the USA, with increasing numbers of new festivals starting up in Europe, Australia and Israel.

Mainstream businesses have now recognized the importance of the rapidly expanding vegan demographic and are offering a wide range of vegan food and drink, clothing and cosmetics in their outlets.

As more and more people have become vegan, the diet and lifestyle have got easier to follow. An increasing number of choices are now available to vegans, from the food they buy and the restaurants they can eat in, to the clothes they wear and the household products they use.

Above: The quality and diversity of vegan food have increased in recent years and it is now served in mainstream delicatessens, street food stores and cafes.

Why go vegan?

The decision to become a vegan is a very personal one, and there is a huge variety of reasons why people choose to adopt a vegan lifestyle. The health benefits of a vegan diet are a big attraction to many people. Others are impressed by the vegan philosophy of an ethical and moral life. Some also wish to follow a more environmentally friendly and ecological way of life. Spiritual factors also come into play as some religions dictate veganism as part of their doctrine.

A NUTRITIOUS VEGAN DIET

Tom Sanders, Emeritus Professor of Nutrition and Dietetics at Kings College, London, has spent his career researching the healthiest diets for humans. He says that providing vegans find reliable sources of nutrients such as vitamin B12 and essential fats, and avoid over-indulgence in new high-fat, high-sugar, high-salt, highly processed vegan convenience foods, there is no reason why vegans can't be the healthiest group on the planet. A well-planned vegan diet is perfectly compatible with his research findings. Similarly, studies such as the EPIC-Oxford Study and other research on Seventh-day Adventists in the United States have shown that a varied and properly balanced plant-based diet can provide an optimum mix of nutrients for a healthy body.

Above: Vegans can still enjoy luxurious treats such as these chocolate brownies.

A well-balanced vegan diet is naturally lower in saturated fats, higher in essential fats, higher in fibre and antioxidants and potentially lower in toxins, due to eating lower down the food chain. Eating meat and dairy has been linked to various cancers, digestive disorders, deteriorating heart health, Alzheimer's, osteoporosis, stroke, arthritis, diabetes and high blood pressure.

Proven health benefits One of the biggest studies on the vegan population, the EPIC-Oxford Study, showed that vegans were at least as healthy as those meat-eaters that had a balanced diet with reduced meat consumption and a higher than average amount of fruit and vegetables. Other positive findings of the study include the fact that vegetarians, and especially vegans, have a lower prevalence of hypertension and lower blood pressure than meat-eaters.

Just like any other individual, maintaining a well-balanced intake of plant-based foods is vital for good health in vegans. Apart from the extra fibre, and a reduced risk of cancer from processed meat (World Health Organization), and the reduced toxin risks by eating lower down the food chain, a vegan processed junk-food diet is unlikely to be substantially better for health than a meat-based one.

Vegans are constantly reminded that if they just cut out meat, dairy, eggs and fish from their diet without introducing new nutrient-dense plant-based foods that they could risk deficiencies of key vitamins and nutrients. But many non-vegans are found to be short on key nutrients (often due to a lack of fruit and vegetables). So if you have a hectic lifestyle and struggle to plan a varied and nutritious diet, you could always carefully choose a reputable brand of plant-based multivitamin/mineral supplements.

EPIC

The European Prospective Investigation into Cancer and Nutrition (EPIC) was initiated in 1992 and is the largest detailed study of diet and health ever undertaken. It involves over 500,000 people in ten European countries and is co-ordinated by the World Health Organization.

The EPIC-Oxford Study group recruited people between 1993 and 1999, and targeted vegetarians and vegans. The results are of great scientific value because the diets of vegetarians, and especially vegans, differ substantially from those of meat-eaters, and many positive findings were concluded regarding eating a plant-based diet.

In addition, many vegan foods such as soya milks and spreads are fortified with calcium, vitamin D, and vitamin B2 in the same way that white bread flour is fortified to partly compensate for the nutrients lost in processing it from wholemeal to white.

Reduced risk of risks to health Eating vegan can lessen the risk of food poisoning. Although reheated rice can be very dangerous, most of the worst cases of food poisoning are from animal foods, such as red meat, pork, chicken, fish, eggs, cheese and milk-based foods.

Eggs, dairy and fish are also common allergens with typical symptoms displaying as asthma, eczema and intestinal

Left: If nutritionally well-balanced, a vegan diet could lead to increased health and vitality in everybody.

upsets, amongst others. In addition, it is estimated that around two-thirds of the world's population are lactose-intolerant. This is not an allergic reaction but occurs because the body lacks (or does not produce enough of) an enzyme called lactase, which is normally active in the intestinal wall. The function of lactase is to break down lactose (milk sugar) into simpler sugars that can be absorbed by the body. If this doesn't happen, the undigested lactose passes into the large intestine (colon) where it causes irritation. This condition is most common in non-dairy consuming societies and can lead to severe bloating and abdominal pain.

Nutritional balance Like other nutrition and dietetic bodies around the world, the British Dietetic Association has affirmed that a well-planned vegan diet can "support healthy living in people of all ages." It reiterated that a balanced vegan diet can be enjoyed by children and adults, including during pregnancy and breastfeeding, if the nutritional intake is well-planned.

Nutritional therapist Yvonne Bishop-Weston confirms that "The ideal is to nourish your body from food, but even if you need therapeutic-grade vitamins, plant-based versions of these are now produced to get your body back in balance. Vegan vitamin D3, omega 3 essential fats EPA and DHA (from algae), amino acids, as well as highly absorbable multivitamins and minerals with iodine, selenium, zinc, iron and powerful plant-based probiotics are all available."

Below left: Green vegetables, such as spinach, cabbage and broccoli, are a great source of iron and calcium.
Below: Lentils are a rich source of dietary fibre and protein.

Above: A recently cut and burned rainforest now turned into a cattle ranch in the Brazilian Amazon, where cattle ranching is the biggest cause of deforestation.

ETHICAL VEGANISM

There are vegans who have chosen their lifestyle for ethical, moral or religious reasons. For many, one of the essential aspects of adopting a vegan diet is the basic belief that harming a living creature is wrong.

Religious ethics The spiritual basis for a vegan diet can be traced back many thousands of years and is seen in the doctrines of various ancient religions. In India, both Hindus, who hold vegetarianism as an ideal, and Jains, for whom vegetarianism is mandatory, avoid eggs and regard cows as sacred, giving them more legal rights than many people. Jain monks follow a strict vegan lifestyle and even brush the path in front of them and wear masks to avoid harming insects and bugs. Buddhism, which prohibits killing, has varying attitudes toward vegetarianism and veganism throughout the world.

The Essenes, a reclusive Jewish sect in the 2nd century BCE, who claimed to be the source of early Christianity, were also virtually vegan on religious grounds. The first chapter in the Bible speaks of plants, seeds and fruit as food for all life and calls for respect and responsibility for all living things. Many Seventh-day Adventists and Quakers are vegan, and veganism is increasingly popular in Humanist and Scientology circles too.

The Rastafari tradition of *ital*, meaning the foods that are approved, is based on dietary laws of the Old Testament. Interpretation of the laws varies but the general principle is that food should be natural, or pure, and from the earth. Therefore chemically modified foods or those with artificial additives are avoided, and foods produced with chemicals such as pesticides are often not considered *ital*. In common with religions such as Judaism, Islam and Ethiopian Christianity, *ital* prohibits the eating of pork, and most Rastas do not eat red meat or shellfish. There are many, however, who restrict what is *ital* to the extent that they are on a vegan diet, and many more are vegetarians.

Philosophical ethics The non-religious debate regarding the moral right or wrong of consuming meat has been around for thousands of years as well. Greek philosophers, such as Pythagoras, the father of mathematics, and Hippocrates, the father of modern medicine, preached the virtues of eating a diet which does not cause suffering to an animal.

Many vegans, along with animal rights supporters and a lot of vegetarians, hold the basic philosophical position that animals possess certain rights – or that humans have particular responsibilities – which means that we have a duty to avoid inflicting any unnecessary pain on them or cause them any suffering.

Many vegans and other vegetarians maintain that harming a living animal is as wrong as harming a human. This is because animals and humans share certain qualities, such as the instinct to survive and the capacity to feel happiness and pleasure as well as fear and pain. They believe that no animal should suffer harm or death unnecessarily and since we can follow a plant-based diet without detriment, killing and consuming an animal is not justifiable.

The argument against killing for food is extended by vegans to include the use of animals for any human purpose. The rights of animals, it is said, are still infringed whether they are in a dairy farm or on a sheep farm producing wool.

Active committed vegans often go beyond just food and clothing, challenging both the pharmaceutical and cosmetics industries. They argue that companies frivolously and repeatedly choose animal testing without any true benefit to mankind. They believe it is often to human detriment, and certainly to the detriment of many animals.

ENVIRONMENTAL VEGANISM

Many people choose to adopt a vegan lifestyle because they believe that it is better for the environment. They hold the view that a vegan diet uses far fewer resources and causes much less damage to the planet than an animal-based diet.

Although arguments about the unsustainability of meat and dairy production were around before Donald Watson's

Above: Shrimps are intensively farmed in the Phang Nga bay area, Thailand. This system relies heavily on industrial fishmeal, and the discharges from these farms pollute adjacent rivers.

first editorial in *The Vegan News* in 1944, it is only relatively recently that it has begun to filter into governmental thinking.

In 2006, the United Nations published a 400-page report called *Livestock's Long Shadow*, in an attempt to "assess the full impact of the livestock sector on environmental problems". It was provoked by growing concerns about global warming and carbon emissions along with other environmental problems. The report confirmed that livestock production is responsible for land degradation, climate change, air pollution, water shortage, water pollution and loss of biodiversity. It was deduced from the report that by raising animals for food, livestock farmers produce more climate change gases than all the motor vehicles in the world. Steak from a grain-fed cow requires 35 calories of fossil fuel for every 1 calorie of consumable meat.

In response to the *Livestock's Long Shadow* report, the International Water Institute in Stockholm concluded that unless we change our reliance on animal-derived foods, we will run out of water. They claim that 1kg/2¼lb of wheat takes 120 litres/32 gallons of water to produce, while an equal amount of beef requires 3,700 litres/978 gallons.

Vegans maintain that feeding grain to animals to produce protein for humans is both inefficient and a waste of precious resources. Up to ten times as many people could be fed on a plant-based diet compared to a diet of beef.

Seventy per cent of the Amazon deforestation is attributable to livestock production. It is often argued that soya, a popular component of many vegan diets, is also partly responsible for rainforest devastation. However, it is important to remember that 90 per cent of the world's soya is used for feeding animals, not humans.

The planet's marine ecosystems are being adversely affected due to overfishing, not just for food but also for oil, which is used in both cosmetic and pharmaceutical products. Biologists worry that it is the largest fish that are most scarce, and it is these larger game fish that guide the smaller fish to spawning grounds. With the important discovery of complex omega 3 oils in sustainably grown algae, the need to source these oils from fish stocks could be halted over time.

In today's society, when people are concerned about carbon emissions and their own 'carbon footprint', a University of Chicago study in 2006 is enlightening. It found that switching from an average American diet to a plant-based vegan one would reduce each person's carbon dioxide emissions by 1,485kg/3,275lb a year – a significant difference bearing in mind that the average car generates about 3,000kg/6,600lb per year.

Right: Most commercial pigs reared for meat are kept indoors in intensive units or 'factory farms'. The pigs are closely confined throughout their lives and are unable to carry out basic pig-specific behaviours such as exercizing, socializing, exploration and foraging, which lead to serious welfare issues.

Essentials of nutrition

A balanced plant-based diet is naturally abundant in the nutrients we require. Like all diets it does, however, require knowledge to ensure you provide yourself with all you need. The best place to start is with the key nutrient groups, known as the macro-nutrients: the carbohydrates, proteins and fats we should ensure we have plentiful supplies of. In turn, opting for the best macro-nutrients will help to give us the micro-nutrients essential to good health. The micro-nutrients includes vitamins, minerals and antioxidants and are just as vital for our well-being.

CARBOHYDRATES

For years carbohydrates have been much-criticised as being the foods that make us gain weight and feel bloated, but it is not the carbs at fault, it is the way we process them and over-use them that brings the health risks.

When chosen as close to their natural state as possible, carbohydrates are the body's key fuel supplier and provide vitamins, minerals, amino acids and fibre. They come in a number of different forms; some are great for our health, others are to be minimized. Carbohydrates get defined into three groups; sugar, starch and fibre.

Above: A well-balanced vegan lunch or supper should allow for approximately one quarter complex carbohydrates, one quarter protein (including a small amount of omega-rich nuts and seeds) and one half vegetables and fruit. The inner circle represents calcium-rich foods from all the food groups that will help keep bones healthy.

Sugars can occur naturally in food such as fruits and vegetables and even as the grass we know as sugar cane. The more we process these foods, the more fast-release and available they are, and the less healthy the sugars in them become. We are better off eating fruit than drinking fruit juice, and it is better to sweeten foods with fruit rather than refined sugar. The blood sugar peaks and troughs which are caused by eating too much available sugar has been associated with a whole host of health problems – from excess weight gain and type 2 diabetes to arthritis.

Starch is made up of the individual sugar units bonded together, and the more complex and unrefined starchy foods such as bread, rice and pasta we choose, the better. These carbohydrates release their sugars more slowly than the refined and more processed versions, giving us steady energy we can burn rather than the destructive highs and lows.

Fibre is found in the cell walls of plant foods. It doesn't bring us nutrition but is vital for all-round digestive health. Choose wholegrain carbohydrates, have a variety of

Left: There are many wholegrains now on the market including rolled oats, barley flakes, rye flakes and quinoa flakes, all of which will release a steady flow of energy to the body.

Above: Olive oil contains 'good' cholesterol that can help protect the heart against disease.

Above: Peanut butter is a great source of protein for vegans and a firm favourite amongst most children.

carbohydrates rather than over-rely on bread, and have the right portion for your activity level. For most adults that is about half your breakfast plate made up of a slow-released starchy carbohydrate and a quarter fruit or vegetable, leaving a quarter for protein and a little essential fat. At lunch and dinner have a quarter plate of starchy carbohydrate and a half plate of vegetables, leaving a quarter plate for protein. If you need to lose weight, reduce the starchy carbohydrate portion for your evening meal. For intense sporty types and young children these ratios will be a little different.

Choosing wholegrain starchy carbohydrates and having your fruits and vegetables with the skin on helps to keep your fibre levels topped up. Fibre comes in soluble and insoluble forms. The soluble forms, such as in oats, helps to reduce cholesterol levels and cleanse the bowel. The insoluble, such as in wheat, helps bulk, facilitating a smooth exit for your food once all the nutrients have been removed. Fibre not only supports our daily cleanse, but also supports the gut bacteria which play a vital role in health and immunity and may help protect against cancer of the colon.

PROTEIN AND AMINO ACIDS

Although cases of protein deficiency are rare, it is important not to overlook this macro-nutrient. The amino acid building blocks are responsible for so much more than growth and repair. They play a role in the immune system, support good mood and aid the slow release of energy in our foods, assisting us to have energy to use, rather than store, and allowing us to feel fuller for longer, thus helping prevent cravings for quick-fix sugary snacks.

Protein is made up of amino acids of which there are 20 in total, nine of which are essential for adults. Shortages of these key amino acids have been implicated in a number of health issues, such as infertility, weight problems and depression. A food containing all nine amino acids is known as a 'complete' protein. Vegan sources of complete proteins include soya (edamame beans, tofu, tempeh), hemp seeds, quinoa, amaranth and buckwheat. For those plant-based foods that do not have all the amino acids a complete protein can be constructed by combining a grain and a pulse, and even better by adding nuts or seeds. Together the full spectrum of amino acids will be provided. Easy meals such as beans on toast, rice and beans, and hummus would all provide the full complement of essential amino acids.

We need about a quarter of our lunch and dinner plates to have a good protein source, and add some to breakfast too. If we compare a plant-based plate to one with meat it will be lower in protein, but there is increasing evidence that people are eating more meat and dairy than is healthy, and serious health risks are associated with processed meat products.

FATS

The fats we choose to put into our bodies can help optimize our health or increase our health risk. Fats can be split into saturated, monounsaturated and polyunsaturated fats. Saturated fats are solid at room temperature and are considered to be harmful to the cardiovascular system and trigger inflammatory responses. There are plant-based saturated fats, such as coconut, but coconut oil has medium- and short-chain fatty acids that are digested and absorbed differently to the harmful long-chain fatty acids of animal fat, and are considered healthier.

Unsaturated fats, including both polyunsaturated and monounsaturated, can help to reduce harmful LDL (low density lipoprotein) cholesterol – the type that furs up arteries – and, importantly, increase the beneficial HDL (high density lipoprotein) cholesterol, which is thought to reduce the cholesterol levels in the body.

Monounsaturated fats, such as olive oil, which is rich in omega 9, sesame oil and rapeseed (canola) oil, are less

Above and above right: Choosing a range of types and colours of vegetables in your daily diet will help to maximize your intake of vitamins.

vulnerable to oxidation than polyunsaturated fats, are more stable and thus better for cooking purposes. Polyunsaturated fats provide the essential fatty acids, omega 3 and omega 6, which are called essential because they cannot be made in the body, and therefore must be obtained as part of the diet. Omega 3, which is found in chia seeds, walnuts, soya beans, hemp and rapeseed oil, has been found to reduce the risk of heart disease, while omega 6 (linoleic acid), which is found in nuts, seeds and plant oils, is thought to reduce blood cholesterol.

The ideal ratio for these essential fats is often argued about but generally regarded to be around 4:1 (omega 6:omega 3). A healthy person can then process the basic omega 3 fats into the brain-building and brain-fuelling fatty acids DHA (docosahexanoic acid) and EPA (eicosapentaenoic acid). Lack of nutrients, digestive imbalances, liver problems and stress can all thwart the body's ability to do this. In this instance you may consider pure EPA and DHA derived from special strains of algae, otherwise a daily tablespoon of hemp oil is a good balanced way to boost your levels of omega 6, omega 3 and omega 9.

VITAMINS

These nutrients are vital for good health and the functioning of our bodies and, with a few exceptions, must be supplied by diet. The levels required by our bodies vary depending on health, lifestyle and age. Vitamins and minerals do not provide energy but assist in the release of energy provided by carbohydrates, fat and protein.

Vitamins are either water-soluble or fat-soluble. Fat-soluble vitamins A, D, E and K are stored in the liver for some time. Water-soluble vitamins, B complex and C, cannot be stored by our bodies and therefore must be replaced on a daily basis. Drinking alcohol and smoking will increase your

body's need for vitamin B- and C-rich foods as your body tries to cope with these toxins. In addition to protecting the nervous system, vitamin B12 is now realized to be also vitally important for a healthy heart by moderating homocysteine, which is a powerful risk factor for cardiovascular disease.

Vitamin D is now claimed to be even more important than vitamin C in boosting your immune system and fighting disease. It is thought to protect against skin cancer, which is slightly ironic since the body makes it from exposure to sunshine. Vitamin D can also be found in fortified cereals, fortified soya milk and margarine.

MINERALS

There are 16 essential minerals. Some, such as calcium and magnesium, are required in relatively large amounts, while trace elements such as selenium and molybdenum are needed in tiny quantities. Minerals have various functions but predominantly regulate and balance the body and maintain a healthy immune system.

The World Health Organization claims iron deficiency is the most common and widespread nutritional disorder in the world. It is the only nutrient deficiency which is also significantly prevalent in industrialized countries. Over 2 billion people (over 30% of the world's population) are anaemic, many due to iron deficiency. Make sure you have enough dark green leafy vegetables, lentils and beans in your diet, especially if you have to take anti-inflammatory painkillers. More detailed information on vitamins and minerals are found on pages 20–23.

WATER

The importance of water is often taken for granted, yet it is vital to all life. Although it is possible for a human to survive for weeks without food, we can live for only a few days without taking in water.

Water plays a vital role in the body. It transports nutrients, regulates the body temperature, transports waste via the kidneys, and also acts as a lubricating fluid. Most people do not drink enough water: it is thought that an adult requires up to 1.2 litres/2 pints per day, including water from foods, and this should be increased in hot weather or after exercise. In the USA the guidance is 1.9 litres/3.5 pints. A shortage of water can provoke headaches, tiredness and loss of concentration. Alcohol, tea and coffee can all act as diuretics and speed up the loss of water and cause dehydration.

HOW TO PRESERVE NUTRIENTS

The nutrients in food, particularly fruits and vegetables, are diminished by time, preparation methods and cooking. If a piece of cut fruit or a sliced potato is left exposed to air or soaked in water, its vitamin and mineral levels will plummet. Old, wilted or damaged produce also has reduced levels of vitamins and minerals. The following tips will ensure you get the most from your fruit and vegetables:

• Buy fruits and vegetables that are as fresh as possible in small quantities and do not keep them for too long.
• Avoid fruits and vegetables that have been stored under fluorescent light, as this can set off a chemical reaction that depletes nutrients.
• Buy loose fresh produce where possible, as it is much easier to check for quality than pre-packed foods.
• Depending on the type of fruit or vegetable, store in a cool larder or in the bottom of the refrigerator.
• Where possible include raw vegetables each day as many are higher in nutrients when raw.
• Avoid peeling fruits and vegetables, if possible, and do not prepare them too far in advance of cooking, as nutrients, for example vitamin C, will be depleted.

• Do not store fruits and vegetables in plastic bags.
• Avoid boiling vegetables. This method of cooking destroys water-soluble vitamins, such as thiamine and vitamins B and C. If you must boil vegetables, use as little water as possible and do not overcook them.

Above: Drink plenty of water to maximize health.
Below left: Nuts provide the essential fatty acids omega 3 and omega 6 in a vegan diet.
Below: Fruit are at their most nutritious when eaten raw.

Minerals and vitamins

We all need to obtain the vital macro- and micro-nutrients from our diets. We also need to minimize the health-hindering foods on offer. The balance between these two is what helps define our wellness. The vegan diet avoids some dietary risks but there are also a few nutrients which may be in less abundant supply and need to be focused on.

CALCIUM

The mineral calcium is essential for building and strengthening bones and teeth. An adequate intake from infancy and throughout life can help to prevent fractures and the brittle bone disease, osteoporosis, which mainly affects post-menopausal women.

Calcium is also needed in the body for normal blood clotting, muscle contraction (including regulating heartbeat) and nerve impulse transmission, as well as for certain digestive processes. Vitamin D, which is produced by the action of sunlight on the skin, is also needed for the absorption of calcium from food into the body.

Vegan sources of calcium are plentiful and can add up to fulfilling everyday needs; post-menopausal women may however also benefit from supplementation. Include plenty of dark green leafy vegetables, nuts and seeds, especially sesame seeds and tahini, and tofu which has been made with calcium. Fortified milks are also great calcium providers.

Vegan sources Dark green leafy vegetables (kale, spring greens, Chinese leaves, spinach, broccoli), beans, peas, lentils, nuts (especially almonds and brazil nuts), sesame and sunflower seeds, dried figs and fortified soya products.

Above: Substitute cow's milk with fortified soya milk or with one of the many nut, seed and plant milks now available.

IRON

This mineral is needed to help the body convert food into energy and to make haemoglobin, which is the pigment in red blood cells that carries oxygen around the body in the blood. It is also essential for many other functions, including keeping your immune system in good order. Iron requirements vary depending on your age and sex, and menstruating women in particular should be sure they are getting enough.

There are two types of iron in food: haem iron that comes from meat and non-haem iron from plants and grains. Haem iron is better absorbed by the body, but absorption of non-haem iron can be boosted by eating a food or drink rich in vitamin C at the same time. Vitamin C-rich foods are plentiful in a well-balanced vegan diet. Iron deficiency is the most common cause of anaemia in women of child-bearing age around the world.

Vegan sources Fortified breakfast cereals, oatmeal, beans, peas, lentils, dried fruits, nuts and dark green leafy vegetables, such as Savoy cabbage, spinach, chard and kale.

VITAMIN B12

Low levels of vitamin B12 can lead to anaemia and damage to the nervous system. Symptoms of anaemia include excessive tiredness, breathlessness and poor resistance to infection. A regular supplement is advised on a vegan diet.

Left: Fortified soya yogurt is a low-fat source of calcium.

Above: Dried fruits are a nutritious source of iron and calcium.
Above right: Edamame beans are rich in folic acid and are a complete protein source.

Vegan sources Foods fortified with vitamin B12, such as soya milk, yeast extract and breakfast cereals.

ZINC
This trace mineral is involved in the metabolism of carbohydrates, proteins and fats, as well as the basic processes of cell reproduction, tissue growth and damage healing. A deficiency in zinc is characterized by slow wound healing, impaired growth and a loss of taste.
Vegan sources Most nuts, tofu, wholegrains, pumpkin seeds, sesame seeds and tahini, beans and lentils.

IODINE
A study funded by the Clinical Endocrinology Trust led researchers from the Royal Free Hampstead NHS Trust in London and other universities from the UK, Ireland and Denmark to claim their findings suggest that the UK is iodine-deficient, with 51% of teenage girls having iodine deficiency. Their findings are of major public health importance, since iodine deficiency can lead to an underactive thyroid, which has been found to have an effect on the development of the foetal nervous system. An underactive thyroid can also cause weight gain, depression, constipation, and tiredness. On the other hand, too much iodine in the diet can result in a hyperactive thyroid, which could accelerate the metabolism, causing (unhealthy) weight loss, a rapid heartbeat, sweating and irritability.

Vegan sources Seaweed can be an excellent source of iodine but the levels of iodine vary dramatically from type to type (5g is the recommended daily amount). Kelp in particular should be eaten in moderation, since this contains the highest levels of iodine. As with vitamin B12, The Vegan Society recommend a trusted regular supplement to guarantee a reliable and safe supply of iodine.

FOLATE (FOLIC ACID)
This B vitamin is essential for the production of red blood cells and is particularly important for women who are trying to conceive, to help protect against neural tube defects. It is not considered to be a nutrient-deficiency risk in a vegan diet but is recommended to be taken as a supplement by all women planning a pregnancy.
Vegan sources Green leafy vegetables, beetroot (beets), beans, peas, lentils, wholegrains, citrus fruits, bananas and nuts. It is used to fortify some breakfast cereals and yeast extract.

VITAMIN D
Between September and April the sun isn't strong enough for the body to make vitamin D in much of the Northern hemisphere; it is therefore recommended that everyone (including pregnant and breastfeeding women) should consider taking a daily supplement containing 10mcg of vitamin D during the autumn and winter. Vegan vitamin D3 (which is stronger than vegan vitamin D2) is now available as a handy oral spray. Some foods, such as cereal and margarine, are fortified with vitamin D2 and vitamin D, and UV-exposed mushrooms are becoming popular too.

Table of minerals and vitamins

Regular intake of a wide range of minerals and vitamins is essential for general good health. By eating enough of the correct foods, including seven portions of vegetables and three portions of fruit every day, most vegans will find that they are getting plenty of these essential vitamins and minerals to maintain their wellbeing. Try to eat a variety of different types and colours of produce, in particular brightly coloured and dark green fruit and vegetables, to ensure that you are obtaining as wide a range of nutrients and beneficial compounds as possible. This handy chart describes which foods are the richest sources of each nutrient, the role the mineral or vitamin plays in maintaining good health, and the signs that may suggest that you have a deficiency of one of these in your diet.

Mineral	Best Sources	Role in Health	Deficiency
Calcium	Green leafy vegetables, orange juice, sesame seeds and tahini, fortified soya milk, almonds, dried figs and brazil nuts.	Essential for building and maintaining strong bones and teeth, muscle function and the nervous system.	Deficiency is characterized by soft and brittle bones, osteoporosis, fractures and muscle weakness.
Chloride	Nuts, wholegrains, beans, peas, lentils, tofu and black tea.	Regulates and maintains the balance of fluids in the body.	Deficiency is rare.
Iodine	Seaweed, cranberries and iodized salt.	In the correct dose it promotes a healthy thyroid function and foetal cognitive development.	Deficiency can lead to sluggish metabolism, and dry skin and hair.
Iron	Fortified cereals, green leafy vegetables, dried fruit, nuts, seeds, beans, peas and tofu.	Essential for healthy blood and muscles.	Deficiency is characterized by anaemia, fatigue and low resistance to infection.
Magnesium	Nuts, seeds, wholegrains, beans, peas, lentils, tofu, dried figs and apricots, and green vegetables.	Essential for healthy muscles, bones and teeth, normal growth, and nerves.	Deficiency is characterized by lethargy, weak bones and muscles, depression and irritability.
Manganese	Nuts, wholegrains, beans, lentils, brown rice, tofu and black tea.	Essential component of enzymes involved in energy production.	Deficiency is not characterized by any specific symptoms.
Phosphorus	Found in many foods, especially wholegrains, lentils, beans, peas, peanuts and nuts.	Essential for healthy bones and teeth, energy production and the absorption of many nutrients.	Deficiency is rare.
Potassium	Bananas, beans, peas, lentils, Brazil nuts, seeds, wholegrains, potatoes and root vegetables.	Essential for water balance, regulating blood pressure, and nerve transmission.	Deficiency is characterized by weakness, thirst, fatigue, mental confusion and raised blood pressure.
Selenium	Avocados, lentils, Brazil nuts, wholegrains, yeast extract, chickpeas and seaweed.	Essential for protecting against free radical damage and may protect against cancer.	Deficiency is characterized by reduced antioxidant protection.
Sodium	Found in most foods, but comes mainly from processed foods.	Essential for nerve and muscle function and body fluid regulation.	Deficiency is unlikely but can lead to dehydration and cramps.
Zinc	Most nuts, wholegrains, tofu, pumpkin seeds, sesame seeds and tahini, beans and lentils.	Essential for a healthy immune system, normal growth, wound healing and reproduction.	Deficiency is characterized by impaired growth, slow wound healing and loss of taste.

Vitamin	Best Sources	Role in Health	Deficiency
A (as beta-carotene)	Carrots, dried fruit, red and orange bell peppers, broccoli, green leafy vegetables, tomatoes, mangoes, sweet potatoes and squash.	Essential for vision, bone growth, and skin and tissue repair. Beta-carotene acts as an antioxidant and protects the immune system.	Deficiency is characterized by poor night vision, dry skin and lower resistance to infection, especially respiratory disorders.
B1 (thiamin)	Wholegrain and fortified bread and cereals, fortified yeast extract, potatoes, nuts, beans, peas, lentils and sunflower seeds.	Essential for energy production, the nervous system, muscles and heart. Promotes growth and boosts mental ability.	Deficiency is characterized by depression, irritability, nervous disorders, loss of memory. Common among alcoholics.
B2 (riboflavin)	Fortified bread and cereals, yeast extract, dried prunes, mushrooms, almonds and avocados.	Essential for energy production and for the functioning of vitamin B6 and niacin, as well as tissue repair.	Deficiency is characterized by lack of energy, dry cracked lips, numbness and itchy eyes.
Niacin (nicotinic acid, also called B3)	Beans, peas, lentils, potatoes, fortified breakfast cereals, yeast extract, wheatgerm, nuts, peas, mushrooms, green leafy vegetables, figs and prunes.	Essential for a healthy digestive system, skin and circulation. It is also needed for the release of energy.	Deficiency is unusual, but characterized by lack of energy, depression and scaly skin.
B6 (piridoxine)	Wholegrain cereals, brown rice, hazelnuts, bananas and cruciferous vegetables, such as broccoli, cabbage and cauliflower.	Essential for assimilating protein and fat, for making red blood cells and maintaining a healthy immune system.	Deficiency is characterized by anaemia, dermatitis and depression.
B12 (cyano-cobalamin)	Fortified breakfast cereals, yeast extract, fortified soya milk and fortified margarine.	Essential for growth, formation of red blood cells and maintaining a healthy nervous system.	Deficiency is characterized by fatigue, increased risk of infection, and anaemia.
Folate (folic acid)	Dark green leafy vegetables, wholegrain and fortified breakfast cereals, bread, nuts, beans, peas, lentils, bananas and yeast extract.	Essential for cell division; especially needed before conception and during pregnancy.	Deficiency is characterized by anaemia and appetite loss. Linked with neural tube defects in babies.
C (ascorbic acid)	Citrus fruit, melons, strawberries, tomatoes, broccoli, potatoes, bell peppers and green vegetables.	Essential for the absorption of iron, healthy skin, teeth and bones. Strengthens the immune system and helps to fight infection.	Deficiency is characterized by increased susceptibility to infection, fatigue, poor sleep and depression.
D (calciferol)	Mainly exposure to sunlight. Also fortified breakfast cereals, fortified soya milk and margarine.	Essential for bone and tooth formation; helps the body to absorb calcium and phosphorus; aids the immune system.	Deficiency is characterized by softening of the bones, muscle weakness and anaemia. Shortage in children can cause rickets.
E (tocopherols)	Seeds, nuts, vegetable oils, green leafy vegetables, avocados, and wholemeal (wholewheat) bread.	Essential for healthy skin, circulation and maintaining cells – an antioxidant.	Deficiency is characterized by increased risk of heart attack, strokes and certain cancers.

Vegan and ethical shopping

There are many factors to take into consideration when shopping as a vegan, which go far beyond the plant-based diet. From the clothes on your back to the shoes on your feet and the cleaning products you use, the ethos of veganism is excluding all forms of exploitation or cruelty to animals and should dictate which products you buy.

Beyond this, the wider philosophy of veganism aims to promote the welfare of people, animals and the environment, which will also affect what products you buy and the way you buy them. It could be argued that vegans are failing to live up to their basic vegan principles if, for example, they buy non-leather shoes made by sweat-shop child labour, or use bio-fuel made from a crop responsible for devastating the rainforests.

There are a number of schemes designed to help vegan and other environmentally concerned shoppers to choose more ethically but caution is often advised. Something labelled 'carbon neutral' could still contain chemicals that harm the environment, or a fair-trade product may be fairer for people but involve cruelty to animals.

If you cannot find what you are looking for in your local stores then the Internet is an excellent resource. There are dedicated online retailers selling everything from vegan marshmallows to vegan condoms. Up-to-date lists of products are also published by a number of organizations. In the UK, the *Animal Free Shopper* is a useful guide and is published every couple of years by The Vegan Society. For vegans in the USA, PETA (People for the Ethical Treatment of Animals) publish a cruelty-free shopping guide to help

Above: If you can, buy your fruit and vegetables from local growers, or join a box scheme to get fresh seasonal produce.

consumers find products that are not tested on animals. Vegetarian and vegan magazines also have a useful classified section in the back.

FOOD
The vegan diet and the plant-based alternatives available will be looked at in detail in the following pages. However, many vegans have a number of other concerns about the origin, processing and transportation of the food they buy.

Organic farming This is a system of agriculture in which organic products and techniques are used, such as when the soil is treated with manure rather than with chemical fertilizers, or when plant pests are eliminated by introducing insects that prey on them rather than by spraying chemical insecticides. The market for organic produce has increased hugely in the last ten years as consumers recognize the environmental damage caused by some methods used in conventional farming, as well as the nutritional value of organic produce.

Stock-free farming This system, also known as vegan-organic growing, avoids all artificial chemical products (synthetic fertilizer, pesticides, growth regulators), genetically modified organisms, animal manures and slaughterhouse by-products (blood, fish meal, bone meal, etc).

Advocates of stock-free farming argue it is more natural to use crop rotation, composting, soil replenishment crops and mulching as a synergistic means of managing the soil quality. It is suggested that manure and other waste products such as feathers not only support factory farming but compromise health and contamination concerns.

Fair trade There are various fair trade or equal exchange schemes. The idea is that the organization tries to bring producers closer to their market, cutting out the middle-men, so that they get a bigger share of the price of the final product. This was extremely successful with commodities such as tea and coffee where, despite their high final price, only a tiny fraction of the profits was going to the farmers who grew the product. Fair trade schemes have helped many communities climb out of poverty and inspired a slightly more responsible attitude among the giant international food manufacturers.

Co-ops These are customer- or producer-owned schemes where all profits are shared out or ploughed back into the business to allow more ethical practices and decisions unmotivated by profit. Many retail co-operative societies have an honest labelling policy and have pioneered new fair trade categories. Many label products such as wine and beer with the true ingredients, including production aids, such as gelatine.

Vegetable box schemes These schemes were introduced in an attempt to support organic, local farming. Consumers order seasonal produce directly from the local farmers and growers, and this is delivered to their homes or picked up, often within a matter of hours after harvesting. As well as supplying the consumer with fresh, seasonal produce these schemes also support the local economy, reduce transportation of food, and decrease unnecessary packaging.

Community supported agriculture Often referred to as CSAs, these are systems of buying local produce that are popular in the USA. Like the box scheme, this is a direct relationship between the consumer and the farmer. The arrangement is usually based on the farmer taking a 'subscription' or offering 'shares' in their crops. After harvesting, the subscribers or shareholders receive fresh, seasonal produce.

Right: Many banana growers have benefited from fair trade schemes and now receive a fair price for their produce.

Environmental concerns when shopping
Vegans try to act in a way that is beneficial to the environment. Think about these factors when buying your food:
- **Production** - How is the food you eat grown? Is it organically produced? Or is it from a farm using synthetic fertilizers, chemicals and pesticides?
- **Transportation** - How far has the food you are buying had to travel? Can it be bought nearer home? Do you really need it?
- **Producers** - Are the people who grow your food free from exploitation and receiving a fair price for their work? Can you buy the same product in a fair trade system? Can you buy the same thing from your local farmer?
- **Packaging** - Is it necessary to wrap the food you buy in plastic? Choose loose fruit and vegetables or join a box scheme. Take reusable bags to the store.
- **Recycling** - Is the packaging you use able to be recycled locally? If not, try and avoid it.

Farmers' markets These are public markets where farmers and other vendors can sell their products directly to the consumer. These markets are becoming increasingly popular in many countries around the world. It is another way of buying fresh, seasonal produce directly from the grower, and many of the farmers will be using organic methods.

Health-food stores The local independent health-food store is a great resource for buying vegan products that supermarkets do not think viable. They are also a good source of advice, as well as support in obtaining an item even if it is not already stocked.

FOOTWEAR

Vegetarian and vegan shoes have been available to the animal-free shopper for a long time, though they were not always the most fashionable. However, the variety available to the modern vegan means that there is a comfortable and stylish shoe suitable for any occasion. From workboots and hiking shoes to running shoes and fashionable footwear for nights out, there is now no design, style or type of shoe for which there is not a vegan equivalent.

Artificial leather, often made from a textile treated with an oil-based coating, has been used by vegan shoemakers for many years. Modern advances in 'pleather' (a slang term for 'plastic leather') means that the comfort and durability of animal-free shoes is just as good as leather. There are now a number of top designers creating smart shoes in 'pleather' and other fabrics so that vegans need never feel they are missing out on the latest stylish footwear.

CLOTHING

There is a huge variety of animal-free clothing available in mainstream stores, which means that avoiding animal-derived clothing, such as leather, silk, wool and fur, should not cause you any serious problems. Organic and fairtrade cotton, linen and man-made fibres are available in normal clothing outlets, and new ethical and sustainable

Above: Many medicines are now available in plant cellulose or vegetable starch capsules, rather than gelatine.

materials for making fashion items are surfacing all the time. Thankfully the fish-skin silk alternative didn't catch on but mushroom leather, leaf leather, hemp, bamboo and waste products from the food industry are gathering fans and gaining momentum. The recycling of waste packaging such as durable bags made from plastic bags or foil drinks pouches is an encouraging trend and a step forward from great grandma's rag rugs and patchwork quilts. Fashion.net, one of the world's most influential fashion news websites, has been working behind the scenes to encourage vegan alternatives, incorporate them into designers' creations and reward innovators through the star-studded Fashion.net Industry Awards.

COSMETICS AND TOILETRIES

The horrors of animal testing to test the safety of cosmetics for humans to adjust their looks and smell led to nearly as many protests as the barbaric fur industry provoked. In the UK, alongside The Body Shop, one of the most outspoken companies to stand up against animal testing was Lush Cosmetics. They pioneered new technologies and travelled around the world to find the most ethically and sustainably produced ingredients. When no truly sustainable ethically produced palm oil could be found in the quantities they needed, they developed their own alternative from a mixture of sustainably grown plant oils. Many smaller companies followed their lead and today there is a wide variety of animal-free options.

Left: Soft and durable materials made from hemp, bamboo and other plants are now widely available.

Above: There are many opportunities to buy soap products that are made entirely using natural plant materials.

PHARMACEUTICALS AND SUPPLEMENTS

Animal-based ingredients are sometimes used by pharmaceutical manufacturers, such as bile from the stomach of calves. Pharmaceutical companies are usually secretive about their product ingredients, however many medicines will have been tested on animals.

For many years vegetarians had to squeeze medications and supplements from their capsules as they contained gelatine. Many companies are now using animal-free versions such as plant cellulose or vegetable starch capsules for their medicinal products.

If you are at all concerned about obtaining all the essential nutrients you need for optimum health, take a food supplement. There are plant-based versions of all therapeutic grade supplements now. Vegan long-chain omega 3 essential fats EPA and DHA are made from algae (which is where the fish get it from). Vegan vitamin D3 (traditionally made from sheep's wool) is made from fungus and lichen. D2 is ubiquitously available – it's just less potent so you need more of it.

HOUSEHOLD GOODS AND CLEANING PRODUCTS

Most mainstream household chemicals and cleaning products are in some way linked to animal testing. Even well-known eco-friendly brands, who make products rich in natural ingredients, test on animals in order to establish that their products are safer than others for animal life.

There are, however, many companies who go the extra mile to make products that are not only effective but are not tested on animals and so are suitable for vegans. These companies can be found online or in vegan shopping guides.

> **Some animal products used in cosmetics**
> Below are listed a few ingredients to watch out for when buying cosmetics and toiletries (a full list can be found from The Vegan Society or other vegan charities):
> - Tallow (hard animal fat) – used in soaps.
> - Lanolin (a fatty substance derived from wool) or beeswax – used in lipsticks.
> - Shellac (resin secreted by insects) – used in nail varnish.
> - Castoreum (secretion from gland of the beaver) – used in perfume.
> - Musk (from gland of male musk deer) – used in perfume.
> - Keratin (protein from hair, horn, hoof and feathers) – used in shampoos, conditioners and skincare products.
> - Civet (from anal pouch of civet cat) – used in perfume.
> - Gelatine (from animal bones, skin and hide) – general use.
> - Propolis (tree sap used as a glue by bees) – general use.
> - Chitin (hard substance from insects and crustaceans) – general use.
> - Squalene (derived from shark liver) – used in skin moisturizers.

There is a surprisingly large amount of household products to avoid, so always ensure you check what the item contains before buying it. Many paints contain shellac, and gardening products often contain manure or other animal products such as bone meal and blood. Even matches use gelatine in the explosive bit on the end.

CONSUMER POWER

One of the aspects of veganism that has the greatest impact is the power that you wield as a consumer. By simply refusing to buy a product due to its animal-based status you send a loud, clear message to companies that they are losing profits to their more ethical and conscientious competitors.

You may consider there is no ethical or economic impact to be made from throwing out a perfectly good leather, feather or animal-derived product just because it is not vegan. You may even feel it is a bit of an insult to the animal.

It is certainly not very environmentally friendly and perhaps you should use it until it needs replacing, or give it away. These are decisions to be made by individuals, and vegans will vary on what they do.

The important thing is to avoid supporting or encouraging, either morally or financially, those companies who thrive or profit from harmful practices to animals, people or the environment.

The daily vegan diet

If you are thinking of following a vegan diet or are still adjusting to one, then it is a good idea to plan out your meals in advance. Once you are a seasoned vegan, a daily menu will still be a great way to explore and experiment with new dishes and to ensure that you are getting all the nutrients you need. The basic rules of health are:

• Eat a rainbow every day – at least seven portions of vegetables and three of fruit every day.

• Keep hydrated – drink enough water and avoid caffeinated and sugary drinks.

• Eat wholefoods not half foods – avoid sugary or artificially sweetened, salty, fat and chemical-laden processed foods, and ensure a source of essential fats for repair.

• Exercise – regularly use all of your muscles, get your heart pumping faster and get sunshine on your skin.

• Make time for sleep and fun – happy people live longer – laugh, sing, dance, do yoga.

Remember, vegans are human too. Vegans need the same nutrients that everyone else needs and bearing in mind the average popular diet is seriously lacking, just the extra vegetables that a vegan invariably eats will give optimal health a good start. As long as you incorporate reliable adequate sources of vitamins such as vitamin B12 (eg yeast extract, chlorella, fortified plant milks and foods), iodine (eg certain seaweeds), Vitamin D (eg sunshine, mushrooms), calcium (eg beans, vegetables, nuts, seeds), essential fats (eg seeds, nuts, cress, purslane), selenium (eg Brazil nuts), and zinc (eg pumpkin seeds) into your diet, under normal circumstances, you should thrive.

If you just can't be bothered to plan your diet, or lead a stressful lifestyle and simply don't have the time to plan,

Above: An ideal vegan meal would contain one-quarter protein, one-quarter carbohydrates and one-half vegetables and fruits.

then just take a good multivitamin and mineral. Choose your vitamins carefully though; the cheapest may not always be the best value due to fillers and less absorbable versions of minerals.

Breakfasts Always start the day with a balanced breakfast, including at least one piece of fruit. Stick to one or two regular weekday cereals if that is easy and healthy – homemade muesli, granola or porridge with a sprinkling of seeds and berries is perfect. Do check out the ingredients lists on cereal packets as many seemingly healthy products contain large amounts of sugar.

• Wholemeal (wholewheat) toast is good as long as you include some protein-rich nut butter, or a sprinkle of seeds to keep you going longer.

• Rolled oats are good raw or cooked. Mix them with dried fruit and flaked (sliced) almonds or chopped nuts.

• Try all the dairy-free milks until you find a sugar-free one that you like. If you have an uncompromising sweet tooth, try the apple-sweetened varieties.

• Add diced fresh fruit, berries, dried fruit, nuts and seeds to live soya yogurt.

• Try scrambled tofu with parsley and red onions on a field or portobello mushroom sprinkled with hemp seeds.

Left: Toasted wholewheat toast with hummus makes a filling and nutritious snack.

Right: Vegan takeaway food is now widely available from street stalls, cafés and markets.

Lunches and light meals The lunchtime meal at work is fast becoming a sandwich at the desk or food grabbed on the go. It is vital to take time out of your working day to enjoy your lunch and refuel and re-energize for the rest of the day. Although there are many more vegan soup and sandwich choices than there used to be, you may find it more rewarding to pack your own picnic the night before instead.

If you have cooking facilities at work, reheated baked potatoes or sweet potatoes with baked beans or leftover lasagne can be a great lunch if you add a salad, watercress, beetroot and seeds on top,

When catering for children who need packed lunches to take to school, ensure that you fill their lunchboxes with plenty of variety and only just enough, so they are hungry enough to finish all the veg. Make their choices as interesting as possible so that they will not feel they are missing out on the foods that their friends are eating. A good trick is to get children a multi-compartment lunch box so you can start teaching them ratios of fruit and vegetables, carbohydrates and protein. Rules are drink water, eat veg first, protein and carbohydrates next, then, if (because everyone else has one) they need a reward, a 'no benefit' (treat) food.

Main meals When planning your main meal, a high-protein complex carbohydrate makes an excellent nutritious base, such as buckwheat pasta, quinoa, barley, basmati rice, mung bean noodles, beansprouts or a whole-meal pancake.

With the base and bulk of the meal decided, choose the vegetables to accompany it from the huge range of options available. Make sure you choose a good variety.

Once you have your vegetables, then consider adding a protein element to your meal. Options include soya, baked tempeh, marinated and grilled tofu, seitan, chopped nuts or seeds, falafel, nut roast, bean burgers or bean salad.

Snacks Dried fruit, seeds and nuts are far better than confectionery or processed snacks. Make up your own mix of lightly roasted cashew nuts, walnuts, Brazil nuts and hazelnuts, with quartered dried apricots and raisins. Lay the nuts out on a baking tray and roast slowly in the oven, then allow them to cool completely before storing with the fruit in an airtight jar.

Sugar Processed white sugar often used to be refined using animal bone char. We can't find anyone that admits to doing that in the UK. In the US it may still sometimes be imported from places that do use bone char to refine it. Best to check the country of origin if it's not a well-known brand and look it up online.

Alcohol The vegan problems with alcohol are the manufacturing processes, which often use isinglass (from a fish swim bladder), gelatin, milk protein, and eggs or chitin from shellfish to speed up the clearing and fining process of beers and wines. Manufacturers are not obliged to label ingredients so it is difficult to tell a vegan wine or beer from a non-vegan one. The good news is that today many manufacturers are using clay-based fining agents such as bentonite, which are particularly efficient at fining out unwanted proteins. Activated charcoal is another vegan-friendly agent that is also used. Vegan charity websites will direct you to the most likely sources. Most spirits, however, are vegan.

Takeaways and meals out A vegan diet is not the end to dining in restaurants and cafés. The restaurant trade has recently become more aware that they need to provide food for people who follow different diets. A vegetarian option has been widely available for many years but, thanks to a better understanding of various food allergies and intolerances, restaurants are now accustomed to accommodating people on various other special diets. The popularity of restaurants serving various world cuisines also provides good opportunities for seeking out a vegan-friendly meal. Vegan restaurants are opening all the time so there has never been an easier time to enjoy vegan food.

Pregnancy and children

Many health professionals recognize a balanced and varied vegan diet to be not only nutritionally adequate for people of all ages but positively beneficial. As with any diet it takes a little health-conscious effort to provide protection at key life stages, such as pregnancy and during infancy, childhood and adolescence. The body is working at its hardest at these times and its nutritional needs should be given special priority. A diverse and well-balanced vegan diet can easily satisfy the body's nutritional needs to promote normal growth.

PRE-CONCEPTION
In addition to following a healthy vegan diet, with plenty of fruits and vegetables, you should ensure adequate intake of folic acid and vitamin B12, iron and essential fats. You should try to avoid coffee and alcohol.

PREGNANCY
For all women, the recommended intake of vitamins and minerals is higher than normal during pregnancy. Increase your intake of folic acid, vitamin A (beta carotene), B1 (thiamine), niacin, riboflavin, B12, D2, calcium, iron, zinc and essential fats – particularly DHA (docosahexaenoic acid), which is needed to build babies' eyes and brains.

During pregnancy the mother's store of vitamin B12 is not readily available to the developing baby. The baby builds up its supply of vitamin B12 from the mother's daily intake. The mother must thus ensure she has enough in her diet for both of them. If vitamin B12 intake is low during pregnancy, the developing baby will struggle to have adequate stores of the vitamin, and this may lead to a deficiency in the child at some point after birth.

Adequate zinc intake should also be ensured otherwise human milk may not be a rich enough source of zinc. Breast-feeding infants would then have to draw on their own body reserves, laid down during the last three months in the womb.

The increase in calorie requirements during pregnancy is relatively small. There is little increase in calorie need during the first six months of pregnancy, but an extra 200 calories per day should be consumed during the third trimester. However, you need to ensure that each calorie counts and that the calories you consume are dense in nutrients, as being pregnant places greater demands upon your body.

Extra water is required by the body for making additional blood for the mother, the baby and for the amniotic fluid. Aim to drink at least six 200ml/7fl oz glasses per day of filtered water. Pregnancy-safe herbal teas, soya milk or vegetable juice could count toward this. Avoid coffee and tea, as caffeine has been associated with various problems during pregnancy, and avoid alcohol.

The basic advice for pregnant women on a vegan diet is to follow the nutritional guidelines established for all adults, ensuring an increased quantity of a mixture of vegan wholefoods. Many women (not just vegans) take a daily multivitamin and mineral supplement during pregnancy as extra insurance to compensate for times when either healthy eating just will not fit into the day or food aversions develop. With a nutritionally balanced diet, typical pregnancy symptoms, such as food cravings, sickness, stress, fatigue and constipation, may be avoided.

FEEDING YOUR NEWBORN
After giving birth it is important to maintain a healthy diet to keep your energy levels high and to help you cope with your new baby. There is no problem with your baby following a vegan diet too. You simply need to make sure that you are covering all their nutritional needs – check with a healthcare professional if you are at all unsure.

Breastfeeding The diet to follow when breastfeeding your baby is similar to the diet that is recommended for pregnancy, although the intakes of calories, protein, calcium, magnesium, zinc, copper, selenium and vitamin B12 should be slightly higher. Eating an increased quantity of vegan wholefoods is an ideal way to give yourself a nutritional

Left: Getting the correct nutritional balance while pregnant is very important for you and your child. In particular, vegans should aim to increase their intake of wholefoods.

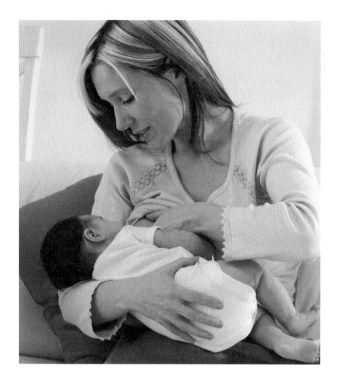

Above: Being vegan is no barrier to breastfeeding. Ensure you are eating a well-balanced diet to see to your baby's needs to ensure they are well-nourished and content.

boost while breastfeeding. In particular, ensure a regular intake of vitamin B12, D2 and essential fats at this time. During the first six months of your baby's life, all its basic nutritional needs will be met by regular feeds of breast milk. Breast milk provides a young baby with a natural and nutritionally balanced diet. Your baby will gradually move away from milk as the main source of nutrition, toward his or her first taste of solid foods.

Bottle-feeding If you opt to bottle-feed, it is possible to purchase a vegan formula. Ask any vegan organization, health-food store or pharmacy for details of vegan formulas currently available. Soya-based infant formulas can be used from birth onward. Infant formulas are often lacking in the DHA needed for brain building, so consult a healthcare professional about essential nutrients and algae-based fatty acids. As is the case with dairy milk, standard soya milks, which are consumed by adults, should never be used as a straight replacement for breast milk or infant formula. They are lacking in the correct amount of nutrients that are required by a baby, which natural human breast milk contains.

First foods The classic 'first food' should be organic baby rice, cooked millet or quinoa, or mashed banana. This can be followed by various vegetable purées such as cauliflower, broccoli, peas, carrot, avocado and then small pieces of fruit. Persevere a number of times with a food that your child seems to be rejecting, as taste buds are constantly changing as they mature.

Begin feeds with breast or bottle milk and gradually increase the amount of solid food afterward. Solids should never be added to a bottle of milk. Do not add salt, sugar or spice to food. Move from solid food at one feed per day to solids at two feeds and so on, following and responding to the baby's appetite and pace. Remember that after four or five months of age, your baby may not receive enough vitamin B12 or D2 from breast milk if your body's stores are depleted. Fortified soya milks intended for infants must contain vitamin B12 and D2 by law.

Seven to nine months By this stage, your baby will be becoming more active and will be ready to try slightly more lumpy foods with more variety of taste. In addition to breast or bottled milk, you can introduce blended oats, millet, rice, quinoa or buckwheat breakfast cereal to the baby's diet, and a variety of vegetables, such as avocado, cooked and mashed broccoli, carrots, sweet potatoes and parsnips. Your baby will now be ready for small pieces of fresh fruits, such as chopped-up pears, peaches, apricots, figs, plums and melons. You can also try finger foods.

Below: Young children may need more frequent meals or snacks as they use up a large amount of energy every day.

Ten to twelve months Foods should be chopped, finely grated or blended. Your baby will be more inclined to hold a spoon, and may be moving toward eating on her or his own. A greater variety of vegetables should be offered at this point. Only introduce nut butters on the advice of your healthcare professional if you have a family history of nut allergies. As your baby starts to become more mobile, aim to boost greater energy needs from fat, such as coconut, hemp oil and avocado, rather than sugary foods and fruit juice.

Twelve months plus From twelve months of age your infant can share the same meals as the rest of the family, with additional snacks to keep their energy levels up. Keep in mind the following key points, which will help to ensure that your child's diet has the optimum balance of nutrients that are necessary for their growth and development:

Use energy-dense foods These will help keep up with your child's growing demands.
• Fruit smoothies, concentrated fruit spreads and dried figs.
• Fortified plant-milks or infant formula.
• Thick porridge with a little additional vegetable oil.
• Nut butters, tahini and hummus (providing there is no genetic history of allergies to these foods).
• Coconut milk.
• Avocados.

Use soya and rapeseed (canola) oils These will encourage your child's brain and visual development.
• Use more rapeseed oil or hemp oil.
• Add a little flax oil to sunflower oil.

Boost vitamins and minerals
• Use black treacle (molasses) to increase iron intake.
• Use tofu prepared with calcium sulphate, which contains more calcium than cow's milk.
• Ensure access to sunshine and intake of foods fortified with vitamin D2 .
• Ensure adequate vitamin B12 intake.
• Include foods in a meal that are rich in vitamin C to enhance iron absorption.

OLDER CHILDREN AND TEENAGERS
Vegetarianism among children is common, but you may encounter some people and health professionals that still feel veganism is a drastic step for a child or growing teenager. Arm yourself with the facts and key sources of nutrients, and your child's radiant health should speak for itself.

The diet recommendations for older children and teenagers are the same as for all vegans, though children may require more frequent meals or snacks due to their high energy needs. A wide variety of wholefoods should be eaten daily, including fruits, vegetables, plenty of leafy greens, as well as wholegrain products, cereals, nuts, seeds, beans, peas and lentils. Ensure they have a reliable source of calcium and supporting vitamins and minerals (especially during growth spurts) and encourage regular weight-bearing exercise to help to build healthy bones.

INTRODUCING A VEGAN DIET
You may be in a position where you are adopting a vegan diet for children who have been raised to some extent on animal-based foods, or perhaps you have older children and have decided to make the lifestyle change to veganism as a family.

In this situation you should take time to plan how and when you are going to substitute animal-derived products in your children's diets, rather than making a hurried overnight decision. It is important to think about what nutrients you are cutting out by eliminating all animal-derived products, and in what vegan form you can replace them in your diet.

Take the time to learn what specific nutrients are important at your child's stage of development and how you can make sure they get sufficient through their new diet. Start children with familiar foods, such as peanut butter sandwiches, and gradually introduce new vegan foods.

Left: Teenagers following a vegan diet should ensure they get enough of the vitamins and minerals needed for growth.

Vegan alternatives

One of the common questions for those starting a vegan diet is, 'How do I cope without milk and eggs?'. It is, however, surprisingly easy to replace dairy products and eggs. There seems no end to the plant-based alternatives to dairy these days, from the long-standing traditional Africa, Oriental, Asian and Caribbean use of coconut milk and coconut cream to the use of other nuts, pulses and cereals. It now seems nothing is impossible, even vegan camembert-style cheese with an authentic rind is on offer.

You can make quiches using tofu, whisk ice cream using soya milk, set jellies using agar-agar and sprinkle a variety of nut cheeses on your food. The options available will ensure that you will barely notice the absence of dairy and eggs.

WHAT IS SOYA?

The most popular and prolific dairy and meat replacer is soya. Soya is a bean related to clover, peas and alfalfa. It contains an excellent balance of amino acids, and is considered the equivalent in protein quality to meat, milk and eggs, which is one reason it has become so popular. Soya has made an enormous impact on the processed food market in the West in recent years and is now used in a variety of products. Many foods have been developed from soya, but the most popular are miso, soya milk, soy sauce, tempeh and tofu. Soya beans and their derivatives are also used for a huge variety of non-food products such as paints, soaps, plastics, adhesives, candles and fabrics.

For centuries, the soya bean has been the basis of Asian cuisine, and is thought to have been cultivated in China for

Above left: Soya beans have been grown for over 5,000 years.
Above: There is a wide range of soya products available, which are perfect vegan substitutes for dairy equivalents.

over 5,000 years. More soya beans are now grown in the USA than anywhere else in the world, though over 90 per cent of them are used to facilitate the production of meat and dairy rather than to directly feed people. Other producers include Brazil, Argentina and China.

Soya beans are unique among beans as they contain compounds called isoflavones. These molecules have structures similar to the oestrogens produced in the body, hence the name plant- or phytoestrogen. There are many classes of active non-nutrients with oestrogenic activity, but interest has focused on the beneficial effects of a group of compounds belonging to the isoflavones. The two primary isoflavones in soya beans are daidzein and genistein. Research suggests soya may offer health benefits relating to heart disease, osteoporosis, menopause symptom relief and, possibly, cancer.

Soya beans are high in protein and are classed as a complete protein – meaning that they contain all the essential amino acids the human body needs. The beans also contain iron, calcium, zinc, B vitamins, vitamin E and fibre. Steamed tofu made with calcium sulphate contains over five times as much calcium as whole pasteurized cow's milk. Soya oil also contains the beneficial polyunsaturated fat. It is free from cholesterol and contains both linoleic and linolenic essential fatty acids.

VEGAN MILKS

There are easily over 25 different sorts of soy milk and then there are other bean milks like edamame and pea milk; nut milks such as coconut, cashew, almond, macadamia, hazelnut, and tiger nut; seed milks such as hemp and flax; cereal milks such as rice, oat, barley, and quinoa; and the mixtures such as coconut and rice, sweetened and unsweetened, flavoured with vanilla or chocolate – the choice is now mind-boggling. They all have their different characteristics. Rice milk is thin, like sterilized or UHT milk; oat milk is perfect for sauces and custard; coconut milk is good in tea; hazelnut or almond is good in coffee; hemp milk makes a great protein shake; soya makes great mayo and ice cream and 'cheesy' sauces.

Whether you make nut products or buy store-bought ones is up to you. Making your own is as simple as blending soaked nuts in water to produce nut milks, or grinding nuts to a paste for nut butters, with or without flavourings. The results are fresh and delicious products, that can be more economical than ready-prepared ones. You can also tailor them to suit your own preferences.

Simple cashew nut milk

This method of making a basic nut milk can be applied to most types of nuts, although the soaking time for each may vary.

175g/6oz/1¼ cups raw unsalted
    cashew nuts
750ml/1¼ pints/3 cups filtered water,
    plus soaking water
pinch of sea salt (optional)

1 Put the cashew nuts in a large glass, ceramic or stainless steel bowl. Pour over enough water to cover by about 2.5cm/1in. Filtered water is preferable, as filtering removes impurities that may spoil the flavour of the milk, but you can use bottled or tap water. Add a small pinch of sea salt as well if you like; this will help soften the nuts, but isn't essential and should be left out if you are on a low-sodium diet. Leave to soak at room temperature for 3–6 hours.

2 After soaking, strain the cashew nuts, then rinse them and tip them into a blender with a capacity of at least 1.5 litres/2½ pints/6¼ cups.

3 Add about a third of the water (250ml/8fl oz/1 cup) to the blender. Pulse a few times to break up the nuts, then blend continuously for about 1 minute. Add a further 250ml/8fl oz/1 cup water and blend for a further minute, until the mixture is smooth. A high-powered blender is preferable to finely pulverize the nuts. If you are using a less powerful machine, blend the mixture for 1–2 minutes more.

4 Strain the liquid to give it a silkier texture and remove any fine pieces of nuts that haven't completely blended. Pour the mixture through a very fine-meshed plastic or stainless steel sieve or strainer into a large bowl. For a smoother end result, line the sieve with a layer of muslin or cheesecloth, or pour the liquid through a re-usable nut bag placed over a bowl, jug or pitcher. Leave it to filter for a few minutes, then gently stir the pulp to encourage the liquid to pass through more quickly. To extract a little more nut milk, slowly pour the remaining water over the pulp and leave it to drain again.

5 Squeeze the last of the milk from the nut pulp. When the milk has filtered through, gather up the corners of the muslin or nut bag and squeeze it with clean hands to extract the last few drops of milk.

Above and above right: Nut milk, butter and yogurt are easy to make and are delicious dairy-free inclusions for everyday recipes.

6 If you want to serve the nut milk at once as a drink, pour it over a few ice cubes in a glass. Otherwise pour the milk into a glass jug, cover and store it in the refrigerator.

VEGAN YOGURT

Making your own yogurt is easy. If you don't have a yogurt maker you can use an insulated soup flask (with a wide top). Then all you need is some freshly-made nut milk and a non-dairy starter culture. Vegan yogurt drinks can also be made with water-grown kefir grains or kombucha as a starter.

Nut milk yogurt

This yogurt will not naturally thicken like dairy yogurt, so here nut milk is first thickened with cornflour (cornstarch). A little sugar, agave or maple syrup is essential as the probiotics 'feed' on this; the sweet taste will disappear by the end of the process. Flavour the yogurt after making it.

10ml/2 tsp cornflour (cornstarch)
7.5ml/1½ tsp caster (superfine) sugar, agave or maple syrup
475ml/16fl oz/2 cups freshly-made nut milk
two vegan probiotic capsules (acidophilus 40ml) or
  1 sachet non-dairy yogurt starter

1 Blend the cornflour and sugar, agave or maple syrup in a pan with 30ml/2 tbsp of the milk until smooth, then stir in the rest of the milk. Bring to the boil and simmer for 1 minute, whisking until the mixture is thickened. Turn off the heat and leave to cool until the temperature falls to 32°C/90°F on a thermometer. Stir occasionally as it cools.

2 Open the probiotic capsules and sprinkle the powder over the warm milk (or add the sachet of yogurt starter, following the instructions on the packet) and whisk well.

3 Pour the mixture into a yogurt maker or a sterilized and cooled flask. Leave it to stand for 8–10 hours; after 8 hours the yogurt will have a mild flavour, so if you prefer it a little more tangy, leave it a little longer. Transfer it from the flask to a bowl and chill it, covered, in the refrigerator. It will thicken further as it chills. Use within 3 days of making.

4 For thicker yogurt, strain it after chilling. Line a plastic or stainless-steel sieve or strainer, large enough to hold all the yogurt, with a piece of muslin or cheesecloth and place it over a bowl. Tip the yogurt into the muslin and leave it to drain for 1–2 hours. The thin liquid will drain away, leaving a thicker yogurt behind in the muslin. Discard the liquid and tip the yogurt into the bowl. Sweeten or flavour if you like, then cover and chill until needed.

VEGAN CHEESE, BUTTER AND CREAM

Plant milks (whether home-made or shop-bought) can also be used to make vegan cheese, butter and cream, so if the thought of having to give up traditional dairy products is stopping you going vegan, think again.

Vegan cheese Getting a vegan cheese to have it all – taste and texture, nutritional value and the ability to melt at high temperatures into a sticky, gloopy, stretchy sticky topping for nachos or pizza – has proved a challenge. Luckily, the easiest to achieve, a mild-flavoured easily melted piece of yellow squidgy combination of potato or starchy grain with coconut fat, seems to be the most popular choice, amongst young consumers anyway.

But for those who love traditional artisan dairy cheeses, these too now have delicious equivalents. By tweaking expert cheesemaking methods and finding key strains of fermenting probiotic bacteria, leaps forward in cheesemaking have been achieved over the past few years. Even vegan blue cheeses are taking their place on the vegan cheeseboard.

'Cheesy' topping

The easiest way to make a delicious cheesy topping for vegan lasagne, moussaka, potato-topped pies, pizza, quiche or cheese on toast, is to blend equal quantities of hot apple-sweetened soya milk and cold vegetable oil with an added teaspoon or two of cider vinegar to emulsify. Then add flavourings such as mustard, yeast extract, garlic and herbs, and yeast flakes.

Below: Hemp seed crackers spread with a home-made soft almond cheese and red pickle relish makes a tasty snack.

Vegan butter If the thought of vegetable margarine is not to your taste, vegan butter is easy to make. Simmer a cup of apple-sweetened soya milk in a pan with some chopped carrots until the milk takes on a pale yellow colour. Remove the carrots and blend the milk with equal quantities of coconut oil and a couple of teaspoons of lemon juice to emulsify it. Add salt to taste and allow to cool. You can replace up to half of the coconut oil with omega 3-rich oil but the more you add the less firm the butter will be. There are also plenty of nut and seed butters on the market but it is quick and easy to make your own.

Almond butter

An increasingly popular nut butter, almonds are very hard so will take slightly longer to process than some other nuts. If you are making the butter in an ordinary food processor, it's a good idea to warm the almonds in the oven for a few minutes first to soften them and start releasing the oils (you can leave this step out if you are using a high-powered blender). If you make this nut butter with blanched almonds (where the skin has been taken off, see page 71) it will have a light, creamy colour, whereas using nuts with their skins on produces a darker, slightly speckled spread.

400g/14oz/2⅓ cups raw unsalted almonds
pinch of salt (optional)
5–10ml/1–2 tsp agave or maple syrup (optional)
5–10m/1–2 tsp almond or sunflower oil (optional)

1 Spread the almonds in a single layer on a baking sheet and put in a cold oven. Turn on the oven to 150°C/300°F/Gas 2. Heat for 4–5 minutes or until the almonds are warm.

2 Remove the almonds from the oven and tip them into a food processor. Sprinkle over the salt, if using. Process for 1–2 minutes, until finely ground.

3 Scrape the sides with a rubber spatula, then add the sweetener and 5ml/1 tsp of the oil, if using. Blend for a few minutes or until the nuts come together in a clumpy paste. Stop and scrape down the sides again.

4 Add the remaining 5ml/1 tsp of oil, if using. Continue processing for 12–15 minutes, until smooth and creamy. The heat of the machine will help the nuts to soften and blend, but if using a low-powered one, take care not to burn out the engine; pause if necessary.

5 Transfer the butter to a clean container or sterilized jar. Store, chilled, for up to 4 weeks.

Vegan ice cream The secret to a good dairy-free ice cream is either fat, fibre or sugar – anything that stops the water in the recipe from turning too hard. So coconut fat, bananas or dried fruit (fibre) or nuts (fats and fibre) are a good starting point. For example, banana, peanut butter, and chocolate ice cream is delightful. Avocado, dried apricots, tofu, and chocolate ice cream is not bad either. Or why not try the recipes for Date and Tofu Ice Cream, and Maple Syrup Ice Cream, both of which feature in the desserts chapter?

Vegan cream When it comes to dairy-free cream, the accepted standby for vegans is creamed coconut or chopped cashew nuts blended with a little water and maple syrup. Oat cream is also easy to make by blending oats with a little water, oil and maple syrup. If it's too 'porridgey' for you, you can sieve out the fibre before adding the oil and syrup. There are all sorts of vegan creams for sale from frothy 'squirty' cream and pouring creams to thick whipping cream and crème fraîche. You can of course also make your own.

Whipped coconut cream

As whipped coconut cream is smoother in texture than nut creams, it may be preferable for some desserts. It makes a great accompaniment to fresh berries. It is very rich, so serve in small helpings. This method does not work as well with canned coconut cream, so use the cream spooned from the top of coconut milk, as outlined below.

400ml/14fl oz can full-fat coconut milk, chilled overnight
5ml/1 tsp vanilla extract

1 Chill the coconut milk in the refrigerator for several hours or overnight. Carefully open the can; the coconut cream will be at the top. Spoon out the coconut cream and place it in a glass bowl, preferably chilled, keeping the more watery coconut milk for other recipes.

2 Add the vanilla extract, then whisk for a few minutes with an electric beater, until the mixture is light and soft peaks form.

3 Serve the cream immediately or store it in the bowl, covered with clear film or plastic wrap, in the refrigerator. It will keep for 2–3 days.

Below: Vanilla-flavoured whipped coconut cream looks and tastes delicious. You honestly won't know that it is dairy-free.

VEGAN EGGS

Substituting eggs in vegan cuisine depends on its function in the recipe: to bind, to trap air, to add fat and enrich, to add protein, sometimes to help emulsify. Mashed potato or thick stocks can be used to bind vegetarian burger mixes; and banana, soya milk or soya can bind sweet dishes or cakes. Baking powder or a mix of cider vinegar and bicarbonate of soda (which is ideal for chocolate cakes) are successful raising agents. In varying degrees, tofu, banana, soy flour, chia seeds, chocolate, soy yogurt, xanthan gum, carob, coconut oil, flour, arrowroot, agar agar, avocado and ackee can all do the job of an egg. On top of this the market has exploded with exciting vegan egg substitutes. Suddenly foods such as custards, scrambles and frittatas are all being mastered using plant-based foods.

Aquafaba Even meringues and raised batter puddings can now be achieved thanks to 'aquafaba', which is bean juice, usually chickpea juice, that's whisked for 5 minutes to a whisked egg white consistency, many times its original volume and which can form 'peaks'. Once simply a liquid that you would pour down the sink, it is now making all kinds of baking recipes possible for vegans.

Right: Tempeh and textured vegetable protein are both useful nutritional meat substitutes for vegans.

Left: Aquafaba is the juice from a humble can of chickpeas that can be used to make meringues and raised batter puddings.

OTHER SOY PRODUCTS

Apart from edamame beans, fermented miso, soy nut butter, and other types of soy designed as meat alternatives, there are other soy products that sit somewhere between meat replacements and dairy replacements, namely tofu, tempeh and soya TVP (textured vegetable protein).

Tofu This is made from soaked, mashed and strained soya beans. It is white, milky and set in custard-like squares. Its texture can be soft (silken tofu) or firm. Fresh tofu should be kept covered with water in the refrigerator. Change the water daily and use the tofu within a week. Vacuum-packed, long-life tofu can be stored unopened at room temperature. Freezing is not recommended as this alters the texture of the tofu. One of the joys of cooking with plain tofu is that it absorbs the flavours of other ingredients well during cooking. Smoked and marinated tofu are also available.

Firm tofu: This lightly pressed product is stored in cakes or blocks, either submerged in water or vacuum-packed, and can be cubed or sliced. It can be stir-fried, used in stews and soups, crumbled into salads or barbecued. It is also excellent as a substitute for scrambled eggs.

Silken tofu: This product is the softest, most delicate form of tofu. A creamy version comes in tubs and can be used for

dips, dressings or sweet dishes, such as fruit fools and non-dairy ice cream. A slightly firmer type of silken tofu comes in cubes, which break down very easily, so handle carefully.
Fried tofu: At first glance, this doesn't look much like tofu. Slice the nut-brown block, however, and the white interior is exposed. The outer colour is the result of deep-frying in vegetable oil, a process that not only adds flavour, but also makes the beancurd more robust.

Tempeh This is made by fermenting cooked whole soya beans in banana leaves, which gives the product a nutty, savoury flavour and causes it to solidify so that it can be cut into blocks. The beans remain visible under a velvety coating. It is available chilled or frozen. Like firm tofu, tempeh benefits from marinating and can be used in many of the same ways – in stir-fries and kebabs, for example. However, its firmer texture also makes it an excellent meat rather than dairy substitute, so it is perfect in casseroles and baked dishes such as pies.

Textured vegetable protein (TVP) This is manufactured from soya beans into different shapes and forms. It has a firm, sponge-like texture and can be flavoured to resemble meat or, alternatively, can be left as a natural soya product. TVP needs to be rehydrated with water or stock before being

Below: A selection of silken, fried and firm tofu.

Phytoestrogens
Naturally occurring plant derivatives called phytoestrogens, such as isoflavones, are found in soya beans, as well as chickpeas and other legumes. Flax seeds are another source. They mimic oestrogen in the body and are particularly useful for menopausal women. A lot of research is taking place into their effect on health, and they have been associated with the following benefits:
· Improved symptoms for people suffering with osteoporosis, which is possibly due to the slowing of bone demineralization.
· A reduced risk of cardio-vascular disease due to a lowering effect on cholesterol.
· A lower risk of some cancers, such as breast and prostate cancer.
· The improvement of menstrual symptoms.
· The reduction of hot flushes in menopausal women.

incorporated into recipes. It is fortified with vitamin B12 and is therefore a nutritious alternative to meat.

Miso This Japanese paste is made from fermented soya beans. It is very salty and should be used sparingly, for example in stews or spread on vegetables before grilling or broiling.

BREAKFASTS, JUICES AND SMOOTHIES

Famously the most important meal of the day, there are so many choices
here for your vegan breakfast, from grab-and-go options to more leisurely weekend brunch
extravaganzas. Choose from luxurious twists on the traditional bowl of muesli; hearty
pancakes with various fruit accompaniments; refreshing juices and smoothies; or
indulge in the classic cooked breakfast with all the trimmings, vegan-style.

Multi-grain fruit and nut bowl

Make up an airtight jar of this multi-grain mix to keep handy, and have sliced bananas and blueberries in the freezer ready and waiting, so that you can rustle up this warming and super-satisfying breakfast in no time.

40g/1¹/₂oz/¹/₃ cup multi-grain mix, see below
250ml/8 fl oz/1 cup unsweetened plant milk

For the topping
1 small banana, sliced
a few dried cranberries
a handful of blueberries
4 pecan nuts
a handful of pine nuts
a few pumpkin seeds

SERVES 1

1 Add the multi-grain mix and plant milk to a small pan and bring the milk just to the boil, then reduce the heat and simmer for about 5 minutes, stirring from time to time until the grains are soft and have absorbed most of the liquid. Add a little extra milk or water, if needed, to get the consistency that you like.

2 Mash half the banana and stir into the porridge to sweeten, then spoon into a serving bowl. Arrange the remaining banana slices, the cranberries, blueberries, nuts and seeds in rows for visual appeal. Serve immediately.

Multi-grain mix
(Makes 200g/7oz or 5 portions)

Add 50g/2oz/¹/₂ cup each of rolled oats, barley flakes and rye flakes and 50g/2oz/generous ¹/₂ cup quinoa flakes to a bowl and stir together, then spoon into a screw-topped jar and store.

Variations
• Use gluten-free oats and replace barley and rye flakes with buckwheat, popcorn and popped amaranth for a gluten-free version.
• Add in de-hulled hempseed hearts or chia seeds for an omega 3 essential fat boost.

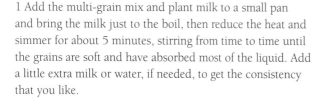

Energy 534kcal/2241kJ; Protein 14.7g; Carbohydrate 67.4g, of which sugars 34.2g; Fat 24.7g, of which saturates 2.1g; Cholesterol 0mg; Calcium 89mg; Fibre 8.7g; Sodium 97mg.

Very berry oatmeal

You might not find this in a 'traditional recipes of the Scottish Highlands' cookbook, but it's worth a shot on a cold winter's day. If you don't fancy the beetroot and kale, try replacing with a little fresh turmeric, ginger, a clove and a pinch of cinnamon to make a wintery version.

25g/1oz/scant ¼ cup medium oatmeal
250ml/8fl oz/1 cup water
75g/3oz/1 small trimmed beetroot (beet), peeled and diced
15g/½oz/½ cup shredded kale
50g/2oz/½ cup fresh or frozen raspberries
50g/2oz/½ cup fresh or frozen blackberries
100ml/3½fl oz/scant ½ cup coconut milk

For the topping
50ml/2oz mixed berries, defrosted if frozen
10ml/2 tsp pumpkin seeds
5ml/1 tsp sunflower seeds
15ml/1 tbsp ground flaxseeds
a few toasted coconut shavings

SERVES 1

1 Add the oatmeal and water to a small pan, bring to the boil, then simmer gently for 15–20 minutes, stirring until the oatmeal is tender and almost all the liquid has been absorbed.

2 Add the beetroot, kale, berries and coconut milk to a blender goblet. Screw on the lid and blitz until smooth. Stir into the oatmeal and warm through.

3 Pour into a bowl and top with the extra berries, whole and ground seeds and a few coconut shavings.

Oatmeal v porridge oats
Oatmeal is the whole oat groat or grain that is cut either with metal blades or in Scotland by stones; sometimes called pinhead oatmeal it can be bought in different grades, coarse, medium or fine. Rolled oats are steamed then rolled flat; quick-cook oats have just been steamed for longer before rolling. Both are rich in fibre, which can help to lower cholesterol, plus they contain protein, B vitamins, vitamin E, calcium, iron and potassium.

Energy 260kcal/1100kJ; Protein 10g; Carbohydrate 38g, of which sugars 17.6g; Fat 8.7g, of which saturates 1.2g; Cholesterol 0mg; Calcium 127mg; Fibre 11g; Sodium 180mg.

Bircher muesli pots

These delicious energy-giving porridge and fruit pots are easy to make and will fill you up until lunchtime. Make the pots the day before, even two days in advance, add a well-fitting lid and keep in the refrigerator. Add a colourful fruit topping of your choice from the selection below just before serving.

50g/2oz/¹/₃ cup mixed unblanched hazelnuts, almonds and Brazil nuts, roughly chopped
20ml/4 tsp ground flaxseeds
110g/4oz/1 cup rolled oats
1.5ml/¹/₄ tsp ground cinnamon

1 dessert apple, cored and coarsely grated, no need to peel
250ml/8 floz/1 cup dairy-free yogurt
60ml/4 tbsp fresh orange juice

MAKES 6

1 Add the nuts, seeds, oats and cinnamon to a bowl and stir together. Add the grated apple, yogurt and orange juice then stir together.

2 Divide the mixture evenly between six small glass pots with lids and smooth the tops level. Cover and chill in the refrigerator until ready to serve.

Toppings, each enough for 2 pots
Very berrytastic: Purée 100g/3¹/₄ oz hulled strawberries in a blender until smooth. Spoon over the two pots and top with 5 blueberries and 2 blackberries each.
Mango and chia: Purée 100g/3¹/₄ oz prepared mango flesh with 30ml/2 tbsp lime or orange juice or water in a blender until smooth. Stir in 2.5ml/¹/₂ tsp chia seeds then spoon over the top of the pots and decorate with a few pomegranates.
Banana, cacao and coconut: Mix 60ml/4 tbsp dairy-free yogurt with 15ml/1 tbsp cacao powder and 10ml/2 tsp date syrup, and spoon over the pots. Top each pot with ¹/₄ small sliced banana, a few roughly chopped goji berries and a sprinkling of coconut flakes.
Green dream: Peel and dice 1 kiwi fruit and mix with 25g/1 oz/8 green seedless grapes, halved. Spoon over the top of the pots.
Red delight: Purée 100g/3¹/₄ oz hulled strawberries in a blender until smooth. Spoon over the pots and top each with 4 raspberries and a couple of hulled and halved strawberries.

Cook's tip
If you find your Bircher pots are a little too thick for your taste, just add a little extra plant milk to the mix.

Base: Energy 28kcal/119kJ; Protein 1.1g; Carbohydrate 3.4g, of which sugars 0.9g; Fat 1.2g, of which saturates 0.1g; Cholesterol 0mg; Calcium 16mg; Fibre 0.5g; Sodium 7.6mg.
Berrytastic: Energy 10.5kcal/44kJ; Protein 0.25g; Carbohydrate 2.4g, of which sugars 2.2g; Fat 0.05g, of which saturates 0g; Cholesterol 0mg; Calcium 6.5mg; Fibre 0.75g; Sodium 2mg.
Mango: Energy 18kcal/76kJ; Protein 0.35g; Carbohydrate 3.7g, of which sugars 3.6g; Fat 0.3g, of which saturates 0.05g; Cholesterol 0mg; Calcium 7mg; Fibre 1.2g; Sodium 7mg.
Banana: Energy 34kcal/143.5kJ; Protein 1.25g; Carbohydrate 6.8g, of which sugars 6.35g; Fat 0.4g, of which saturates 0.05g; Cholesterol 0mg; Calcium 27mg; Fibre 0.4g; Sodium 2.5mg.
Green: Energy 11kcal/47kJ; Protein 0.2g; Carbohydrate 2.55g, of which sugars 2.5g; Fat 0.1g, of which saturates 0g; Cholesterol 0mg; Calcium 4.5mg; Fibre 0.45g; Sodium 1mg.
Red: Energy 9kcal/37kJ; Protein 0.3g; Carbohydrate 1.9g, of which sugars 1/9g; Fat 0.05g, of which saturates 0g; Cholesterol 0mg; Calcium 6mg; Fibre 0.65g; Sodium 2mg.

Pecan crunch

Pecan nuts are high in healthy unsaturated fat and just a handful a day can help
to lower 'bad' cholesterol. They also contain more than 19 vitamins and minerals so are
a super-nutritious way to start the day. Serve this tasty crunchy cereal simply with soya
or rice milk or, for a real treat, with soya yogurt and a handful of seasonal fresh fruits.

200g/7oz/1³/₄ cups rolled oats
150g/5oz/1¹/₄ cups pecan nuts,
  roughly chopped
90ml/6 tbsp agave syrup
75g/3oz/6 tbsp dairy-free margarine

SERVES 6

1 Preheat the oven to 160°C/325°F/ Gas 3. Put all the
ingredients together into a bowl and mix well.

2 Spread the mixture on to a large baking tray. Bake for
30–35 minutes, or until golden and crunchy. Leave to cool,
then break up into clumps and serve.

Cook's tip
This crunchy oat cereal will keep in an airtight container for
up to two weeks. Store the container in a cool, dry place.

Variations
• For a gluten-free version, use a mixture of buckwheat,
quinoa flakes and puffed rice in place of the rolled oats.
• Use walnuts in place of pecans for an omega 3 boost.

Energy 245kcal/1016kJ; Protein 3.5g; Carbohydrate 26.4g, of which sugars 7.8g; Fat 14.1g, of which saturates 1.4g; Cholesterol 0mg; Calcium 64mg; Fibre 2.8g; Sodium 402mg.

Chestnut mushrooms on toast

There is nothing more satisfying – and quick to prepare – than a couple of rounds of toast topped with delicious fried mushrooms. You can use any mushrooms in this recipe, but chestnut mushrooms are slightly darker in colour and have a richer flavour than white ones. Oat milk makes a fabulously rich and tasty sauce.

250g/9oz chestnut mushrooms
15ml/1 tbsp avocado or nut oil
120ml/4fl oz/$^1/_2$ cup oat milk
salt and ground black pepper
2 thick slices of wholemeal (wholewheat) bread
chopped chives, to garnish

SERVES 2

1 Pick over and trim the mushrooms, wipe them clean with kitchen paper if necessary, then cut them into thick slices.

2 Heat the oil in a non-stick pan, add the mushrooms and cook quickly for about 3 minutes, stirring frequently.

3 Tip the mushrooms into a bowl and set aside. Add the oat milk to the pan. Simmer for 4–5 minutes or until reduced by half. Add the mushrooms, season with salt and pepper and simmer for 2 minutes.

4 Toast the bread. Divide the mixture between the two pieces of toast, garnish with chopped chives and serve.

Other toast toppings
• In a bowl, roughly smash a ripe avocado with a fork, season with plenty of salt and black pepper, and generously spread on sourdough toast to make a great breakfast treat.
• Spread blackbean hummus thickly onto lightly toasted wholemeal bread, sprinkle with sesame seeds and slices of cucumber.
• Cream together 2 tablespoons of dairy-free margarine with 2 teaspoons ground cinnamon, 1 tablespoon agave syrup and 1 teaspoon of tahini and spread on lightly toasted bread, served with chopped fresh fruit, if you like.

Energy 199kcal/838kJ; Protein 7.9g; Carbohydrate 25.5g, of which sugars 1.7g; Fat 8.1g, of which saturates 1.2g; Cholesterol 0mg; Calcium 71mg; Fibre 3.2g; Sodium 286mg.

Pecan nut and caramel banana pancakes

These pancakes are more like drop scones than the classic thin French crêpes.
Bananas and pecan nuts, cooked in maple syrup, make a sweet and delicious topping.

75g/3oz/²/3 cup plain (all-purpose) flour
50g/2oz/¹/2 cup wholemeal
(wholewheat) flour
50g/2oz/generous ¹/2 cup rolled oats
5ml/1 tsp baking powder
25g/1oz/2 tbsp soft light brown sugar
15ml/1 tbsp rapeseed (canola) oil,
plus extra for frying
250ml/8fl oz/1 cup plant milk
pinch of salt

For the caramel nut bananas
50g/2oz/¹/4 cup dairy-free margarine
15ml/1 tbsp maple syrup
3 bananas, halved and quartered lengthways
25g/1oz/¹/4 cup pecan nuts

SERVES 4

1 To make the pancakes, mix together the two flours, oats, baking powder, sugar and a pinch of salt in a bowl.

2 Make a well in the centre of the flour mixture and add the oil and a quarter of the milk. Mix well, then gradually add the rest of the plant milk to make a thick batter. Leave to rest for 20 minutes in the refrigerator.

3 Heat a large, heavy, lightly oiled frying pan. Using about 30ml/2 tbsp of batter for each pancake, cook two to three pancakes in the pan at a time. Cook for about 3 minutes on each side or until golden. Keep warm while you cook the remaining pancakes.

4 To make the caramel bananas and pecan nuts, wipe out the frying pan and add the dairy-free margarine. Heat gently until the margarine melts, then add the maple syrup and stir well. Add the bananas and pecan nuts to the pan.

5 Cook, turning once, for about 4 minutes or until the bananas have just started to soften and the sauce has caramelized.

6 To serve, place two pancakes on each of five warm plates and top with the caramel bananas and pecan nuts. Serve immediately.

Nutrition note
Bananas are a good source of energy, making them an excellent food to start the day. They also contain potassium, which is essential for the functioning of cells in our bodies.

Energy 417kcal/1744kJ; Protein 6.8g; Carbohydrate 48.8g, of which sugars 21.3g; Fat 22.8g, of which saturates 5.1g; Cholesterol 2mg; Calcium 42mg; Fibre 3.2g; Sodium 109mg.

Buckwheat pancakes with apple and cinnamon

Buckwheat is a great source of all eight essential amino acids. Spiced pan-fried apple slices create a scrumptious topping for these nutritious pancakes.

50g/2oz/¹/2 cup buckwheat flour
50g/2oz/¹/2 cup rice flour
15ml/1 tbsp coconut oil
300ml/¹/2 pint/1¹/4 cups plant milk
10ml/2 tsp arrowroot
rapeseed (canola oil), for frying
pinch of salt

For the spiced apple slices
3 cooking apples, peeled, cored and sliced
50ml/2fl oz/¹/4 cup agave syrup
60ml/4 tbsp dairy-free margarine
30-45ml/2-3 tbsp lemon juice
5-10ml/1-2 tsp ground cinnamon
dairy-free cream cheese, to serve
fresh mint sprigs, to garnish

SERVES 4

1 To make the pancakes, place the buckwheat flour, rice flour and a pinch of salt in a bowl and make a well in the centre of the flour. Add the coconut oil and a little of the plant milk, beating well with a wooden spoon.

2 Gradually beat in the remaining milk, drawing the flour in from the sides to make a smooth batter.

3 Heat a little rapeseed oil in a large, heavy, lightly oiled frying pan. Pour in enough batter to coat the base of the pan thinly. Cook until golden brown, then turn the pancake over and cook on the other side.

4 Transfer the cooked pancake to a warmed plate and keep warm while you cook the remaining pancakes.

5 Toss the apple slices in the agave syrup in a mixing bowl until the pieces are evenly coated.

6 Melt the dairy-free margarine in a large frying pan, add the apple slices to the pan and cook over a high heat, stirring frequently for about 5 minutes, or until the apple slices have softened slightly and the sugar has caramelized.

7 Remove the pan from the heat and sprinkle the cooked apple slices with the lemon juice and the cinnamon.

8 Place the warm pancakes on plates, allowing two per person. Top with the cooked apples and some dairy-free cream cheese sprinkled with a little extra ground cinnamon, if you like. Serve immediately, garnished with a few fresh mint leaves.

Variation
Use pears in place of the apples and mixed (apple pie) spice instead of the cinnamon. Fresh apricots work well in this recipe too.

Energy 355kcal/1487kJ; Protein 13.5g; Carbohydrate 49.2g, of which sugars 5.3g; Fat 12.2g, of which saturates 1.2g; Cholesterol 0mg; Calcium 85mg; Fibre 4.7g; Sodium 25mg.

Granola breakfast bars

A gloriously dense fruity, nutty and oaty mixture, packed with goodness and delicious too, these bars are an ideal grab-and-go breakfast when you are short of time in the morning.

175g/6oz/³/4 cup dairy-free margarine, diced
150ml/¹/4 pint/²/3 cup agave syrup
250g/9oz/generous 1 cup demerara (raw) sugar
350g/12oz/3 cups rolled oats
5ml/1 tsp ground cinnamon
75g/3oz/³/4 cup pecan nut halves
75g/3oz/generous ¹/2 cup raisins

75g/3oz/³/4 cup ready-to-eat dried papaya, chopped
75g/3oz/scant ¹/2 cup ready-to-eat dried apricots, chopped
50g/2oz/scant ¹/2 cup pumpkin seeds
50g/2oz/scant ¹/2 cup sunflower seeds
50g/2oz/4 tbsp sesame seeds
45ml/3 tbsp ground almonds

MAKES 6

1 Preheat the oven to 190°C/375°F/Gas 5. Line a 23cm/9in square cake tin or pan with baking parchment.

2 Put the margarine and agave syrup in a large heavy pan and heat gently until the margarine has melted and the mixture is completely smooth.

3 Add the demerara sugar to the pan and heat very gently, stirring the mixture constantly, until the sugar has completely dissolved.

4 Bring the mixture to the boil and continue to boil for 1–2 minutes. Stir the mixture constantly to prevent it sticking until it has formed a smooth caramel sauce.

5 Add the remaining ingredients and mix together. Transfer the mixture to the tin and press down with a spoon. Bake for 15 minutes until the edges turn brown.

6 Place in the refrigerator and chill well. Turn out of the tin, peel off the parchment and cut into bars.

Variations
• To make this recipe lower in fat, swap the margarine for grated carrot.
• To reduce the sugar content slightly, use apricot purée (blend dried apricots in a little orange juice) in place of the agave syrup.
• Add in 2 tablespoons of hempseed to up the omega 3 content.

Energy 522kcal/2189kJ; Protein 8.4g; Carbohydrate 63.8g, of which sugars 40.9g; Fat 27.7g, of which saturates 8.9g; Cholesterol 31mg; Calcium 93mg; Fibre 4.3g; Sodium 108mg.

Prune double deckers

Prunes reputedly have more antioxidants than blueberries, although wild blueberries come a close second. Don't think of them just as a laxative, they are also rich in potassium, which helps to regulate blood pressure. Figs would also work well in this recipe.

200g/7oz/1 cup ready-to-eat pitted prunes
90ml/6 tbsp water
5ml/1 tsp vanilla extract
100g/3³/₄oz/¹/₂ cup dairy-free margarine
30ml/2 tbsp smooth unsweetened peanut butter
50g/2oz/¹/₃ cup light muscovado (brown) sugar

1 medium banana
100g/3³/₄oz/1 cup quinoa flakes
150g/5oz/1¹/₂ cups rolled oats
40g/1¹/₂oz/¹/₄ cup sunflower seeds

MAKES 12

1 Preheat the oven to 180°C/350°F/Gas 4. Line a shallow square 20cm/8in cake tin or pan with a larger piece of baking parchment, snip into the corners of the paper and press down to line the base and sides.

2 Add the prunes, water and vanilla to a food processor and blend until a coarse purée.

3 Melt the margarine in a medium pan then stir in the peanut butter and sugar. Mash the banana with a fork then add to the pan with the quinoa, oats and sunflower seeds. Stir the mixture together then spoon two-thirds into the prepared tin and spread into an even thickness.

4 Spoon the prune purée over the top and spread into an even layer then sprinkle with the remaining oat mixture and lightly press into the prunes. Bake for about 25 minutes until the top is golden brown.

5 Mark into 12 pieces then leave to cool in the tin. Remove from the tin, peel off the paper and pack into a plastic container. Eat within 2 days.

Nutrition note
Oats contain a high level of soluble fibre, one of which is called beta-glucan, which has been proven to reduce overall cholesterol levels. Another effect of the soluble fibre is to slow down the energy release from the oats, which makes you feel fuller for longer.

Variation
The peanut butter can be replaced with any other nut butter of your choice.

Energy 18kcal/74kJ; Protein 0.4g; Carbohydrate 25.3g, of which sugars 2.1g; Fat 0.9g, of which saturates 0.2g; Cholesterol 0mg; Calcium 1.8mg; Fibre 0.4g; Sodium 12mg.

Double peanut protein balls

These power balls are flecked with chunky pieces of roasted peanut and make a great protein- and energy-booster when you feel yourself flagging. Expensive to buy, they are really simple to make your own. They will keep a week in the refrigerator, or freeze them and add to your packed lunch to help keep your lunch cool.

5 Medjool dates, stoned (pitted)
110g/4oz/1 cup rolled oats
30ml/2 tbsp ground flaxseeds
30ml/2 tbsp unsweetened crunchy peanut butter
75g/3oz/¹/₂ cup roasted salted peanuts
45ml/3 tbsp unsweetened almond milk

MAKES 16

1 Add the dates and oats to a food processor and blitz until finely chopped.

2 Add the flaxseeds, peanut butter and peanuts then add the almond milk and blend briefly until the mixture begins to clump together and the nuts are still quite chunky.

3 Squeeze the mixture into a ball, take out of the processor, roll into a thick sausage and cut into 16 even pieces. Roll each piece in the palm of your hands to make a smooth ball. Pack into a plastic container, interleaving with layers of baking parchment. Store in the refrigerator for up to 3 days.

Nutrition note
A jar of good peanut butter will contain 26.9g of protein per 100g which is pretty good. Choose a brand without added sugar, salt or palm oil. Peanuts are also a good source of B vitamins and minerals, copper, phosphorous, magnesium and zinc.

Cook's tip
To make them into an indulgent treat, put half a date in the middle and cover them in dark chocolate.

Energy 94kcal/394kJ; Protein 3.1g; Carbohydrate 11.2g, of which sugars 5.1g; Fat 4.4g, of which saturates 0.7g; Cholesterol 0mg; Calcium 10mg; Fibre 1.8g; Sodium 17mg.

Gingered apricot energy balls

This healthier take on chocolate truffles is packed with slow-release carbs for sustained energy, and essential fatty acids and minerals.

50g/2oz/^{1}/$_3$ cup mixed pumpkin and sunflower seeds
50g/2oz/^{1}/$_2$ cup rolled oats
100g/3^3/$_4$oz/^{1}/$_2$ cup ready-to-eat dried apricots
25g/1 oz dried goji berries
10g/^{1}/$_4$oz root ginger, peeled and finely chopped
45ml/3 tbsp quinoa flakes
30ml/2 tbsp pressed cloudy apple juice
20ml/4 tsp hemp oil
20ml/4 tsp maple syrup
10ml/2 tsp raw cacao powder, for dusting

MAKES 12

1 Add the seeds and oats to a blender or food processor and roughly chop. If using a blender, tip the mixture into a bowl then finely chop the apricots, goji berries and ginger and stir into the oats, along with the quinoa flakes. Add the apple juice, oil and syrup and mix together with a spoon then your hands to make a coarse paste.

2 If using a food processor, add the apricots, goji berries and ginger to the chopped seeds and oats in the food processor and blitz until the apricots are chopped. Add the quinoa flakes, apple juice, oil and maple syrup and blitz again until the mixture binds together.

3 Divide the mixture into 12 even-sized mounds then roll in your hands to make small balls. Put the cacao powder on a sheet of baking parchment and roll the truffles in the cacao until lightly dusted. Store in a plastic container in the refrigerator for up to 3 days.

Cook's tips
• If you don't have any hemp oil then use omega 3 rich rapeseed (canola) oil or walnut oil, or melt 20ml/4 tsp coconut oil and then stir into the mixture.
• If you want them gluten-free, just use gluten-free oats (that have been kept away from other grains).

Variations
Variety is the spice of life. Vary your balls so you don't get bored with them. Swap apricots with prunes, sunflower seeds with de-hulled hemp seed hearts, ginger with fresh turmeric – you will soon find your perfect version.

Energy 9.25kcal/27.5kJ; Protein 0.2g; Carbohydrate 0.97g, of which sugars 0.5g; Fat 0.3g, of which saturates 0.04g; Cholesterol 0mg; Calcium 1mg; Fibre 0.15g; Sodium 2mg.

Mushroom and pine nut muffins

These light savoury muffins are an attractive breakfast or weekend brunch treat.
The pine nuts are decorative as well as adding texture and crunch, and a warm nutty flavour.
Serve them freshly baked and warm to enjoy them at their best.

30ml/2 tbsp apple cider vinegar
10ml/2 tsp bicarbonate of soda (baking soda)
250g/9oz/2$\frac{1}{2}$ cups plain (all-purpose) flour
15ml/3 tsp baking powder
150g/5oz mixed mushrooms
90ml/6 tbsp/scant $\frac{1}{2}$ cup vegetable oil,
for frying

large pinch cayenne pepper
large pinch mace
75g/3oz/$\frac{3}{4}$ cup pine nuts
90ml/6 tbsp plant milk
75g/3oz/6 tbsp dairy-free margarine, melted

MAKES 6-7 LARGE MUFFINS

1 Preheat the oven to 180°C/350°F/Gas 4. Lightly grease the cups of a muffin tin or pan.

2 In a small bowl, mix together the apple cider vinegar and bicarbonate of soda and set aside while it bubbles.

3 In a large bowl, sift the flour and baking powder and set aside.

4 Clean and slice the mushrooms. In a frying pan, heat 75ml/3oz/6 tbsp of the vegetable oil over a medium heat. When it is just bubbling, add the mushrooms. Season with cayenne pepper and mace. Fry gently, stirring, until just softened. Scrape into a bowl and set aside to cool.

5 Fry the pine nuts in the remaining vegetable oil for 30 seconds. Add to the mushrooms.

6 Beat together the milk, melted margarine and vinegar mixture in a bowl. Stir into the dry ingredients with the mushrooms and pine nuts.

7 Spoon the batter into the muffin tins and bake for 25 minutes until the tops are golden.

Cook's tip
Buy a packet of wild mushrooms for the best flavour and taste.

Energy 399kcal/1660kJ; Protein 6.9g; Carbohydrate 28g, of which sugars 1.4g; Fat 29.6g, of which saturates 14.2g; Cholesterol 109mg; Calcium 154mg; Fibre 1.5g; Sodium 334mg.

Classic cooked breakfast

There are few more famous – or more filling – breakfasts than the classic full breakfast. Thankfully there is no need to give up this traditional favourite because there are vegan versions of everything from vegan bacon and sausages to black pudding and haggis. This version also features a delicious tofu and corn mixture, soya cheese on toast and smoked tempeh. Feel free to use ingredients based on your preferences or what is available.

1 large fresh tomato
30ml/2 tbsp olive oil
15ml/1 tbsp soy sauce
2 vegan sausages
2 frozen potato croquettes or potato waffles
6 medium mushrooms
2 slices smoked soya tempeh
15ml/1 tbsp soya cream cheese
15ml/1 tbsp tomato ketchup
2.5ml/¹/₂ tsp yeast extract

2.5ml/¹/₂ tsp mustard
2 slices wholemeal (wholewheat) bread
20g/³/₄ oz fresh tofu
25g/1 oz frozen or canned corn
5ml/1 tsp dairy-free margarine
200g/7oz can baked beans
salt and ground black pepper

SERVES 2

1 Preheat the oven to 180°C/350°F/Gas 4. Cut the tomato in half and season with salt and pepper.

2 Mix the olive oil with the soy sauce in a cup and lightly brush the mix on to the sausages. Place the sausages on a baking tray with the tomato halves and the potato croquettes or waffles and bake for 10 minutes in the oven.

3 Meanwhile, lightly brush the oil mixture over the mushrooms and the soya tempeh.

4 Mix the soya cream cheese with the tomato ketchup, yeast extract and mustard until well blended.

5 When the sausages have been in the oven for 10 minutes, turn them over. Add the mushrooms, tempeh and both slices of bread and return everything to the oven. Cook for another 10–15 minutes until everything is golden brown and tender.

6 Blend together the tofu and the corn with the margarine. Season with salt and pepper. Place the mixture in a pan and simmer gently, stirring frequently, until heated through.

7 In a separate pan, simmer the baked beans for about 5 minutes until piping hot.

8 Meanwhile, toast the bread and spread the soya cheese and tomato ketchup mixture evenly over both slices. Cut the toasted bread slices in half diagonally and divide everything between two plates. Serve immediately with freshly squeezed juice, herb tea, tomato ketchup, brown sauce and mustard.

Cook's tip

Spread some yeast extract onto your toast to sneak in some vitamin B12, sprinkle on some hemp seeds to up the omega 3 levels, and add some seaweed culinary seasoning into the scrambled tofu to boost your iodine levels. You can make bubble and squeak with sweet potato as a base or add smashed avocado.

Energy 526kcal/2205kJ; Protein 23.8g; Carbohydrate 53.9g, of which sugars 9.7g; Fat 27.8g, of which saturates 4.7g; Cholesterol 0mg; Calcium 409mg; Fibre 9.2g; Sodium 1744mg.

Muesli smoothie

A great breakfast booster, this store-cupboard smoothie can be a vegan's lifesaver if you have run out of fresh fruit.

1 piece preserved stem ginger, plus
    30ml/2 tbsp syrup from the
    ginger jar
50g/2oz/½ cup ready-to-eat dried
    apricots, halved or quartered
40g/1½oz/scant ½ cup natural
    muesli (granola)
200ml/7fl oz/scant 1 cup plant milk

SERVES 2

1 Chop the ginger and put it in a food processor or blender with the syrup, apricots, muesli and milk.

2 Process the mixture until smooth, adding more milk if necessary. Pour into glasses and serve immediately.

Cook's tip
You can try adding in a little chlorella algae or green drink powder made from freeze-dried plant extracts; just add a little at a time so you do not overpower it.

Vitamin C supercharge

For people that don't like kale, sneaking it into a smoothie with lots of berries may be the perfect solution to increase your green consumption.

a handful of shredded kale
50g/2oz/½ cup blueberries
75g/3oz or 3 strawberries, hulled and quartered
120ml/4 fl oz/½ cup dairy-free yogurt
15ml/1 tbsp ground seed mix, see below
120ml/4fl oz/½ cup water, or to taste

SERVES 1

1 Add all the ingredients to a blender, add the lid and blitz until smooth and frothy. Stir in a little extra water if needed then pour into a tall glass.

Ground seed mix
(Makes 125g/4¼ oz/generous 1 cup):
Add 45g/3 tbsp each of sesame, sunflower, pumpkin and golden flaxseeds to a blender or spice mill, and blend until finely ground. Scoop out and store in a sealed plastic container in the refrigerator for up to 2 weeks.

Muesli: Energy 203kcal/862kJ; Protein 6.4g; Carbohydrate 40.1g, of which sugars 30.9g; Fat 3.2g, of which saturates 1.3g; Cholesterol 6mg; Calcium 163mg; Fibre 2.9g; Sodium 163mg.
Vitamin C: Energy 209kcal/875kJ; Protein 9.9g; Carbohydrate 23.8g, of which sugars 19g; Fat 8.9g, of which saturates 1.8g; Cholesterol 2mg; Calcium 247mg; Fibre 4.9g; Sodium 89mg.

Red berry smoothie

Cranberries make a tasty dairy-free shake when combined with soya milk. This blend is packed with natural sugars, and essential nutrients.

25g/1oz/¹/₄ cup dried cranberries
150g/5oz/1¹/₄ cups redcurrants, plus extra
  to decorate
10ml/2 tsp agave syrup
50ml/2fl oz/¹/₄ cup soya milk
sparkling mineral water

SERVES 1

1 Put the cranberries in a small bowl, pour over 90ml/6 tbsp boiling water and leave to stand for 10 minutes.

2 Put the redcurrants in a food processor or blender with the cranberries and soaking water. Blend well until smooth.

3 Add the agave syrup and milk to the processor or blender and whizz briefly to combine the ingredients.

4 Pour the berry mixture into a large glass, then top up with a little sparkling mineral water to lighten the drink and add a little fizz. Decorate with redcurrants draped over the glass.

Cacao comforter

You don't need to miss out on a chocolate fix when eating more healthily. This super-filling meal in a glass will sustain you until lunchtime.

10ml/2 tsp raw cacao powder
pinch ground cinnamon
250ml/8fl oz/1 cup unsweetened almond milk
50g/2oz or 3 cauliflower florets
a handful of shredded kale
1 large date, stoned (pitted)
¹/₂ banana

SERVES 1

1 Add all the ingredients to a blender, add the lid and blitz until smooth and frothy. Adjust the consistency with a little water or extra almond milk if needed then pour into a tall glass to serve.

Cook's tip
Unsweetened almond milk has been suggested in this recipe but rice milk or oat milk would also work just well. They are all fortified with extra calcium, vitamin B12 and vitamin D, plus they are low in fat and lactose-free, although calorie counts vary slightly.

Red berry: Energy 126kcal/539kJ; Protein 3.8g; Carbohydrate 27.1g, of which sugars 27.1g; Fat 0.9g, of which saturates 0.2g; Cholesterol 0mg; Calcium 115mg; Fibre 7g; Sodium 25mg.
Cacao: Energy 242kcal/1023kJ; Protein 6.5g; Carbohydrate 47.7g, of which sugars 44.7g; Fat 4.2g, of which saturates 0.8g; Cholesterol 0mg; Calcium 65mg; Fibre 5.7g; Sodium 223mg.

SOUPS AND SNACKS

Whether you want a warming soup, a tempting appetizer or a party
snack, this chapter is full of delicious ideas for plant-based comfort food
at its very best. Roasted Butternut Squash Soup or Red Bean Soup with
Salsa provide a simple and satisfying way to get lots of essential nutrients.
Hummus or Aubergine Dip make a great snack with pitta bread, or
for a special occasion you can impress guests by serving Tofu
Dragon Balls or Coconut Patties.

Country lentil soup

The secret of a good lentil soup is to be generous with the olive oil.
This dish can serve as a main meal, accompanied by bread and olives.

275g/10oz/1¼ cups brown or green lentils
150ml/¼ pint/⅔ cup extra virgin olive oil
1 onion, thinly sliced
2 garlic cloves, sliced into thin batons
1 carrot, thinly sliced
400g/14oz can chopped tomatoes
15ml/1 tbsp tomato purée (paste)

2.5ml/½ tsp dried oregano
salt and ground black pepper
25g/1oz roughly chopped fresh herbs,
  to garnish

SERVES 4

1 Rinse the lentils, drain them and put them in a large pan with enough cold water to cover. Bring to the boil and boil for 3–4 minutes. Strain, discarding the liquid, and set the lentils aside.

2 Wipe the pan clean, heat the olive oil in it, then add the onion and sauté until translucent. Stir in the garlic, then, as soon as it becomes aromatic, return the lentils to the pan. Add the carrot, tomatoes, tomato purée and oregano. Stir in 1 litre/1¾ pints/4 cups hot water and a little pepper to taste.

3 Bring to the boil, then lower the heat, cover the pan and cook gently for 20–30 minutes until the lentils feel soft but have not begun to disintegrate. Add salt and the chopped herbs just before serving.

Nutrition note
These little pulses are oozing with goodness. They contain high levels of soluble fibre, thereby helping to lower cholesterol. They are a good source of iron and protein, are low in calories and have virtually no fat. It would be a crime not to include them in your weekly meal plans.

Energy 463kcal/1937kJ; Protein 17.9g; Carbohydrate 40.4g, of which sugars 7.2g; Fat 26.7g, of which saturates 3.9g; Cholesterol 0mg; Calcium 67mg; Fibre 8g; Sodium 33mg.

Vegetable seaweed soup

Over 50% of people could be low in iodine. Eating seaweed may help. This soup is also a good way to use up leftover vegetables and reach the seven-a-day vegetable target. Sea spaghetti lends substance as well as flavour and, if you choose not to blend the soup, makes a vegetable alternative to noodles.

**75g/3oz fresh sea spaghetti or
10g/¹/₄oz dried sea spaghetti
glug of olive oil
2 leeks, sliced
2 courgettes (zucchini), diced
200g/7oz/1³/₄ cups frozen peas
15ml/1 tbsp mixed seaweeds**

**200g/7oz spinach
200g/7oz spring greens or cabbage, diced
1.3 litres/2¹/₄ pints/5¹/₂ cups vegetable stock
a couple of handfuls of fresh basil
seaweed salt and ground black pepper, to taste**

SERVES 4

1 If using dried sea spaghetti, rehydrate it in cold water for 10 minutes prior to cooking. The water can be used to make up some of the stock.

2 Heat the olive oil in a large pan, then add the leeks and fry gently for a few minutes, until starting to soften. Add the courgettes and cook until they and the leeks are softened.

3 Add the peas, sea spaghetti, mixed seaweeds, spinach and spring greens or cabbage, then cover with the stock.

4 Bring to the boil and simmer for 20 minutes or until everything is very soft.

5 Add the fresh basil and blend until smooth, or leave it chunky, if you prefer. Season to taste with salt and ground black pepper and serve immediately.

Nutrition note
Sea spaghetti tastes like mildly salted asparagus when young and fresh. It adds a meaty flavour to stocks and soups and is packed full of calcium, magnesium, zinc, iodine and vitamins A, E, C and B.

Energy 145kcal/603kJ; Protein 8.2g; Carbohydrate 12.1g, of which sugars 7.9g; Fat 7.3g, of which saturates 1.1g; Cholesterol 0mg; Calcium 183mg; Fibre 12.9g; Sodium 90mg.

Curried cauliflower and nut milk soup

This lightly spiced soup is both simple and satisfying. Serve with warm, crusty bread or with naan bread, and garnish with sprigs of fresh coriander.

750ml/1¼ pints/3 cups cashew nut milk
1 large cauliflower, broken or cut into florets
15ml/1 tbsp garam masala
salt and ground black pepper, to taste
fresh coriander (cilantro) leaves, to garnish

SERVES 4

1 Put the milk, cauliflower, garam masala and seasoning in a pan and place over a medium heat. Bring to the boil, then reduce the heat, partially cover the pan and simmer for 20 minutes, until the cauliflower is tender.

2 Leave to cool for a few minutes, then process until smooth. Heat through without boiling.

3 Ladle the soup into warmed bowls. Sprinkle with a few fresh coriander leaves and serve immediately.

Cook's tip
This soup would work equally well with other nut soups such as almond or chestnut. For information on making your own nut milks turn to page 34 of the introduction.

Nutrition note
Cashew nuts are especially good for vegans as they contain high amounts of both iron and zinc. As zinc is not stored in the body, a daily intake is needed. Cashews are also rich in protein, potassium, magnesium, vitamin B6, and folate, which is important for pregnant women.

Energy 197kcal/823kJ; Protein 10.1g; Carbohydrate 17.6g, of which sugars 10.1g; Fat 10.5g, of which saturates 2g; Cholesterol 0mg; Calcium 68mg; Fibre 5.2g; Sodium 175mg.

Saffron, almond and onion soup

The combination of onions and saffron gives this pale yellow soup a beguiling and distinctive flavour. It will make the perfect appetizer for a special vegan meal for friends or family.

45ml/3 tbsp coconut oil
2 large yellow onions, thinly sliced
1 small garlic clove, finely chopped
pinch of saffron threads
50g/2oz blanched almonds,
toasted and finely ground
750ml/1^1/$_4$ pints/3 cups vegetable stock
2.5ml/^{1}/$_2$ tsp paprika
salt and ground black pepper
25g/1oz flaked or sliced almonds, toasted and
chopped fresh parsley, to garnish

SERVES 4

1 Heat the coconut oil in a heavy pan over a low heat. Add the onions and garlic, stirring to ensure that they are thoroughly coated in the oil.

2 Cover the pan and cook very gently, stirring frequently, for about 20 minutes, or until the onions have softened and turned golden yellow.

3 Add the saffron threads to the pan and cook, uncovered, for 3–4 minutes, then add the finely ground almonds and cook, stirring the ingredients constantly, for a further 2–3 minutes.

4 Pour the vegetable stock into the pan and stir in 5ml/1 tsp salt and the paprika. Season with plenty of black pepper. Bring to the boil, then lower the heat and simmer gently for about 10 minutes.

5 Pour the soup into a food processor or blender and process until smooth, then return it to the rinsed pan. Reheat slowly, without allowing the soup to boil, stirring occasionally. Taste for seasoning, adding more salt and pepper if required.

6 Ladle the soup into warmed bowls. Garnish each serving with the toasted flaked almonds and a little chopped fresh parsley and serve immediately.

Blanching almonds
Removing the brown papery skins from almonds is known as 'blanching'. Put the almonds in a heatproof bowl and pour over enough boiling water to cover the nuts by about 2.5cm/1in. Leave to soak until the water is tepid and the almonds cool enough to handle. Drain the almonds, then squeeze the nuts out of the brown skins; they should slide out easily. Discard the skins. The blanched almonds can now be toasted, ground or soaked to make milk.

Energy 255kcal/1054kJ; Protein 5.8g; Carbohydrate 11.5g, of which sugars 8.1g; Fat 19.6g, of which saturates 6.1g; Cholesterol 21mg; Calcium 82mg; Fibre 3.2g; Sodium 68mg.

Miso mushroom and roasted squash ramen

Quick, sustaining and delicious, ramen is low-fat, healthy and full of deep and satisfying flavours. In its simplest form, ramen combines wheat noodles, a tasty base broth, a salt or soy 'tare', and carefully selected toppings, and is ideally suited to vegan cuisine. In this recipe the miso adds plenty of umami flavouring which marries perfectly with sweet roasted squash.

1 butternut squash, peeled, halved, seeds removed and cubed
15ml/1 tbsp olive oil
pinch of sea salt
freshly ground black pepper
pinch of chilli flakes
30ml/2 tbsp white miso
30ml/2 tbsp mirin
15ml/1 tbsp rice vinegar

1.75 litres/3 pints/7½ cups vegetable stock
500g/1¼lb ramen noodles
200g/7oz chestnut mushrooms, sliced
2-3 spring onions (scallions), green parts only, finely sliced
1 fresh red chilli, sliced
a handful of purple shiso leaves
10ml/2 tsp sesame seeds, toasted

SERVES 4

1 Preheat the oven to 200°C/400°F/Gas 6. Add the squash to a large roasting pan, sprinkle with the olive oil, season with sea salt and black pepper and scatter over the chilli flakes. Toss together using your hands. Put in the oven and cook for about 30–35 minutes or until the squash is golden and tender.

2 While that is cooking, mix together the white miso, mirin and rice vinegar and add to the stock in a pan, bring to the boil then reduce to a simmer and cook for 5 minutes. Taste and adjust the seasoning as needed.

3 Add the noodles to a separate pan of boiling water and cook for 2–3 minutes, remove with a slotted spoon and transfer to serving bowls.

4 Ladle over the piping hot broth, add the squash to the bowls then top with mushrooms, spring onions, chilli and shiso leaves. Sprinkle over sesame seeds to serve.

Cook's tip
You could add the mushrooms to the roasting pan for the last 15 minutes of cooking; this will result in them tasting much richer as opposed to the more earthy flavour of the raw mushrooms.

Nutrition note
As its bright orange colour might suggest, butternut squash is packed full of carotenoids, which not only are full of vitamin A, they are also strong antioxidants. As with carrots, the availability of these carotenoids is increased by chopping or mashing, which releases them from the cell structure. Butternut squash also contains a decent amount of vitamin C, manganese and potassium.

Energy 499kcal/2112kJ; Protein 16g; Carbohydrate 84.3g, of which sugars 7.9g; Fat 13.3g, of which saturates 3g; Cholesterol 30mg; Calcium 116mg; Fibre 7.7g; Sodium 462mg.

Corn and pineapple sunshine soup

A great way to brighten up your day on a summer lunchtime and top up on the yellow spectrum of your rainbow diet. Try this with some seeded corn bread.

400ml/14 fl oz/1^1/$_3$ cups water
600ml/1 pint/2^1/$_2$ cups coconut milk
150g/5oz/^{2}/$_3$ cup frozen corn
2 small yellow bell peppers, cored, deseeded and diced
4 slices of pineapple, peel cut away, cored and diced
20ml/4 tsp chia seeds

1 fresh lime
8 cauliflower florets, cut into small pieces
40g/1^1/$_2$oz roughly chopped pistachio nuts
torn nasturtium or English marigold petals, optional
a few small rocket (arugula) leaves, optional

SERVES 4

1 Heat the water, coconut milk and corn in a small pan and simmer for 3 minutes until the corn is hot.

2 Reserve a little of the yellow pepper for the topping then add the rest to a blender with the pineapple. Pour in the coconut and corn mix, screw on the lid and blend until smooth. Stir in the chia seeds and add lime juice to taste.

3 Pour into bowls, and top with the reserved yellow pepper, cauliflower florets, pistachio nuts, flower petals and rocket leaves, if using.

Cook's tips
• If this soup is left to stand the chia seeds will swell and it will take on a jelly-like texture, so serve it as soon as it is made.
• You could also replace the chia seeds with hemp seeds.

Energy 183kcal/773kJ; Protein 6.1g; Carbohydrate 27.6g, of which sugars 20.9g; Fat 6g, of which saturates 0.9g; Cholesterol 0mg; Calcium 81mg; Fibre 8.2g; Sodium 138mg.

Roasted butternut squash soup

Butternut squash are grown throughout the summer months, then harvested and stored to eat through the winter. Roasting the squash gives it a greater intensity of flavour, and toasted pumpkin seeds give a lovely crunch to the creamy soup. Obviously if it is anywhere near Halloween then use pumpkin instead.

3 red onions, peeled and quartered
500g/1¹/₄lb/2¹/₄ cups butternut squash, peeled and chopped
30ml/2 tbsp olive oil
1 fresh red chilli, deseeded and chopped
3 garlic cloves, crushed
2.5ml/¹/₂ tsp ground cinnamon
5ml/1 tsp ground coriander
2.5ml/¹/₂ tsp ground ginger

900ml/1¹/₂ pints/3³/₄ cups hot vegetable stock
1 small ripe mango, peeled and diced
salt and black pepper
45g/1¹/₂ oz toasted pumpkin seeds, chopped fresh coriander (cilantro), lime juice and dairy-free yogurt or cashew nut or coconut cream, to serve

SERVES 6

1 Preheat the oven to 200°C/400°F/Gas 6. Place the onions and squash in a deep heavy roasting pan and drizzle with the olive oil. Season with a little salt to help crisp the edges. Roast for 15–20 minutes, until the vegetables are golden and tender.

2 Remove the roasting pan from the oven and place on the top of the stove over a low heat. Add the chilli, garlic and spices and cook, stirring, for 2 minutes until the oil and spices have coated the vegetables.

3 Add the a little of the stock to the roasting pan, stirring to remove any traces from the bottom, and transfer the contents into a medium-sized pan. Add the rest of the stock, gently bring to the boil and simmer for 10 minutes until the vegetables are tender.

4 Remove from the heat and add the diced mango. Blend with a stick blender, or transfer to a food processor, until smooth. Ladle into bowls and serve with toasted pumpkin seeds, lots of chopped coriander, lime juice, black pepper, and a swirl of dairy-free yogurt or cashew nut or coconut cream.

Kale and shiitake soup

Shiitake mushrooms are usually much more nutrient-dense than button mushrooms and kale is, well, just splendid. As well as setting you up for the winter months, the soup has a vibrant green colour and strong nutty, smoky taste, brought on by smoked salt, walnut oil and dry-fried kale. It is smart enough to wow any dinner party, but simple enough for a cosy night in.

16 shiitake mushrooms
200g/7oz shallots, peeled and halved
4 garlic cloves
30ml/2 tbsp walnut or vegetable oil
600g/1lb 6oz kale, rinsed and roughly chopped
1 litre/1³/4 pints/4 cups mushroom stock (see tip below)
juice of ¹/2 lemon

2.5ml/¹/2 tsp sugar
smoked sea salt and cracked pink peppercorns
dairy-free yogurt or cashew nut cream, to serve

SERVES 4

1 Preheat the oven to 190°C/375°F/Gas 5. On a baking sheet, place the shiitake mushrooms, shallots and garlic cloves and sprinkle over the walnut or vegetable oil. Season with the salt and roast for 15–20 minutes, until the shallots are softened.

2 In the meantime, in a large heavy pan, dry-fry the kale, in batches if needed, until the kale is moist and softened (about 3–5 minutes).

3 Add the roasted shallots and its juices to the kale, then peel the roasted garlic and add to the mixture. Add 4 shiitake mushrooms, then simmer, stirring, for 2 minutes. Slice the remaining 12 roasted shiitake and set aside.

4 Pour the stock into the pan and add the lemon juice and sugar, then bring to the boil. Simmer for 15 minutes, then allow to cool slightly, before using a stick blender to blend the soup in the pan, or liquidize, in batches if necessary.

5 Return the liquidized soup to the pan, then add the sliced shiitake mushrooms and pink peppercorns. Simmer for 2 minutes, then serve with a swirl of dairy-free yogurt or cashew nut cream.

Cook's tips
• To make mushroom stock, place 400g/14oz dried mushrooms in a bowl and cover with 1 litre/1¾ pints/ 4 cups boiling water. Leave to soak for 15 minutes. Drain into a jug or pitcher – you can reserve the rehydrated mushrooms to use in another recipe. Reduce or enlarge quantities as required.
• If you have lots of kale try rubbing with oil, dusting with salt, pepper and garlic granules, and roasting in the oven until crispy. It would make a great low-carb, gluten-free accompaniment to this soup.

Energy 116kcal/484kJ; protein 6.8g; carbohydrate 4g, of which sugars 3.7g; fat 8.3g, of which saturates 0.9g; cholesterol 0mg; calcium 210mg; fibre 7.9g; sodium 72mg.

Red bean soup with salsa

This mildly spiced soup is perfect for lunch on a lovely summer's day. A delicious cooling salsa of avocado and lime is added as a garnish for a special finishing touch.

30ml/2 tbsp olive oil
2 onions, chopped
2 garlic cloves, chopped
10ml/2 tsp ground cumin
1.5ml/¼ tsp cayenne pepper
15ml/1 tbsp paprika
15ml/1 tbsp tomato purée (paste)
2.5ml/½ tsp dried oregano
400g/14oz can chopped tomatoes
2 x 400g/14oz cans red kidney beans, drained and rinsed
900ml/1½ pints/3¾ cups vegetable stock

salt and ground black pepper
chilli sauce, to serve

For the guacamole salsa
2 avocados
1 small red onion, finely chopped
1 fresh green chilli, seeded and finely chopped
15g/½ oz chopped fresh coriander (cilantro)
juice of 1 lime

SERVES 6

1 Heat the oil in a large, heavy pan and add the onions and garlic. Cook for about 4–5 minutes, until softened. Add the cumin, cayenne and paprika, and cook for 1 minute, stirring continuously.

2 Stir the tomato purée into the pan and cook for a few seconds, then stir in the oregano. Add the chopped tomatoes and kidney beans, and then pour in the vegetable stock.

3 Bring the tomato and bean mixture to the boil and simmer for 15–20 minutes. Cool the soup slightly, then purée it in a food processor or with a stick blender until smooth. Return to the rinsed-out pan and add seasoning to taste.

4 To make the guacamole salsa, halve, stone (pit) and peel the avocados, then dice them finely. Place in a small bowl and gently, but thoroughly, mix with the finely chopped red onion and chilli, and the fresh coriander and lime juice.

5 Reheat the soup and ladle into bowls. Spoon a little guacamole salsa into the middle of each and serve, offering a chilli sauce for those who want to spice up their soup.

Cook's tip

This is the perfect soup to make in a big batch and freeze in small portions ready to thaw when needed.

Energy 302kcal/1265kJ; Protein 11.7g; Carbohydrate 33.2g, of which sugars 11.8g; Fat 14.5g, of which saturates 2.8g; Cholesterol 0mg; Calcium 125mg; Fibre 11.8g; Sodium 537mg.

Pearl barley and haricot bean soup

This hearty main meal vegetable soup is perfect on a freezing cold day.
Serve in warmed bowls, with plenty of rye or pumpernickel bread on the side.

40g/1¹/₂ oz haricot (navy) beans, soaked overnight
2 litres/3¹/₂ pints/8 cups water or
vegetable stock
45ml/3 tbsp green split peas
45ml/3 tbsp yellow split peas
90ml/6 tbsp pearl barley
1 onion, chopped
3 celery sticks, diced or sliced
5 garlic cloves, sliced
2 carrots, sliced
1 large potato, peeled and cut
into chunks
10g/¹/₄oz mixed dried mushrooms
ground black pepper
chopped fresh parsley, to garnish

SERVES 6

1 Put the beans in a large pan, cover with water or vegetable stock and bring to the boil. Boil for 10 minutes, then skim any froth from the surface. Add the green and yellow split peas, pearl barley, onion, celery and garlic.

2 Bring the mixture to the boil, then reduce the heat, cover and simmer gently for about 1¹/₂ hours, or until the beans are tender.

3 Add the carrots, potato and dried mushrooms and cook for a further 30 minutes, or until the beans and vegetables are tender.

4 Season to taste, then ladle into bowls, garnish with parsley and serve.

Cook's tip
Dried beans should be soaked in a bowl of cold water overnight to reduce the cooking time.

Energy 162kcal/689kJ; Protein 6.8g; Carbohydrate 34.1g, of which sugars 4.3g; Fat 0.8g, of which saturates 0.1g; Cholesterol 0mg; Calcium 34mg; Fibre 2.9g; Sodium 30mg.

Classic hummus

Chickpeas make a great and cheap storecupboard standby and can be easily transformed into a versatile dish that is so much more than a dip. Customize this basic recipe to suit your tastes: add more tahini or finely chopped garlic, or less lemon juice, as you prefer.

200g/7oz/1 cup dried chickpeas, soaked overnight in cold water
2 litres/3¹/₂ pints/8 cups water
2.5ml/¹/₂ tsp bicarbonate of soda (baking soda)
30-60ml/2-4 tbsp tahini
juice of 1 lemon
salt and cayenne pepper
30ml/2 tbsp olive oil
pinch of paprika

SERVES 6-8

1 Drain the soaked chickpeas and add to a large pan. Pour in the measured water then stir in the bicarbonate of soda and slowly bring to the boil.

2 Skim off any scum with a spoon then half-cover the top of the pan with a lid and simmer for 45–75 minutes until the chickpeas are soft and can be pressed between two fingers.

3 Drain the chickpeas into a colander, reserving the cooking water for later, loosely cover the colander with a clean dish towel and leave the chickpeas to cool for 30 minutes.

4 Add the chickpeas to a food processor and spoon in 30ml/ 2 tbsp of tahini. Add the lemon juice and a little salt and cayenne pepper. Blitz for 2–3 minutes until finely blended.

5 Gradually mix in enough of the reserved cooking water or fresh water if preferred to give a smooth spoonable hummus – usually about 125ml/4fl oz/¹/₂ cup. Taste and adjust with extra tahini and seasoning if needed.

6 Spoon into a shallow bowl, swirl with the back of a spoon then drizzle with olive oil and sprinkle with the paprika. Serve with warm pitta bread or other accompaniment.

Cook's tips
• Keep an eye on the chickpeas as they cook, as you want to maintain a steady, even heat. While it is tempting to cover the pan completely, it will always boil over, so keep the lid half on and half off the pan.
• Try blending the chickpeas for much longer than usual for that authentic, Middle Eastern creamy-smooth consistency.
• Buy the best olive oil you can afford rather than blended oil, to serve with this dish.

Energy 152kcal/635kJ; Protein 7.1g; Carbohydrate 12.5g, of which sugars 0.7g; Fat 8.5g, of which saturates 1.2g; Cholesterol 0mg; Calcium 64mg; Fibre 0.8g; Sodium 11mg.

Black bean and black olive hummus

Packed with Mediterranean tastes, this unusually coloured hummus is infused with pesto and fresh basil for the most delicious flavour. But there's no need to stop there. Use any bean; or swap olives for sundried tomatoes, or beetroot, or smoked garlic, or artichoke, or capers or marinated mushrooms. You might also like to serve this with a roasted pepper salad, chargrilled vegetable kebabs or baked potatoes.

100g/3³/₄oz/¹/₂ cup dried black beans, soaked overnight in cold water
1 litre/1³/₄ pints/4 cups water, plus 30-45ml/3-4 tbsp extra
20ml/4 tsp dairy-free vegan pesto
45ml/3 tbsp olive oil

a small handful of fresh basil, plus some tiny leaves for garnish
110g/4oz/scant 1 cup pitted black Kalamata olives
salt and cayenne pepper

SERVES 4

1 Drain the soaked beans and add to a pan with the water, bring to the boil and skim off any scum with a spoon. Cover with a lid and simmer for about 1 hour or until tender.

2 Drain the beans into a colander and leave for 15 minutes then tip into the bowl of a food processor. Mix 5ml/1 tsp of the pesto with 10ml/2 tsp olive oil in a small bowl then set aside. Add the rest of the pesto and oil to the food processor with three-quarters of the basil and three-quarters of the olives. Season with salt and cayenne pepper and blitz until smooth.

3 Taste and adjust the seasoning and add a little water if needed. Spoon into a shallow bowl, swirl with the back of a spoon and garnish with the reserved pesto oil, olives and tiny basil leaves. Serve with warm olive focaccia bread, celery and cucumber sticks.

Cook's tips
• For garlic fans, add 1 or 2 sliced garlic cloves to the food processor when blitzing the beans.
• To make your own home-made vegan pesto, see page 145.

Nutrition note
Olives contain healthy oils just like olive oil, plus small amounts of fibre, iron, calcium and vitamin A. 15ml/1 tbsp of olive oil contains 120 calories, while 4–5 olives around 45 calories.

Energy 205kcal/856kJ; Protein 7.1g; Carbohydrate 13.7g, of which sugars 0.7g; Fat 14g, of which saturates 1.8g; Cholesterol 2mg; Calcium 62mg; Fibre 3.8g; Sodium 640mg.

Avocado guacamole

Often served as a dip with corn chips, this highly nutritious salsa is also great served alongside a main course. It is made from avocados, onion and tomatoes spiked with fresh chilli, crushed garlic, toasted cumin seeds and fresh lime juice.

2 large ripe avocados
1 small red onion, finely chopped
1 fresh red or green chilli, seeded and
**   very finely chopped**
1 garlic clove, crushed
finely shredded rind of 1/2 lime and juice
**   of 1-11/2 limes**
225g/8oz tomatoes, seeded and chopped
25g/1 oz roughly chopped fresh
**   coriander (cilantro)**
2.5-5ml/1/2-1 tsp cumin seeds, toasted then ground
15ml/1 tbsp olive oil
ground black pepper
lime wedges and fresh coriander (cilantro)
**   sprigs, to garnish**

SERVES 4

1 Cut one of the avocados in half and lift out and discard the stone. Scrape the flesh from both halves into a bowl and mash it roughly with a fork.

2 Add the onion, chilli, garlic, lime rind, tomatoes and coriander and stir well. Add the ground cumin seeds and pepper to taste, then stir in the olive oil.

3 Halve and stone the remaining avocado. Dice the flesh and stir it into the guacamole.

4 Squeeze in fresh lime juice to taste, mix well, then cover and leave to stand for 15 minutes so that the flavour develops. Serve with lime wedges and garnish with fresh coriander sprigs.

Energy 187kcal/771kJ; Protein 2.4g; Carbohydrate 4.7g, of which sugars 3.3g; Fat 17.6g, of which saturates 3.5g; Cholesterol 0mg; Calcium 41mg; Fibre 4g; Sodium 14mg.

Aubergine dip with tahini-almond yogurt

This smoky aubergine and tahini dip is also known as baba ganoush. Some cooks add chopped flat leaf parsley and others sharpen it with lemon juice, or make it creamy with thick vegan yogurt. This one contains all of these for maximum flavour.

2 large aubergines (eggplants)
30–45ml/2–3 tbsp tahini
juice of 1–2 lemons
45ml/3 tbsp thick almond milk yogurt
(see cook's tip)
2 garlic cloves, crushed

a bunch of flat leaf parsley, chopped
salt and ground black pepper
olive oil, for drizzling

SERVES 4

1 Place the aubergines on a hot griddle, or directly over a gas flame or charcoal grill, turning them from time to time, until they are soft to the touch and the skin is charred and flaky.

2 Place the charred aubergines in a plastic bag and leave for a few minutes to sweat. When they are cold enough to handle, hold them by the stems under cold running water and peel off and discard the skin. Squeeze out the excess water, then chop the flesh to a pulp.

3 In a bowl, beat the tahini with the lemon juice – the mixture stiffens at first, then loosens to a creamy paste. Beat in the thick almond milk yogurt and then, using a fork, beat in the aubergine pulp until everything is combined.

4 Add the garlic and parsley (reserving a little to garnish), season with salt and pepper and beat the mixture thoroughly.

5 Transfer the dip to a serving dish, drizzle a little olive oil over the top to keep it moist, and sprinkle with the reserved parsley.

Cook's tip
To make thick almond milk yogurt, line a plastic sieve or strainer with a piece of muslin or cheesecloth and place it over a bowl. Spoon in 90ml/6 tbsp almond milk yogurt. Leave the bowl in the refrigerator for 1–2 hours to drain; you should then be left with about 45ml/3 tbsp thick almond milk yogurt in the muslin. Discard the liquid in the bowl. Alternatively you could add 20ml/4 tsp of ground chia seeds to the almond milk to thicken it.

Energy 202kcal/840kJ; Protein 6.6g; Carbohydrate 5.3g, of which sugars 3.4g; Fat 17.5g, of which saturates 2.5g; Cholesterol 0mg; Calcium 206mg; Fibre 6.5g; Sodium 12mg.

Falafel spicy bean balls

Ideal street food, falafel are one of the most popular snacks in Lebanon and Egypt, and now the world. They can be served as a mezze dish with a tahini sauce, with plant-based yogurt and mint or coconut cream and lots of parsley, or with a salad.

250g/9oz/1 cup dried broad (fava) beans, soaked overnight
115g/4oz/1/2 cup chickpeas, soaked overnight
10–15ml/2–3 tsp ground cumin
10ml/2 tsp ground coriander
1 fresh red chilli, seeded and chopped
1/2 onion, chopped
1 red or green bell pepper, chopped
4 garlic cloves, crushed
a small bunch of fresh coriander (cilantro), chopped
a bunch of flat leaf parsley, chopped
5ml/1 tsp bicarbonate of soda (baking soda)
sunflower oil for deep-frying
sea salt and ground black pepper
lemon wedges and plant-based yogurt or coconut cream,
    flavoured with chopped fresh mint, to serve

SERVES 4-6

1 Drain the beans and chickpeas and place in a blender with the ground cumin and coriander. Blend to a paste, then add the chilli, onion, pepper, garlic and herbs. Season well, then whizz until smooth. Transfer to a bowl, beat in the bicarbonate of soda, cover, and leave for 15 minutes.

2 With wet hands, mould the mixture into small, tight balls.

3 Heat enough oil for deep-frying in a pan and when it is hot enough, fry the balls in batches until golden brown.

4 Drain the falafel on kitchen paper and serve them warm or at room temperature, with lemon wedges to squeeze over them, and a dollop of plant-based yogurt or coconut cream, flavoured with chopped fresh mint.

Cook's tip
If you are short of time you can use canned beans and peas instead.

Energy 303kcal/1282kJ; Protein 18.5g; Carbohydrate 44.7g, of which sugars 5.2g; Fat 6.9g, of which saturates 1.2g; Cholesterol 0mg; Calcium 88mg; Fibre 7.2g; Sodium 16mg.

Dolmades

The ultimate picnic food and essential part of a mezze or tapas, try these vine leaves stuffed with spiced brown rice, nuts and fruit. The filling is infused with sumac, which has a sharp lemon flavour. Vacuum-packed vine leaves are available from Middle Eastern food stores, supermarkets and delicatessens.

20 vacuum-packed vine leaves in brine
90g/3$^1/_2$oz/$^1/_2$ cup long grain brown rice
25ml/1$^1/_2$ tbsp olive oil
1 small onion, finely chopped
50g/2oz/$^1/_2$ cup pine nuts
45ml/3 tbsp raisins
25g/1 oz chopped fresh mint
2.5ml/$^1/_2$ tsp ground cinnamon

2.5ml/$^1/_2$ tsp ground allspice
10ml/2 tsp ground sumac
10ml/2 tsp lemon juice
30ml/2 tbsp tomato purée (paste)
salt and ground black pepper
lemon slices and mint sprigs, to garnish

SERVES 4-5

1 Rinse the vine leaves well under cold running water, then drain and put to one side. Bring a pan of lightly salted water to the boil. Add the rice, lower the heat, cover and simmer for 10–12 minutes, or until almost cooked. Drain.

2 Heat 10ml/2 tsp of the olive oil in a non-stick frying pan, add the onion and cook until soft. Stir in the pine nuts and cook until lightly browned, then add the raisins, chopped mint, cinnamon, allspice and sumac, with salt and pepper to taste. Stir in the rice and mix well. Leave to cool.

3 Line a pan with any damaged vine leaves. Trim the stalks from the remaining leaves and lay them flat. Place a little filling on each. Fold the sides over and roll up each leaf neatly. Place the dolmades side by side in the leaf-lined pan, so that they fit tightly.

4 Mix 300ml/$^1/_2$ pint/1$^1/_4$ cups water with the lemon juice and tomato purée in a small bowl. Whisk in the remaining olive oil until the mixture is well blended.

5 Pour the mixture over the dolmades in the pan and place a heatproof plate on top to keep them in place. Cover the pan and simmer the dolmades for about 1 hour, or until all the liquid has been absorbed and the leaves are tender.

6 Transfer the dolmades to a platter, garnish with lemon slices and mint sprigs and serve hot or cold.

Energy 43kcal/181kJ; Protein 0.7g; Carbohydrate 6.7g, of which sugars 1.7g; Fat 1.1g, of which saturates 0.1g; Cholesterol 0mg; Calcium 12mg; Fibre 0.3g; Sodium 2mg.

Spiralized potato latkes

Latkes are usually made in batches in a large frying pan or skillet on the hob.
Oven-baking them will ensure they absorb less oil and are all ready at the same time.
Squeeze out the excess juices from the spiralized potatoes and onions with your hands,
or roll them up in a clean dish towel and wring well.

1 large potato, about 250g/9oz
1 small red onion
30ml/2 tbsp wholemeal (wholewheat) flour
5ml/1 tsp French mustard
10ml/2 tsp chia seeds

15ml/1 tbsp plant-based mayonnaise or
  smooth-blended tofu
salt and ground black pepper

SERVES 4

1 Preheat the oven to 200°C/400°F/Gas 6 and line a baking
sheet with baking parchment. Spiralize the potato and red
onion using the fine (2mm/¹/₁₂in) spiralizer noodle blade.
Cut into shorter lengths about 10cm/4in long with clean
kitchen scissors, then use your hands to squeeze out as much
liquid as possible.

2 Put the vegetable noodles in a bowl and sprinkle over the
flour, French mustard and chia seeds. Mix well, then add the
mayonnaise or tofu and mix again. Season well.

3 Shape into 12 small flat rounds, keeping the edges as neat
as possible and the noodles tucked in (or they may burn).
Place on the baking sheet, loosely cover with foil and bake
for 12 minutes.

4 Turn the latkes over, re-cover with foil and bake for a
further 8 minutes, removing the foil for the last 3–4 minutes
to allow them to brown.

Cook's tip
If you do not have a spiralizer, then slice the potato as finely
as you can using a very sharp knife or a mandoline.

Energy 224kcal/939kJ; Protein 7.8g; Carbohydrate 26.9g, of which sugars 3.7g; Fat 10.2g, of which saturates 2g; Cholesterol 182mg; Calcium 48mg; Fibre 2.5g; Sodium 66mg.

Mushroom parcels

Tofu sheets are made by boiling soya milk and then lifting off the skin that forms on the top and drying it in sheets. They need to be immersed briefly in water before using to wrap around this tasty filling, which features delicately flavoured enokitake mushrooms.

30ml/2 tbsp groundnut (peanut) oil
50g/2oz fresh enokitake mushrooms
1 garlic clove, crushed
5ml/1 tsp grated fresh root ginger
4 spring onions (scallions), finely shredded
1 small carrot, cut into thin matchsticks
115g/4oz bamboo shoots, cut into thin matchsticks

15ml/1 tbsp light soy sauce
15ml/1 tbsp cornflour (cornstarch)
8 tofu sheets (approximately 18 x 23cm/7 x 9in each)
sunflower oil, for deep-frying
dipping sauce, to serve

SERVES 4

1 Heat the groundnut oil in a wok over a high heat. Finely chop the mushrooms and add the garlic, ginger, spring onions, carrot and bamboo shoots. Stir-fry for 2–3 minutes, then add the soy sauce and toss to mix thoroughly.

2 Remove the vegetables from the heat and place in a sieve or strainer to drain off the juices. Set aside to cool.

3 In a small bowl, mix the cornflour with 60ml/4 tbsp of cold water to form a smooth paste. Soak the tofu sheets in a bowl of warm water for 10–15 seconds and then lay them out on a clean work surface and pat dry with kitchen paper.

4 Brush the edges of one of the tofu sheets with the cornflour paste. Place 30ml/2 tbsp of the vegetable mixture at one end of the sheet. Fold the edges over toward the centre and roll up tightly to form a roll. Repeat with the remaining tofu sheets and filling.

5 Place the filled rolls on a baking sheet or tray lined with baking parchment, cover and chill for 3–4 hours.

6 To cook, fill a wok one-third full with sunflower oil and heat to 180°C/350°F or until a cube of bread, dropped into the oil, browns in 45 seconds.

7 Working in batches, deep-fry the rolls for 2–3 minutes, or until they are crisp and golden. Drain on kitchen paper and serve immediately with a dipping sauce of your choice.

Energy 255kcal/1053kJ; Protein 3.8g; Carbohydrate 7.9g, of which sugars 3.4g; Fat 23.4g, of which saturates 2.8g; Cholesterol 0mg; Calcium 144mg; Fibre 1.2g; Sodium 228mg.

Beansprout and cucumber parcels

This is inspired by a typical Vietnamese dish. These delightful rice paper rolls filled with crunchy raw summer vegetables and fresh mint and coriander are light and refreshing, either as a snack or an appetizer to a meal. A great gluten-free option for friends who cannot have wheat.

12 round rice papers
1 medium lettuce, leaves separated and ribs removed
2-3 carrots, cut into julienne strips
1 small cucumber, peeled, halved lengthways and seeded, and cut into julienne strips
3 spring onions (scallions), trimmed and cut into julienne strips

225g/8oz mung beansprouts
a small bunch of fresh mint leaves, roughly chopped
a small bunch of fresh coriander (cilantro) leaves, roughly chopped
dipping sauce, to serve

SERVES 4

1 Pour some lukewarm water into a shallow dish. Soak the rice papers, two or three at a time, for 5 minutes until pliable. Place the soaked papers on a clean dish towel and cover with a second dish towel to keep them moist.

2 Work with one paper at a time. Place a lettuce leaf toward the edge nearest to you, leaving about 2.5cm/1in to fold over. Place a mixture of the different vegetables on top, followed by some mint and coriander leaves.

3 Fold the edge nearest to you over the filling, tuck in the sides, and roll tightly to the edge on the far side. Place the filled roll on a plate and cover with clear film or plastic wrap, so it does not dry out. Repeat with the remaining rice papers and vegetables.

4 Serve the rolls with a dipping sauce of your choice. If you are making these summer rolls ahead of time, keep them in the refrigerator under a damp dish towel, so that they remain moist.

Cook's tip
Rice papers are readily available in Chinese and Asian markets.

Energy 105kcal/441kJ; Protein 4g; Carbohydrate 20g, of which sugars 6.6g; Fat 1g, of which saturates 0.2g; Cholesterol 0mg; Calcium 74mg; Fibre 3.7g; Sodium 23mg.

Courgette fritters

A healthier twist on Japanese tempura, using Indian spices and gram flour – made from chickpeas – in the batter. The result is a wonderful snack that has a light, crispy coating, while the courgette baton inside becomes meltingly tender. They are delicious served with steamed basmatic rice, soya dairy-free yogurt and pickles.

90g/3$^1\!/_2$oz/$^3\!/_4$ cup gram flour
5ml/1 tsp baking powder
2.5ml/$^1\!/_2$ tsp ground turmeric
10ml/2 tsp ground coriander
5ml/1 tsp ground cumin
5ml/1 tsp chilli powder
250ml/8fl oz/1 cup bottled beer
600g/1lb 6oz courgettes (zucchini), cut into batons
sunflower oil, for deep-frying
sea salt

SERVES 4

1 Sift the gram flour, baking powder, turmeric, coriander, cumin and chilli powder into a large bowl. Stir lightly to mix through.

2 Season the mixture with salt and then gradually add the beer, mixing gently as you pour it in, to make a thick batter – be careful not to overmix.

3 Fill a large wok or deep, heavy pan one-third full with sunflower oil and heat to 180°C/350°F or until a cube of bread, dropped into the oil, browns in about 45 seconds.

4 Working in batches, dip the courgette batons in the batter and then deep-fry for 1–2 minutes until crisp and golden. Lift out of the wok using a slotted spoon. Drain on kitchen paper and keep warm.

Energy 207kcal/857kJ; Protein 8.3g; Carbohydrate 10.8g, of which sugars 4.7g; Fat 14.8g, of which saturates 2.4g; Cholesterol 95mg; Calcium 104mg; Fibre 2.1g; Sodium 50mg.

Crispy onion bhajis

These delicious Indian snacks are the perfect gluten-free vegan snack or starter.
They are light, crispy and definitely moreish. Serve with chutney or a
dairy-free yogurt and mint dip.

675g/1¹/₂ lb onions, halved and thinly sliced
5ml/1 tsp sea salt
5ml/1 tsp ground coriander
5ml/1 tsp ground cumin
2.5ml/¹/₂ tsp ground turmeric
1-2 fresh green chillies, seeded and finely chopped
45g/1¹/₂ oz chopped fresh coriander (cilantro)
90g/3¹/₂ oz/³/₄ cup gram flour

2.5ml/¹/₂ tsp baking powder
rapeseed oil, for deep-frying

To serve
lemon wedges (optional)
fresh coriander (cilantro) sprigs
dairy-free yogurt and herb dip (see cook's tip)

SERVES 4-5

1 Place the onion slices in a colander, add the salt and toss.
Place on a plate and leave to stand for 45 minutes, tossing
once or twice. Rinse the onions, then squeeze out any excess
moisture.

2 Place the onions in a bowl. Add the ground coriander,
cumin, turmeric, finely chopped chillies and chopped fresh
coriander. Mix well.

3 Add the gram flour and baking powder to the onion
mixture in the bowl, then use your hand to mix all
the ingredients thoroughly.

4 Shape the mixture by hand into approximately 12–15
fritters, about the size of golf balls.

5 Heat the rapeseed oil for deep-frying to 180–190°C/350–
375°F, or until a cube of day-old bread browns in about 45
seconds. Fry the fritters in batches until golden brown all
over. Remove with a slotted spoon, drain on kitchen paper
and keep warm while the rest are frying.

6 Serve the fritters warm accompanied by lemon wedges and
a herby dip.

Cook's tips
• You can of course spray them lightly with oil and bake
them in a hot oven too.
• To make a herb dip, stir 30ml/2 tbsp each of chopped fresh
coriander and mint into about 225g/8oz/1 cup soya, coconut
or almond yogurt.

Energy 245kcal/1016kJ; Protein 3.5g; Carbohydrate 26.4g, of which sugars 7.8g; Fat 14.1g, of which saturates 1.4g; Cholesterol 0mg; Calcium 64mg; Fibre 2.8g; Sodium 402mg.

Pea and potato baked samosas

Most samosas are deep-fried but these healthier versions are baked in the oven.
They are perfect for parties, since the pastries need no last-minute attention.

1 large potato, about 250g/9oz, diced
15ml/1 tbsp groundnut or peanut oil
2 shallots, finely chopped
1 garlic clove, finely chopped
60ml/4 tbsp coconut milk
5ml/1 tsp hot curry paste
75g/3oz/³/₄ cup peas

juice of ¹/₂ lime
25 samosa wrappers or 10 x 5cm/4 x 2in strips
   of filo pastry
oil, for brushing
salt and ground black pepper

MAKES 25

1 Preheat the oven to 220°C/425°F/Gas 7. Bring a small pan of water to the boil, add the diced potato, cover and cook for 10–15 minutes, until tender. Drain and set aside.

2 Meanwhile, heat the groundnut oil in a wok or large frying pan. Add the shallots and cook over a medium heat, stirring occasionally, for 3–4 minutes.

3 Add the chopped garlic to the wok and cook for a further 2–3 minutes until the shallots are soft and golden.

4 Add the drained diced potato, the coconut milk, curry paste, peas and lime juice to the wok.

5 Mash the mixture coarsely with a wooden spoon. Season to taste with salt and pepper and cook over a low heat for 2–3 minutes. Remove the pan from the heat and set aside until the mixture has cooled a little.

6 Lay a samosa wrapper or filo strip flat on the work surface. Brush with a little oil, then place a generous teaspoonful of the mixture in the middle of one end. Turn one corner diagonally over the filling to meet the long edge.

7 Continue folding over the filling, keeping the triangular shape as you work down the strip. Brush with a little more oil if necessary and place on a baking sheet. Prepare all the other samosas in the same way.

8 Bake the samosas for 15 minutes, or until the pastry is golden and crisp. Leave them to cool for a few minutes before serving.

Energy 42kcal/178kJ; Protein 1.2g; Carbohydrate 8.5g, of which sugars 0.6g; Fat 0.6g, of which saturates 0.1g; Cholesterol 0mg; Calcium 14mg; Fibre 0.5g; Sodium 4mg.

Dragon balls

Tofu is wonderfully healthy and versatile. It is delicious in this Japanese dish, known
as hiryozu, meaning flying dragon's head. They make excellent appetizers or party snacks.

2 x 285g/10¼oz packets firm tofu
1 small carrot, peeled
40g/1½oz green beans
30g/2 tbsp buckwheat flour
30ml/2 tbsp sake
10ml/2 tsp mirin
5ml/1 tsp sea salt
10ml/2 tsp light miso
10ml/2 tsp agave syrup
sunflower oil, for deep-frying
chopped fresh chives, for serving

For the lime sauce
45ml/3 tbsp light miso
juice of ½ lime
5ml/1 tsp rice vinegar or mirin

SERVES 4

1 Drain the tofu and wrap in kitchen paper. Cover and leave
for 2 hours, or until it loses most of its liquid.

2 To make the tofu balls, chop the carrot finely. Trim and cut
the beans into 5mm/¼in lengths. Cook both vegetables for
1 minute in boiling water.

3 In a food processor, blend the tofu, buckwheat flour, sake,
mirin, salt, light miso and agave syrup until smooth. Transfer
to a bowl and mix in the carrot and beans.

4 Soak a piece of kitchen paper with a little vegetable oil,
and lightly moisten your hands with it. Scoop about 40ml/
2½ tbsp of the mixture in one hand and shape into a ball
between your hands.

5 To make the lime sauce mix together the miso, lime juice
and rice vinegar or mirin in a small bowl and set aside.

6 Fill a wok or pan with oil 4cm/1½in deep, and heat to
185°C/365°F.

7 Using a slotted spoon, carefully slide the ball into the oil
and deep-fry until crisp and golden brown. Drain on kitchen
paper. Repeat with the remaining mixture.

8 Arrange the tofu balls on a plate and sprinkle with chives.
Serve the tofu balls with the sauce to be dipped into by each
guest.

Energy 250kcal/1038kJ; Protein 12.4g; Carbohydrate 10.4g, of which sugars 3.1g; Fat 17.1g, of which saturates 2g; Cholesterol 0mg; Calcium 722mg; Fibre 0.5g; Sodium 649mg.

Tangy coconut polenta

Polenta is an excellent wheat-free starchy carbohydrate, here flavoured with chillies, fresh herbs and coconut and served with pebre, a spicy Chilean condiment.

10ml/2 tsp crushed dried chilli flakes
600ml/1 pint/2 ½ cups coconut water
750ml/1¼ pints/3 cups mild vegetable stock
or water
250g/9oz/1¼ cups quick-cook polenta
45ml/3 tbsp coconut oil
25g/1 oz chopped fresh dill
25g/1 oz chopped fresh coriander (cilantro)

SERVES 6

For the pebre
½ red onion, finely chopped
4 drained bottled sweet cherry peppers, finely chopped
1 fresh medium-hot red chilli, seeded and finely chopped
1 small red bell pepper, quartered, seeded and diced
10ml/2 tsp coconut vinegar
30ml/1 tbsp coconut oil
4 tomatoes, cored and choppped
45g/1½ oz chopped fresh coriander (cilantro)

1 Put the chilli flakes in a pan with the coconut water and stock and bring to the boil. Pour in the polenta in a steady stream, whisking all the time. Reduce the heat and continue to whisk for a few minutes. When the polenta is thick, whisk in half the oil and all the herbs. Pour into a greased 33 x 23cm/13 x 9in baking tray and leave to cool. Chill, uncovered, overnight.

2 To make the pebre, place the onion, cherry peppers, chilli and diced pepper in a mortar with the coconut vinegar and coconut oil. Pound with a pestle for 1 minute, then tip into a dish. Stir in the tomatoes and coriander. Cover and leave in a cool place.

3 Bring the polenta to rooom temperature. Cut into 12 even triangles and brush the top with the 3 tbsp of coconut oil.

4 Heat a griddle until drops of water sprinkled on the surface evaporate instantly. Lower the heat to medium and grill or broil the triangles in batches oiled-side down for 1 minute, then turn through 180 degrees and cook for 1 minute more, to achieve a checked effect. Serve immediately, with the pebre.

Energy 273kcal/1139kJ; Protein 7.3g; Carbohydrate 35.8g, of which sugars 11g; Fat 11g, of which saturates 8g; Cholesterol 0mg; Calcium 28mg; Fibre 6.1g; Sodium 264mg.

Coconut patties

These originally hail from India where they are made from grated fresh coconut. Use this if you have time, but for simplicity, here they are made with shredded coconut softened with coconut water.

150g/5oz/2 cups desiccated (dry unsweetened shredded) coconut
150ml/¼ pint/⅔ cup coconut water, warmed
2 slices of bread, crusts removed
75g/3oz/⅔ cup gram flour
1-3 fresh green chillies, roughly chopped
2.5cm/1in fresh root ginger, peeled and roughly chopped
1 large garlic clove, peeled and roughly chopped

15g/1 tbsp fresh coriander (cilantro) leaves and stalks, chopped
2.5ml/½ tsp chilli powder, or to taste
2.5ml/½ tsp salt, or to taste
1 medium onion, finely chopped
coconut oil, for shallow-frying
chutney, to serve

MAKES 16

1 Put the coconut in a large mixing bowl and pour over the warm coconut water. Set aside for 10 minutes for the coconut to absorb the water. Cut the bread into small pieces.

2 Place all the ingredients, except the onion and the oil, in a food processor and blitz to a smooth paste. Transfer the mixture to a bowl and add the onion. Mix thoroughly and divide the mixture into 16 balls, each the size of a lime.

3 Flatten the coconut balls to form 16 smooth, round patties. If the mixture sticks to your fingers, moisten your palms with water between patties.

4 Put 15ml/1 tbsp coconut oil in a non-stick frying pan and heat over a medium-high heat. Fry the patties in batches for 3–4 minutes on each side, until browned all over.

5 Lift out and drain on kitchen paper. Keep warm while you fry the other patties, adding more oil to the pan when necessary. Serve immediately with the chutney.

Cauliflower munchies

These crispy cauliflower bites make a great alternative to carb- and fat-loaded chips, and taste just as good hot or cold. Served with a cool mint-flavoured vegan yogurt, you won't be surprised to see these disappearing all too soon.

30ml/2 tbsp olive oil
15ml/1 tbsp za'atar spice mix
2 garlic cloves, thinly sliced
1 cauliflower, cut into florets,
    core and leaves removed
5ml/1 tsp paprika
a little coarse salt

To serve
200g/7oz/³/₄ cup vegan yogurt
45g/1¹/₂ oz freshly chopped mint

SERVES 4

1 Heat the oil in a large non-stick frying pan, add the za'atar mix and garlic and heat over a low heat for 1 minute to release the flavour of the spices.

2 Add the cauliflower and increase the heat to medium, then stir-fry for 3–4 minutes until the cauliflower is just beginning to brown around the edges and is hot but still crisp.

3 Sprinkle with the paprika and a little salt and serve on their own or with yogurt flavoured with chopped mint.

Cook's tip
Za'atar spice mix is made up of sesame seeds, dried thyme, oregano, sumac and cumin seeds and is now available in most large supermarkets. It is popular all over the Middle East and is often sprinkled over flatbreads before baking.

Energy 96kcal/396kJ; Protein 4.7g; Carbohydrate 4.2g, of which sugars 3.1g; Fat 6.8g, of which saturates 1.1g; Cholesterol 0mg; Calcium 29mg; Fibre 3g; Sodium 12mg.

Roasted kale crisps

All hail the kale. This is a fun and quick way to appreciate this super-nutritious vegetable.
You can buy kale snacks in supermarkets now but they are so easy to make once
you get the knack of not burning them.

175g/6oz/6 large handfuls of kale leaves, washed, drained
well and thickly sliced
15ml/1 tbsp olive oil
30ml/2 tbsp soy sauce
10ml/2 tsp molasses sugar or syrup
2.5cm/1in piece fresh root ginger, peeled,
and coarsely grated

SERVES 4

1 Preheat the oven to 150°C/300°F/Gas 2. Dry the kale well
with kitchen paper then add to a large bowl. Massage the oil
gently onto the kale until all leaves are shiny, then add soy
sauce and molasses over and add the ginger. Toss together to
mix well to dress all the leaves.

2 Divide the flavoured kale mixture between two large
baking sheets and spread into a thin layer.

3 Bake for 4–5 minutes until the kale leaves around the
edges of the baking sheet are beginning to crisp up. Move
the kale from the outer edges into the centre and those in the
centre to the edges and cook for 3–5 minutes more until all
the kale pieces are crisp and dry.

4 Leave to cool for 15 minutes then enjoy while still warm
and crisp, or leave to cool completely and pack into a lidded
plastic container, to store in the refrigerator. However the
kale is best eaten on the day of making.

Cook's tips
• Try to buy whole kale leaves so that you can slice them
thickly; some supermarkets sell bags of thickly sliced kale,
if you can only get bags of thinly sliced kale then reduce the
cooking time down to 3–4 minutes, stir and then cook for a
further 3–4 minutes.

• Kale has become the favourite healthy option and is
available in all supermarkets and farmers' markets, plus it is
easy to grow even for those new to gardening.
• If you have a fan oven with a very low setting you can
dehydrate kale overnight, which leaves it more nutritious.

Energy 72kcal/299kJ; Protein 1.6g; Carbohydrate 2.6g, of which sugars 2.5g; Fat 6.2g, of which saturates 0.9g; Cholesterol 0mg; Calcium 71mg; Fibre 1.8g; Sodium 290mg.

Ruby vegetable crisps

These tasty beetroot crisps make an appealing and healthy alternative to potato crisps, particularly for children, who will love the bright colour of this snack. Serve them with a bowl of creamy, garlicky soya mayonnaise or soya cream cheese, and use the crisps to scoop it up.

1 small fresh beetroot (beet)
fine salt, for sprinkling
olive oil, for frying
coarse sea salt and black pepper

SERVES 4

1 Peel the beetroot and, using a mandoline or a vegetable peeler, cut it into very thin slices.

2 Lay the slices on kitchen paper and sprinkle them with fine salt.

3 Heat 5cm/2in oil in a deep pan until a bread cube turns golden in 1 minute. Cook the slices in batches, until they float to the surface and turn golden at the edge. Drain on kitchen paper and sprinkle with salt and pepper when cool.

Variation
Beetroot crisps are particularly flavoursome, but other naturally sweet root vegetables, such as carrots and sweet potatoes, will also taste delicious when cooked in this way.

Energy 130kcal/537kJ; Protein 0.3g; Carbohydrate 1.4g, of which sugars 1.3g; Fat 13.8g, of which saturates 1.9g; Cholesterol 0mg; Calcium 4mg; Fibre 0.4g; Sodium 13mg.

Roasted coconut cashew nuts

Serve these wok-fried hot and sweet cashew nuts in paper cones at parties. Not only do they look enticing and taste terrific, but the cones help to keep guests' clothes and hands clean and can simply be crumpled up and thrown away afterwards.

15ml/1 tbsp groundnut or peanut oil
30ml/2 tbsp agave syrup
250g/9oz/2 cups cashew nuts
115g/4oz/1¹/₃ cups desiccated (dry unsweetened shredded) coconut
2 fresh red chillies, seeded and finely chopped
salt and ground black pepper

SERVES 6-8

1 Heat the groundnut oil in a wok or large frying pan and then stir in the agave syrup. After a few seconds add the nuts and coconut and stir-fry until both are golden brown.

2 Add the chillies, with salt and black pepper to taste. Toss until all the ingredients are well mixed. Serve the nuts warm or cooled in paper cones or on saucers.

Variation
Reduce the heat of this snack by using paprika instead of chillies.

Energy 301kcal/1247kJ; Protein 7.2g; Carbohydrate 9.7g, of which sugars 5.5g; Fat 26.2g, of which saturates 11.1g; Cholesterol 0mg; Calcium 14mg; Fibre 3g; Sodium 95mg.

SALADS

For tempting, nutritionally balanced salads, this chapter is full of fresh ideas. A vegan diet is a joy to follow, with dishes such as Quinoa, Cucumber and Lime Salad; Aubergine and Pomegranate Seed Salad; or Thai Noodle Salad. Quick to prepare and with plenty of vitamin-packed fruit and vegetables, these versatile dishes can be enjoyed at any time of day, all year round.

Black bean salad

This salad has a fabulously striking appearance. It is rare to find a predominantly black dish and it provides a wonderful contrast to the more common reds and greens on the plate. The pasado chilli adds a subtle citrus flavour. Leave the salad for a day or two after preparing it to allow all the wonderful flavours to develop and mingle fully.

175g/6oz/1 cup black beans, soaked overnight
in water to cover
1 pasado chilli
2 fresh red chillies
1 red onion
grated rind and juice of 1 lime

15ml/1 tbsp olive oil
a small bunch of fresh coriander (cilantro),
finely chopped
pinch of salt

SERVES 4

1 Drain the beans and place in a large pan. Pour in water to cover and place the lid on the pan. Bring to the boil, then simmer for 40 minutes or until tender. They should still have a little bite. Drain, rinse under cold water, then drain again and set aside until cold.

2 Soak the pasado chilli in hot water for about 10 minutes until softened. Drain, remove the stalk, then slit the chilli and scrape out the seeds with a small sharp knife. Chop the flesh finely.

3 Spear the fresno chillies on a long-handled metal skewer and roast them over the flame of a gas burner until the skins blister and darken. Do not let the flesh burn. Alternatively, dry fry them in a griddle pan until the skins are scorched. Then place the roasted chillies in a strong plastic bag and tie the top to keep the steam in. Set aside for 20 minutes.

4 Meanwhile, chop the red onion finely. Remove the chillies from the bag and peel off the skins. Slit them, remove the seeds and chop them finely.

5 Transfer the beans into a bowl and add the onion and both types of chilli. Stir in the lime rind and juice, oil and coriander. Season and mix well. Chill before serving.

Cook's tip
A pasado chilli is a medium-strength dried green chilli. If you can't find it then you can replace it with any other medium-strength dried chilli, such as ancho.

Energy 109kcal/461kJ; Protein 6.6g; Carbohydrate 14g, of which sugars 1.1g; Fat 3.4g, of which saturates 0.5g; Cholesterol 0mg; Calcium 49mg; Fibre 2.7g; Sodium 9mg.

Bean salad with garlic and coriander

This traditional Lebanese salad is popular as a mezze dish and is equally delicious served hot or cold. It is usually made when fresh broad beans are in season, but it is also very good when prepared with frozen beans. Broad beans are a rich source of vegetable protein, fibre, iron, potassium and energy-providing B vitamins.

500g/1¹/₄lb/3¹/₂ cups shelled broad
(fava) beans
5ml/1 tsp sugar
30-45ml/2-3 tbsp olive oil
juice of ¹/₂ lemon
1-2 garlic cloves, crushed
sea salt and ground black pepper
a small bunch of fresh coriander (cilantro), finely chopped

SERVES 4-6

1 Put the shelled beans in a pan with just enough water to cover. Stir in the sugar to preserve the colour of the beans, and bring the water to the boil.

2 Reduce the heat and simmer, uncovered, for about 15 minutes, until the beans are cooked but remain al dente.

3 Drain the beans and refresh them under running cold water, then drain again and put them in a bowl.

4 Toss the beans in the oil, lemon juice and garlic. Season well with salt and pepper to taste, and stir in the chopped coriander, reserving a little to sprinkle over before serving.

Cook's tip
If you wish to eat this salad whilst still warm, simply drain the beans without refreshing under cold water, toss them in the oil, then add the other ingredients and serve immediately.

Energy 111kcal/464kJ; Protein 6.8g; Carbohydrate 10.7g, of which sugars 2g; Fat 4.8g, of which saturates 0.7g; Cholesterol 0mg; Calcium 64mg; Fibre 5.8g; Sodium 10mg.

Thai-style noodle salad

The coconut milk and sesame oil in the dressing gives this salad a delicious nutty flavour. Coconuts are also rich in fibre, vitamins and many minerals, making it a highly nutritious ingredient to add to any salad. This makes an ideal summer treat for a picnic or a leisurely lunch in the garden.

350g/12oz egg-free noodles
1 large carrot, cut into thin shavings
a bunch of asparagus, trimmed and cut into 4cm/1½in lengths
115g/4oz mangetouts (snow peas), trimmed and halved
115g/4oz baby corn cobs, halved lengthways
115g/4oz/½ cup beansprouts
115g/4oz can water chestnuts, drained and finely sliced
50g/2oz roasted peanuts and fresh coriander (cilantro) leaves, to garnish

For the dressing
45g/1½ oz roughly torn fresh basil
75g/3 oz roughly chopped fresh mint
250ml/8fl oz/1 cup coconut milk
30ml/2 tbsp dark sesame oil
15ml/1 tbsp grated fresh root ginger
2 garlic cloves, finely chopped
juice of 1 lime
2 spring onions (scallions), sliced
salt and cayenne pepper

SERVES 4

1 To make the dressing, mix the basil, mint, coconut milk, sesame oil, ginger, garlic, lime juice and spring onions. Season with salt and cayenne pepper.

2 Cook the egg-free noodles in boiling water until just tender, following the instructions on the packet. Drain, rinse under cold running water and drain again, then set aside.

3 Cook the carrot, asparagus, mangetouts, baby corn cobs and water chestnuts in a pan of boiling water for approximately 5 minutes until tender, but still crisp. Drain, plunge them immediately into cold water and drain again.

4 Toss the noodles, vegetables and dressing together to combine. Arrange in individual bowls and garnish with the peanuts and coriander.

Energy 365kcal/1521kJ; Protein 6g; Carbohydrate 55.1g, of which sugars 6.7g; Fat 12.8g, of which saturates 2.3g; Cholesterol 0mg; Calcium 61mg; Fibre 2.5g; Sodium 280mg.

White beans with green pepper salad

This dish mixes cannellini beans in a spicy sauce with peppers. It makes a tasty addition to a packed lunch for school or office, and will keep well in the refrigerator if you wanted to make double quantities and have it again the next day.

750g/1²/₃lb tomatoes, diced
1 onion, finely chopped
1 mild fresh chilli, finely chopped
1 green bell pepper, seeded and chopped
pinch of sugar
4 garlic cloves, chopped
400g/14oz can cannellini beans, drained
45-60ml/3-4 tbsp olive oil
grated rind and juice of 1 lemon
15ml/1 tbsp cider vinegar or wine vinegar
salt and ground black pepper
chopped fresh parsley, to garnish
pitta bread slices, to serve (optional)

SERVES 4

1 Put the tomatoes, onion, chilli, green pepper, sugar, garlic, cannellini beans, salt and plenty of ground black pepper in a large bowl and toss together until well combined.

2 Add the olive oil, grated lemon rind, lemon juice and vinegar to the salad and toss lightly to combine. Chill before serving, garnished with plenty of chopped parsley and slices of pitta bread, if you like.

Nutrition note
Cannellini beans are a good source of protein and dietary fibre and contain a wealth of B vitamins, including B12. They also provide iron, potassium, zinc and manganese.

Energy 391kcal/1654kJ; Protein 24g; Carbohydrate 53.8g, of which sugars 11.8g; Fat 10.4g, of which saturates 1.6g; Cholesterol 0mg; Calcium 120mg; Fibre 18.5g; Sodium 37mg.

Ratatouille salad

Vegetables retain more of their shape and texture when cooked in the oven rather than on the hob. Here, spiralized courgettes and aubergines are roasted with red onions, peppers, tomatoes and garlic until slightly caramelized and tender.

2 large courgettes (zucchini), about 450g/1lb
2 firm medium aubergines (eggplants), about 600g/1lb 5oz
1 red onion, peeled
1 yellow bell pepper, seeded and cut into 2cm/3/4in chunks
2 large beefsteak tomatoes, cut into 2cm/3/4in chunks

3 garlic cloves, unpeeled
60ml/4 tbsp olive oil
15ml/1 tbsp balsamic vinegar
salt and ground black pepper
rustic-style bread, focaccia or flatbread, to serve
fresh basil leaves, to garnish

SERVES 6

1 Preheat the oven to 220°C/425°F/Gas 7. Spiralize the courgettes and aubergines using the medium (3mm/1/8in) noodle blade or preferably a wide (4mm/1/6in) noodle blade if your spiralizer has one. Cut into shorter lengths, about 7.5cm/3in. Slice the onion with the spiralizer slicing blade.

2 Put the courgettes, aubergines, onion, pepper, tomatoes and garlic in a large non-stick roasting pan and drizzle over 30ml/2 tbsp of the oil. Season with salt and pepper. Use your hands to turn over the vegetables and coat in the oil. Place the garlic cloves to one side of the pan.

3 Cook for 20–25 minutes, until the vegetables are tender and the edges tinged golden brown. Turn them once or twice during cooking, so they cook evenly; they should be slightly caramelized and tender. Remove from the oven and transfer to a serving dish, adding any juices from the pan.

4 Remove the garlic cloves and squeeze the roasted garlic into a small bowl. Mash to a paste with the remaining 30ml/ 2 tbsp olive oil, then whisk in the balsamic vinegar. Pour the dressing over the vegetables and gently toss together. Serve at room temperature with bread and garnished with basil leaves.

Cook's tips
• This salad is good with a sprinkling of Mediterranean herbs, such as finely chopped thyme or rosemary leaves (pick them off the woody stems, first), or torn basil leaves.
• If you do not have a spiralizer then chop the vegetables up as finely as you can with a very sharp knife or mandoline.

Energy 119kcal/492kJ; Protein 3.1g; Carbohydrate 8.4g, of which sugars 7.5g; Fat 8.3g, of which saturates 1.3g; Cholesterol 0mg; Calcium 40mg; Fibre 5.1g; Sodium 8mg.

Beetroot and red onion salad

There is a wide range of beetroots available – most are an intense red colour but there are also pink and yellow varieties, which are well worth seeking out. This tangy and refreshing salad looks especially attractive when made with a mixture of the red and yellow types.

500g/1¼lb small red and yellow beetroot (beets)
75ml/5 tbsp water
60ml/4 tbsp olive oil
90g/3½oz/scant 1 cup walnut or pecan halves
10ml/2 tsp agave syrup
30ml/2 tbsp walnut oil
15ml/1 tbsp balsamic vinegar
5ml/1 tsp soy sauce

5ml/1 tsp grated orange rind
2.5ml/½ tsp ground roasted coriander seeds
5-10ml/1-2 tsp orange juice
1 red onion, halved and very thinly sliced
½ fresh fennel bulb, chopped
75g/3oz watercress or mizuna leaves
sea salt and ground black pepper

SERVES 6

1 Preheat the oven to 180°C/350°F/Gas 4. Place the beetroot in a shallow ovenproof dish and add the water. Cover the dish with foil and bake for about 1–1½ hours, or until the beetroot are just cooked and tender.

2 Allow the beetroot to cool. Once cooled, peel them, then slice them into roughly equal strips and place in a large bowl. Add about 15ml/1 tbsp of the olive oil to the bowl and mix thoroughly until the beetroot strips are well coated in oil.

3 Meanwhile, heat 15ml/1 tbsp of the olive oil in a frying pan and cook the walnuts or pecans until they begin to brown.

4 Add 5ml/1 tsp of agave syrup to the pan and cook, stirring, until the nuts begin to caramelize. Season, then turn the nuts out on to a plate and leave to cool.

5 Whisk together the remaining olive oil, the walnut oil, vinegar, soy sauce, orange rind and ground roasted coriander seeds to make the dressing. Season to taste and mix in the rest of the agave syrup. Whisk in orange juice to taste.

6 Separate the red onion slices into half-rings and add them to the strips of beetroot. Add the dressing and toss to mix.

7 When ready to serve, toss the salad with the fennel, watercress or mizuna leaves. Transfer to individual bowls or plates and sprinkle with the caramelized nuts. Serve immediately.

Energy 239kcal/991kJ; Protein 3.3g; Carbohydrate 8.2g, of which sugars 7.2g; Fat 21.7g, of which saturates 2.3g; Cholesterol 0mg; Calcium 50mg; Fibre 2.6g; Sodium 121mg.

Seaweed salad

This salad is a fine example of the traditional Japanese idea of eating: look after your appetite and your health at the same time. Seaweed is a nutritious food which is rich in fibre and iodine. Its unique flavours are a great complement to vegetable and tofu dishes.

5g/¹⁄₈oz each dried wakame, dried arame
and dried hijiki seaweeds
130g/4¹⁄₂oz enokitake mushrooms
2 spring onions (scallions)
¹⁄₂ cucumber, cut lengthways
250g/9oz mixed salad leaves
15ml/1 tbsp rice vinegar
10ml/2 tsp soy sauce

For the dressing
60ml/4 tbsp rice vinegar
7.5ml/1¹⁄₂ tsp toasted sesame oil
15ml/1 tbsp shoyu
15ml/1 tbsp water with a pinch of dashi-no-moto
(dashi)stock granules
2.5cm/1in piece of fresh root ginger, grated

SERVES 4

1 First rehydrate the seaweeds. Soak the dried wakame seaweed for about 10 minutes in one bowl of water and, in a separate bowl of water, soak the dried arame and hijiki seaweeds together for 30 minutes.

2 Trim off the hard end of the enokitake mushroom stalks and discard. Cut the bunch in half and separate the stems.

3 Make the spring onion curls. Slice the spring onions into thin strips about 4cm/1¹⁄₂in long, then place the strips into a bowl of cold water with a few ice cubes added. This will cause the onion strips to curl up. Drain the onions thoroughly. Slice the cucumber into thin slices.

4 Cook the wakame and enokitake in boiling water for 2 minutes, then add the arame and hijiki for a few seconds then remove from the heat. Drain and sprinkle over the 15ml/1 tbsp vinegar and 10ml/2 tsp soy sauce while still warm. Chill.

5 Mix the dressing ingredients in a bowl. Arrange the mixed salad leaves in a large bowl with the cucumber on top, then add the seaweed and enokitake mixture. Decorate the salad with spring onion curls and serve with the dressing.

Nutrition note
The iodine in the seaweed may help to keep your thyroid gland in balance. However, see the cautions on page 21, as too much iodine can have an adverse effect on your thyroid.

Energy 33kcal/139kJ; Protein 2.1g; Carbohydrate 2.2g, of which sugars 1.8g; Fat 1.9g, of which saturates 0.3g; Cholesterol 0mg; Calcium 48mg; Fibre 1.4g; Sodium 237mg.

Toasted mixed grains, fennel and orange salad

Wholegrains such as quinoa and buckwheat are absorbed more slowly than refined grains, so they keep you satisfied for longer. They are easy to prepare, and tasty when combined with other grains such as pearled spelt and wheatberries. Toasting gives a richness and greater depth of flavour.

75g/3oz/^{1}/$_2$ cup wheatberries
175ml/6fl oz/^{3}/$_4$ cup boiling water
75g/3oz/^{1}/$_2$ cup pearled spelt
75g/3oz/^{1}/$_2$ cup buckwheat
115g/4oz/^{2}/$_3$ cup red quinoa, rinsed
750ml/1^1/$_4$ pints/3 cups vegetable stock
50g/2oz/^{1}/$_2$ cup blanched whole almonds, cut in half
1 fennel bulb, outer leaves removed, finely sliced
1 orange, peeled and segmented, all white pith removed

a good handful of parsley, finely chopped
  rocket (arugula) or lettuce leaves, to serve

For the dressing
60ml/4 tbsp olive oil
30ml/2 tbsp cider vinegar
5ml/1 tsp wholegrain mustard
ground black pepper

SERVES 4

1 Place the wheatberries in a small pan and dry-fry for 4–6 minutes, until lightly browned. Add the boiling water, being careful as it hits the hot pan, and simmer for 35–40 minutes until the wheatberries are tender to bite. Drain, discarding any excess water.

2 Meanwhile, in large pan, dry-fry the spelt, buckwheat and quinoa for 4–6 minutes, stirring, until lightly browned. Add the vegetable stock to the pan and simmer for 20–25 minutes, until the grains are tender to bite.

3 Meanwhile, toast the almonds under a medium grill or broiler for 6–8 minutes, until lightly browned. Watch them all the time as it is easy to scorch them.

4 Make the dressing by shaking the ingredients together in a jar, or whisking together in a small bowl.

5 Mix the cooked wheatberries with the other warm grains in a large bowl. Add the toasted almonds along with the fennel, orange and parsley. Pour over the dressing and toss through gently.

6 Serve immediately on a bed of fresh rocket or other fresh lettuce leaves.

Cook's tip
Wheatberries take nearly twice as long to cook compared to the other grains so need to be prepared separately.

Variations
• Use other tangy fruits such as pomegranate seeds, grapefruit or little clementines in place of the orange.
• Serve this salad chilled if you prefer.

Energy 520kcal/2177kJ; 16g; Carbohydrate 61g, of which sugars 4g; Fat 25g, of which saturates 3g; Cholesterol 7mg; Calcium 75mg; Fibre 5g; Sodium 361mg.

Quinoa, cucumber and lime salad

Along with other staple crops such as amaranth, quinoa sustained the ancient American cultures of the Incas, Maya and Aztecs. Quinoa contains all the essential amino acids and can have up to 20 per cent protein. It is also ideal for those who are gluten-intolerant.

175g/6oz/1 cup quinoa
90ml/6 tbsp olive oil
juice of 2 limes
juice of 1 large orange
2 fresh green chillies, finely chopped
2 garlic cloves, crushed
1/2 cucumber, peeled
1 large tomato, seeded and cubed

4 spring onions (scallions), sliced
25g/1 oz chopped fresh mint
15g/1/2 oz chopped fresh flat
   leaf parsley
salt

SERVES 6

1 Put the quinoa in a sieve or strainer, rinse thoroughly under cold water, then transfer to a large pan. Pour in cold water to cover and bring to the boil. Lower the heat and simmer for about 10–12 minutes, until tender. Drain and leave to cool.

2 Make a dressing by whisking the oil with the citrus juices. Stir in the chillies and garlic and season with salt.

3 Cut the cucumber in half lengthways and, using a teaspoon, scoop out and discard the seeds. Cut into 5mm/1/4in slices and add to the cooled quinoa with the tomato, spring onions and herbs. Toss well to combine.

4 Pour the dressing over the salad and toss again until all the ingredients are evenly coated. Check the seasoning, adjusting if necessary, and serve.

Cook's tip
Sprinkle in some hemp seeds to add extra nutrition.

Energy 175kcal/727kJ; Protein 2.7g; Carbohydrate 16.1g, of which sugars 0.6g; Fat 11.5g, of which saturates 1.6g; Cholesterol 0mg; Calcium 31mg; Fibre 0.2g; Sodium 4mg.

Puy lentil and spinach salad

Puy lentils have an excellent, earthy flavour and keep their shape on cooking. This salad is great for a picnic or at a barbecue. It improves with standing and is at its best served at room temperature rather than chilled. Add some toasted croûtes, if you like.

225g/8oz/1 cup Puy lentils
1 fresh bay leaf
1 celery stick
1 fresh thyme sprig
30ml/2 tbsp olive oil
1 onion or 3-4 shallots, finely chopped
10ml/2 tsp cumin seed, toasted and crushed
400g/14oz young spinach
50g/2 oz chopped fresh parsley,
plus a few extra sprigs to garnish
salt and ground black pepper

For the dressing
75ml/5 tbsp extra virgin olive oil
5ml/1 tsp Dijon mustard
15-25ml/3-5 tsp red wine vinegar
1 small garlic clove, finely chopped
2.5ml/$\frac{1}{2}$ tsp finely grated lemon rind

SERVES 6

1 Rinse the lentils and place them in a large pan. Add water to cover. Tie the bay leaf, celery and thyme into a bundle and add to the pan, then bring to the boil. Reduce the heat to a steady boil. Cook for 30–45 minutes, until just tender.

2 Meanwhile, make the dressing. Mix the oil, mustard, 15ml/ 1 tbsp vinegar, garlic and lemon rind, and season well.

3 Thoroughly drain the lentils and turn them into a bowl. Add most of the dressing and toss well, then set the lentils aside, stirring occasionally.

4 Heat the oil in a deep frying pan and cook the onion or shallots over a low heat for about 4–5 minutes, until they are beginning to soften. Add the cumin and cook for 1 minute.

5 Add the spinach and season to taste, cover and cook for 2 minutes. Stir, then cook again briefly until wilted.

6 Stir the spinach into the lentils and leave the salad to cool. Bring back to room temperature if necessary. Stir in the remaining dressing and chopped parsley. Adjust the seasoning, adding extra red wine vinegar if necessary.

7 Turn the salad on to a serving platter and sprinkle over some parsley sprigs.

Cook's tip
Do not add salt when cooking as it toughens the outer skin. Season when cooked.

Energy 248kcal/1037kJ; Protein 11.2g; Carbohydrate 20.3g, of which sugars 2.1g; Fat 14.1g, of which saturates 2g; Cholesterol 0mg; Calcium 150mg; Fibre 5.1g; Sodium 102mg.

Chickpea and bulgur salad with mint

This is a traditional Lebanese salad, using ingredients that are readily available in the hills and valleys of the Middle East and, of course, most good supermarkets. The mixture is also used as a filling for vine leaves or peppers and aubergines. To prepare it as a salad, the ingredients are simply bound with olive oil and lemon juice, then tossed with mint.

150g/5oz/scant 1 cup fine bulgur, rinsed
400g/14oz can chickpeas, drained and rinsed
1 red onion, finely chopped
15-30ml/1-2 tbsp sesame seeds, toasted
2-3 garlic cloves, crushed
60-75ml/4-5 tbsp olive oil

juice of 1-2 lemons
a bunch of flat leaf parsley, finely chopped
a large bunch of mint, coarsely chopped
sea salt and ground black pepper
5ml/1 tsp paprika, to garnish

SERVES 4-6

1 Place the bulgur in a bowl and pour over boiling water to cover. Leave to soak for 10–15 minutes, until it has doubled in volume.

2 Meanwhile, place the chickpeas in a bowl with the onion, sesame seeds and garlic, and bind with the olive oil and lemon juice.

3 When cool enough to handle, squeeze the bulgur to remove any excess water and add it to the chickpeas.

4 Add the chopped parsley and mint to the bowl. Toss well, season with salt and pepper to taste, and sprinkle the paprika over the top before serving.

Cook's tip
To toast sesame seeds, heat a frying pan, pour in enough seeds to just cover the bottom of the pan, then dry-fry over a low heat, stirring constantly, until the seeds turn golden brown. Remove from the pan immediately, and leave to cool. Alternatively, roast in a medium oven for a few minutes until golden brown.

Energy 267kcal/1116kJ; Protein 8.6g; Carbohydrate 34.1g, of which sugars 3.3g; Fat 11.4g, of which saturates 1.4g; Cholesterol 0mg; Calcium 89mg; Fibre 4.1g; Sodium 153mg.

Green soya bean and rocket salad

This quick and simple salad is a refreshing change from simple salad leaves, as the young beans give a lovely texture. As well as being an excellent source of protein, green soya beans are also a good source of cholesterol-reducing isoflavones.

250g/9oz green soya beans
70g/2³/₄oz rocket (arugula) leaves
10ml/2 tsp chopped fresh basil leaves
10ml/2 tsp chopped fresh coriander (cilantro) leaves
1 tbsp olive oil

5ml/1 tsp lemon juice
5ml/1 tsp balsamic vinegar
fresh ground black pepper

SERVES 4

1 Cook the soya beans in boiling water for 5 minutes. Drain, then set aside to cool.

2 To make the dressing, mix together the olive oil, lemon juice and vinegar. Season with ground black pepper.

3 When the beans are cool, pour over the dressing and stir to mix both well together.

4 Toss the dressed beans together with the rocket and chopped herbs. Serve the salad immediately.

Cook's tip
Green soya beans are also known as edamame beans. You can buy them frozen for convenience.

Energy 125Kcal/520kJ; Protein 9g; Carbohydrate 4g, of which sugars 2g; Fat 8g, of which saturates 1g; Cholesterol 0mg; Calcium 59mg; Fibre 4g; Sodium 1mg.

Sprout salad with cashew cream dressing

This interesting salad has contrasting colours, textures and flavours and you can experiment with your own favourite sprout mix. The sprouts are very high in B-vitamins and vitamin C and the cashews and seeds are protein-rich, making this a highly nutritious salad.

130g/4¹/₂oz cashew nuts
1 red bell pepper, seeded
and finely chopped
90g/3¹/₂oz mung or aduki beansprouts
or chickpea sprouts
¹/₂ small cucumber, chopped
juice of ¹/₂ lemon
a small bunch of fresh parsley, coriander (cilantro)
or basil, finely chopped
5ml/1 tsp sesame, sunflower
or pumpkin seeds

SERVES 2

1 Soak the cashew nuts in 90ml/3¹/₂fl oz/6 tbsp of water for a few hours, preferably overnight, until they are plump.

2 Process the nuts with their soaking water in a food processor until you have a smooth sauce. Add more water if necessary.

3 Place the chopped pepper, sprouts, cucumber and lemon juice in a bowl and toss together. Serve with the cashew cream and sprinkle with the herbs and seeds.

Cook's tips
• The cashew cream makes a smooth dressing for many different salads or can be used as a sauce.
• There are all kinds of sprouts, and beansprouts are one of the most readily commercially available. Rinse thoroughly in cold water before using in salads, juices and other recipes. Choose fresh, crisp sprouts with the seed or bean still attached. Avoid any that are slimy or appear musty. Sprouts are best eaten on the day they are bought, but, if fresh, they will keep for 2–3 days wrapped in a plastic bag in the refrigerator.

Nutrition note
Cashews are rich in monounsaturated fatty acids, as found in the Mediterranean diet, and are favoured for their heart-protecting and anti-cancer properties.

Energy 352Kcal/1459kJ; Protein 12g; Carbohydrate 18g; of which sugars 10g; Fat 26g; of which saturates 5g; Cholesterol 0mg; Calcium 78mg; Fibre 4.7g; Sodium 19mg.

Aubergine and pomegranate seed salad

Variations of this dish can be found throughout the eastern Mediterranean.
Serve it either warm or at room temperature to make the most of the subtle, smoky flavour of
the aubergine and the sharp crunch of the pomegranate seeds.

2 aubergines (eggplants)
2 tomatoes, skinned, seeded
and chopped
1 green bell pepper, chopped
1 red onion, finely chopped
a bunch of flat leaf parsley, finely chopped
2 garlic cloves, crushed
30-45ml/2-3 tbsp olive oil

juice of 1 lemon
15-30ml/1-2 tbsp walnuts, finely chopped
15-30ml/1-2 tbsp pomegranate seeds
sea salt and ground black pepper
wedges of pomegranate, to garnish

SERVES 4

1 Place the aubergines on a hot griddle, or directly over a gas flame, and leave to char until soft, turning occasionally.

2 Hold the aubergines by their stems under running cold water and peel off the charred skins, or slit open the skins and scoop out the flesh.

3 Squeeze out the excess water from the aubergine flesh then chop it to a pulp and place it in a bowl with the tomatoes, pepper, onion, parsley and garlic.

4 Add the olive oil and lemon juice and toss thoroughly. Season to taste with salt and pepper, then stir in the walnuts and pomegranate seeds.

5 Turn the salad into a serving dish and garnish with wedges of pomegranate.

Nutrition note

Pomgranate seeds are packed full of vitamin C and are a good source of dietary fibre.

MAIN COURSES

This chapter features dishes that take full advantage of the huge variety of grains, beans, vegetables, pasta and rice that is available. These deliciously diverse main courses are full of mouthwatering flavours, and bring together influences from cuisines across the world to create nourishing and satisfying meals for lunch, midweek family suppers and entertaining with friends.

Tabbouleh with guacamole in a tortilla wrap

Tabbouleh is a classic Middle Eastern dish that is perfect for a vegan diet. The combination of spring onions, guacamole, lemon juice and plenty of fresh herbs creates a refreshing and healthy meal.

175g/6oz/1 cup bulgur wheat
25g/1 oz chopped fresh mint
25g/1 toz chopped fresh flat leaf parsley
1 bunch spring onions (scallions), sliced
1/2 cucumber, diced
50ml/2fl oz/1/4 cup extra-virgin olive oil
juice of 1 large lemon
salt and ground black pepper
4 wheat tortillas
flat leaf parsley, to garnish (optional)

For the guacamole
1 avocado, halved, stoned (pitted) and diced
juice of 1/2 lemon
1/2 red chilli, seeded and sliced (optional)
1 garlic clove, crushed
1/2 red bell pepper, seeded and finely diced

SERVES 4-6

1 To make the tabbouleh, place the bulgur wheat in a large heatproof bowl and pour over enough boiling water to cover. Leave for 30 minutes until the grains are tender but still retain a little resistance to the bite. Drain thoroughly, then place back into the bowl.

2 Add the mint, parsley, spring onions and cucumber to the bulgur wheat and mix thoroughly. Blend together the olive oil and lemon juice and pour over the tabbouleh, season to taste and toss well to mix. Chill for 30 minutes to allow the flavours to mingle.

3 To make the guacamole, place the avocado in a bowl and add the lemon juice, chilli and garlic. Season to taste and mash with a fork to form a smooth purée. Stir in the red pepper.

4 Warm the tortillas in a dry frying pan for about 20 seconds on each side. Serve the tortillas either flat, folded or rolled up with the tabbouleh and guacamole. Garnish with parsley, if liked.

Cook's tip
The soaking time for bulgur wheat can vary. For the best results, follow the instructions on the packet and taste the grain every now and again to check whether it is tender enough.

Variation
Use quinoa instead of bulgur wheat for a tasty and healthy alternative.

Energy 259kcal/1081kJ; Protein 5.1g; Carbohydrate 35g, of which sugars 1.9g; Fat 11.5g, of which saturates 1.9g; Cholesterol 0mg; Calcium 55mg; Fibre 1.7g; Sodium 52mg.

Jackfruit and avocado wrap

Not only is jackfruit delicious and incredibly versatile, it is also an excellent source of B-vitamins and is full of dietary fibre. This tasty wrap will keep you going right through until supper.

15ml/1 tbsp dark soy sauce
juice of 1/2 lime, the remaining 1/2 cut
into fine wedges for serving
5cm/2in piece of fresh ginger, peeled and finely grated
pinch of chilli flakes
565g/20oz can young jackfruit, drained
and roughly shredded
7.5ml/1/2 tbsp rapeseed oil
1/2 red onion, finely sliced
2 avocados, halved, stoned (pitted) and sliced
large handful of salad leaves
4 large wholemeal wraps

SERVES 4

1 In a small bowl, soak the red onion slices in cold water for 10 minutes, drain and set aside.

2 Add the soy sauce, lime juice, ginger and chilli flakes to a large bowl, add the jackfruit and toss to coat.

3 Heat the oil in a pan and add the jackfruit mixture, cook and stir around the pan for 4–5 minutes. Let it bubble a little and cook for a few minutes more.

4 Remove from the heat and stir through the drained onion.

5 Divide the mixture up between the wraps along with the leaves and avocado, then fold or roll and serve with a few lime wedges.

Cook's tip
Canned jackfruit is often packed with water and sometimes some salt so it is a good idea to rinse the jackfruit in cold water and drain prior to cooking.

Nutrition note
In recent years jackfruit has been hailed as a vegetarian meat alternative as it isn't as processed as other vegan 'meats', and when minced or ground the texture resembles that of pulled chicken or pulled pork. However, it is relatively low in protein so shouldn't be used as a regular protein source. Its high number of B vitamins and fibre will keep you fuller for longer though, and support metabolism, blood health and your heart.

Energy 420kcal/1764kJ; Protein 6.9g; Carbohydrate 64.8g, of which sugars 28.5g; Fat 16.6g, of which saturates 3.2g; Cholesterol 0mg; Calcium 110mg; Fibre 6.1g; Sodium 455mg.

Artichokes with beans and almonds

Globe artichokes are a variety of perennial thistle and have been a renowned epicurean delight for hundreds of years. Prized by the ancient Romans and grown in the garden of Henry VIII, they are still well-deserving of a place in every vegan's kitchen. In this dish, the tender bottoms are filled with fresh broad beans and flavoured with dill.

275g/10oz/2 cups shelled broad
(fava) beans
4 large globe artichokes
120ml/4fl oz/¹/₂ cup olive oil
juice of 1 lemon
10ml/2 tsp sugar

75g/3oz/³/₄ cup blanched almonds
a small bunch of fresh dill, chopped
2 tomatoes, skinned, seeded and diced
sea salt

SERVES 4

1 Put the beans in a pan of water and bring to the boil. Lower the heat, then simmer for 10–15 minutes or until tender. Drain and refresh under cold running water, then peel off the skins.

2 Prepare the artichokes. Cut off the stalks and pull off all the leaves. Dig out the hairy choke from the middle using a teaspoon, then cut away any hard bits with a small sharp knife and trim into a neat cup shape. Rub the cup-shaped bases – called bottoms – with a mixture of lemon juice and salt to prevent them from discolouring.

3 Place the prepared artichokes in a large, heavy pan. Mix together the olive oil, lemon juice and 50ml/2fl oz/¹/₄ cup water and pour the mixture over the artichokes.

4 Cover the pan with a tight-fitting lid and bring to a simmer. Cook the artichokes in the lemon juice and olive oil mixture gently for about 20 minutes.

5 Add the sugar, prepared broad beans and blanched almonds to the pan. Cover again with the lid and continue to simmer gently for a further 10 minutes, or until the artichokes are tender.

6 Toss half the chopped dill into the pan and season with sea salt. Mix all the ingredients together, then turn off the heat. Leave the artichokes to cool in the pan.

7 Lift the artichokes out of the pan and place them hollow-side up in a large serving dish. Mix the diced tomatoes with the beans and almonds in the pan.

8 Spoon the bean and vegetable mixture into the middle of the artichokes and all around them. Garnish with the remaining dill. Leave to cool, then serve.

Cook's tip
Fresh globe artichokes should be treated the same as fresh flowers. As soon as you get them home, place them in a jug or pitcher of water until you are ready to use them.

Energy 351kcal/1455kJ; Protein 8.2g; Carbohydrate 13.4g, of which sugars 8.3g; Fat 29.8g, of which saturates 3.6g; Cholesterol 0mg; Calcium 110mg; Fibre 5.5g; Sodium 29mg.

Lentils with mushrooms and anis

Rich in protein, iron, calcium and magnesium, lentils have been shown to be beneficial to heart health. Aniseed liqueur adds a delicious flavour to this nutritious dish.

30ml/2 tbsp olive oil
1 large onion, sliced
2 garlic cloves, finely chopped
250g/9oz/3 cups brown cap
(cremini) mushrooms, sliced
150g/5oz/generous ½ cup brown
or green lentils, soaked overnight
4 tomatoes, cut in eighths

1 bay leaf
175ml/6fl oz/¾ cup vegetable stock
25g/1oz chopped fresh parsley
30ml/2 tbsp anis spirit or anisette
pinch of paprika
sea salt and ground black pepper

SERVES 4

1 Heat the oil in a flameproof casserole. Add the onion and fry gently, with the garlic, until softened but not browned.

2 Add the sliced mushrooms and stir to combine with the onion and garlic. Continue cooking, stirring gently, for a couple of minutes.

3 Add the lentils, tomatoes, bay leaf and the stock. Simmer gently, covered, for 35 minutes until the lentils are soft, and the liquid has almost disappeared.

4 Stir in the parsley and anis. Season with salt, paprika and black pepper. Serve immediately in individual bowls.

Cook's tip

If you prefer not to use alcohol in your cooking, you can replace the anis with natural aniseed essence. Six drops is the equivalent of 15ml/1 tbsp anis.

Energy 216kcal/910kJ; Protein 12.4g; Carbohydrate 29.3g, of which sugars 9.6g; Fat 4.5g, of which saturates 0.7g; Cholesterol 0mg; Calcium 72mg; Fibre 6.9g; Sodium 26mg.

Curried leek and squash gratin

You can use virtually any kind of squash for this tasty gratin, which is perfect for a warming and hearty meal on a chilly day. Patty pans and acorn squash or pumpkins could all be used.

450g/1lb peeled and seeded squash,
cut into 1cm/^{1}/$_2$in slices
60ml/4 tbsp olive oil
450g/1lb leeks, cut into thick, diagonal slices
675g/1^1/$_2$lb tomatoes, peeled and
thickly sliced
2.5ml/^{1}/$_2$ tsp ground nutmeg
2.5ml/^{1}/$_2$ tsp cumin seeds, toasted and ground
300ml/^{1}/$_2$ pint/1^1/$_4$ cups coconut mik
1 fresh red chilli, seeded and sliced
1 garlic clove, finely chopped
15g/^{1}/$_2$ oz chopped fresh mint
25g/1 oz chopped fresh parsley
60ml/4 tbsp rolled oats
salt and ground black pepper

SERVES 4-6

1 Steam the squash over boiling salted water for 10 minutes.

2 Heat half the oil in a frying pan and cook the leeks gently for 5–6 minutes until lightly coloured. Try to keep the slices intact. Preheat the oven to 190°C/375°F/Gas 5.

3 Layer the squash, leeks and tomatoes in a large gratin dish, arranging them in rows. Sprinkle with salt, pepper, nutmeg and toasted cumin.

4 Pour the coconut milk into a small pan and add the sliced chilli and chopped garlic. Bring to the boil over a low heat, then stir in the mint. Pour the mixture evenly over the layered vegetables, using a rubber spatula to scrape all the sauce out of the pan.

5 Cook for about 45–50 minutes, or until the gratin is bubbling and tinged brown. After 25 minutes, sprinkle the parsley and oats on top and drizzle over the remaining oil. Bake for a further 15–20 minutes until the oats have turned brown and crispy. Serve the gratin immediately.

Cook's tip
For a more 'cheesy' flavour add mustard and a teaspoon of yeast extract or yeast flakes to the coconut milk.

Variation
For a curried version of this dish, use ground coriander as well as cumin. Use fresh coriander (cilantro) instead of the mint and parsley.

Energy 248kcal/1032kJ; Protein 5.7g; Carbohydrate 16.7g, of which sugars 7.8g; Fat 18g, of which saturates 7.4g; Cholesterol 28mg; Calcium 126mg; Fibre 3.8g; Sodium 104mg.

Sea aloo stew

This pretty bowl is brimming with goodness and is as pleasing to eat as it is on the eye. Seaweed works brilliantly with most spiced dishes, the earthy umami bringing out the nuances of the other flavours, and in this dish it also perfectly complements the spinach and tender new potatoes.

5ml/1 tsp cumin seeds
5ml/1 tsp mustard seeds
15-30ml/1-2 tbsp vegetable oil
1 large white onion, peeled and sliced
1cm/1/2 in piece of fresh root ginger, finely grated
1cm/1/2 in piece of fresh turmeric, finely grated, or
1.25ml/1/4 tsp ground turmeric
1 fresh chilli, finely chopped (optional)
2 garlic cloves, peeled and crushed
3 tomatoes, diced

500g/11/4lb new potatoes, scrubbed if necessary and halved
seaweed salt and ground black pepper, to taste
15g/1/2 oz dried sea salad, sea greens, or
large handful fresh seaweed, roughly chopped
65g/21/2 oz fresh dulse, roughly chopped or
10g/1/4oz flaked dulse
5ml/1 tsp garam masala
200g/7oz baby leaf spinach

SERVES 4

1 Heat a dry, heavy pan over a low heat, add the cumin and mustard seeds and toast for a couple of minutes, until they start popping and smell aromatic.

2 Remove from the heat and lightly crush the toasted seeds in a pestle and mortar or give them a quick whizz in a spice grinder, until they are coarsely ground.

3 Pour the oil into the pan and place over a medium heat, then add the onion, toasted spices, ginger, turmeric and chilli (if using). Cook until the onions are starting to soften.

4 Add the garlic and tomatoes and cook for a further few minutes, until both are starting to soften. Now add the potatoes, season well and add a splash of water. Put on the lid, turn down the heat and allow the mixture to simmer, stirring regularly and adding water as necessary so that the potatoes don't dry out.

5 When the potatoes are nearly cooked, add the seaweeds. Replace the lid and cook for a couple of minutes so the greens can rehydrate in the steam – make sure there is still moisture in the pan but bear in mind this is traditionally a dry-ish dish.

6 Finally, stir in the garam masala and baby leaf spinach, replace the lid and cook briefly, until the spinach has just wilted over the potatoes. Serve immediately.

Nutrition note
Many different seaweeds are rich in iodine so are a useful source of this nutritious mineral. Care does need to be taken however as excess intake may affect thyroid function. See page 21 for further information.

Energy 190kcal/798kJ; Protein 6g; Carbohydrate 28.2g, of which sugars 8.2g; Fat 6.7g, of which saturates 0.9g; Cholesterol 41mg; Calcium 130mg; Fibre 7.5g; Sodium 122mg.

Baked sweet potato with hummus

A baked potato makes an easy hot lunch, but why not ring the changes by baking a sweet potato and topping it with protein-rich, but low-fat hummus for a healthy mid-week meal.

2 x 350g/12oz sweet potatoes, scrubbed
2 tomatoes, diced
5cm/2in piece of cucumber, deseeded and diced
1/4 red onion, finely chopped or 1 spring onion (scallion), sliced
1/2 yellow bell pepper, cored, deseeded and diced

25g/1 oz chopped fresh parsley
15ml/1 tbsp olive oil
juice of 1/2 lemon
110g/4oz/1/2 cup hummus

SERVES 2

1 Preheat the oven to 200°C/400°F/Gas 6. Prick each potato several times with a fork then put on to a baking sheet and bake in the oven for 45–60 minutes or until soft.

2 Meanwhile mix the tomatoes, cucumber, onion and yellow pepper together in a bowl. Stir in the parsley, oil and lemon and set aside.

3 When the potatoes are cooked, make a slit along the length of each one, open out slightly and put on to 2 serving plates. Spoon the hummus into the centre of each one then top with the salad and serve.

Nutrition note
Sweet potatoes, with their bright orange flesh, are an excellent source of beta-carotene, converted by the body into vitamin A plus vitamin C. Sprinkle with shelled hemp seed hearts for extra protein and omega 3 essential fats.

Cook's tip
To make it a more substantial meal add a green salad or add baked beans, steamed broccoli and some shredded red cabbage sautéed in balsamic vinegar and tamari sauce.

Energy 494kcal/2090kJ; Protein 9.7g; Carbohydrate 88.1g, of which sugars 27.9g; Fat 14g, of which saturates 2.2g; Cholesterol 0mg; Calcium 118mg; Fibre 15.6g; Sodium 518mg.

Grilled vegetable pizza

You really cannot go too far wrong with this classic mixture of grilled vegetables on home-made pizza dough. It is filling and healthy, and is a favourite with children.

4 plum tomatoes, skinned and chopped
60ml/4 tbsp olive oil
1 garlic clove, crushed
25g/1 oz chopped fresh basil
1 courgette (zucchini), sliced
6 mushrooms, sliced
2 baby aubergines (eggplants)
or 1 small aubergine, sliced
1 yellow bell pepper, seeded and sliced
50g/2oz/¹/₂ cup cornmeal
50g/2oz/¹/₂ cup buckwheat flour
100g/4oz/1 cup soya flour

5ml/1 tsp baking powder
50g/2oz/¹/₄ cup dairy-free spread
100ml/3¹/₂ fl oz/scant ¹/₂ cup soya milk
salt and ground black pepper

For the 'cheesy' topping
120ml/4fl oz/¹/₂ cup rapeseed (canola) oil
120ml/4fl oz/¹/₂ cup soya milk
15ml/1 tbsp tomato ketchup
5ml/1 tsp French mustard

SERVES 6

1 In a pan, place the chopped tomatoes, half the olive oil, garlic and the basil and season with salt and pepper. Simmer until reduced to a thick sauce.

2 Preheat the grill or broiler. Brush the courgette, mushrooms aubergine and pepper slices with a little oil and place on a grill rack. Grill until lightly browned.

3 Meanwhile, make the cheesy topping. With a hand blender or liquidizer, blend the oil and soya milk with the tomato ketchup and mustard to form a mayonnaise consistency. If the sauce is too runny, add 15ml/1 tbsp of potato flour.

4 Meanwhile, preheat the oven to 200°C/400°F/Gas 6. Place the cornmeal, buckwheat flour, soya flour, baking powder and 2.5ml/¹/₂ tsp salt in a large mixing bowl and stir until well combined. Lightly rub in the spread until the mixture resembles breadcrumbs, then stir in enough soya milk to make a soft dough.

5 Place the dough on a piece of baking parchment on a baking sheet and roll or gently press it out to form a 25cm/10in round, making the edges thicker than the centre.

6 Brush the dough with the remaining olive oil, then spread the tomato sauce evenly over the dough. Arrange the grilled vegetables on top of the tomato sauce and finish with the 'cheese' topping. Bake for 25–30 minutes until crisp and golden brown, then serve in slices.

Energy 426kcal/1768kJ; Protein 9.2g; Carbohydrate 28.4g, of which sugars 7.1g; Fat 30.8g, of which saturates 5.9g; Cholesterol 1mg; Calcium 47mg; Fibre 4.2g; Sodium 139mg.

Vegetable kebabs with a harissa dip

These skewered vegetables are first coated in a spicy oil and lemon juice marinade before grilling. Serve with a fiery harissa and soya yogurt dip for a flavoursome, healthy meal.

2 aubergines (eggplants), cut into chunks
8 button (white) mushrooms
2 courgettes (zucchini), cut into chunks
2-3 red or green bell peppers, seeded and cut into chunks
12-16 cherry tomatoes
4 small red onions, quartered
60ml/4 tbsp olive oil
juice of 1/2 lemon
1 garlic clove, crushed
5ml/1 tsp ground coriander
5ml/1 tsp ground cinnamon

10ml/2 tsp dark soy sauce
10ml/2 tsp agave syrup
pinch of sea salt

For the harissa and yogurt dip
450g/1lb/2 cups soya yogurt or coconut cream
30-60ml/2-4 tbsp harissa
a small bunch of fresh coriander (cilantro) chopped
a small bunch of mint, finely chopped
salt and ground black pepper

SERVES 4

1 Preheat the grill or broiler on the hottest setting. Put all the vegetables in a large bowl. Mix together the olive oil, lemon juice, garlic, ground coriander, cinnamon, dark soy sauce, agave syrup and sea salt to taste and pour the mixture over the vegetables.

2 Using your hands, turn the vegetables gently in the marinade until they are well coated. Thread them on to metal skewers, alternating the vegetables.

3 Cook the kebabs under the grill, turning them occasionally, until the vegetables are nicely browned all over.

4 Meanwhile make the dip. Put the yogurt in a bowl and beat in the harissa, using as much as you need to suit how fiery you like the taste. Add most of the chopped coriander and mint, reserving a little to garnish, and season well with salt and ground black pepper.

5 Serve the skewers immediately with the dip, garnished with the reserved herbs. While the vegetables are still hot, slide them off the skewers and dip them into the yogurt and harissa dip before eating. Serve with a green salad, brown rice or quinoa if you like, or inside a tortilla wrap.

Cook's tips
• Make sure you cut the vegetables into even chunks, so they will cook at the same time under the grill.
• This works well on a barbecue too.

Energy 305kcal/1267kJ; Protein 9.9g; Carbohydrate 24.8g, of which sugars 22.6g; Fat 19.1g, of which saturates 6.6g; Cholesterol 16mg; Calcium 230mg; Fibre 5.2g; Sodium 181mg.

Sun-dried tomato and herb polenta with fried tomatoes

Golden polenta is a wheat-free vegan favourite but can taste a little bland on its own. Here it is flavoured with fresh summer herbs and then pan-fried and served with tomatoes.

750ml/1¼ pints/3 cups vegetable stock or water
5ml/1 tsp salt
175g/6oz/1 cup polenta
4 sun-dried tomatoes, chopped
25g/1oz/2 tbsp dairy-free margarine
75g/3 oz chopped mixed fresh parsley, thyme, chives and basil, plus extra, to garnish

olive oil, for greasing and brushing
4 large plum or beefsteak tomatoes
salt and ground black pepper

SERVES 4

1 Prepare the polenta in advance. Place the stock or water in a heavy pan, with the salt, and bring to the boil. Lower the heat, slowly pour in the polenta and stir with a wooden spoon.

2 Stir the mixture constantly, using a figure-of-eight action, over a medium heat for 5 minutes, until the polenta begins to thicken and come away from the sides of the pan.

3 Add the sun-dried tomatoes to the polenta. Stir the mixture thoroughly so the tomatoes are well combined.

4 Remove from the heat and continue stirring for another minute or two. Stir in the margarine, freshly chopped parsley, thyme, chives and basil, and season with black pepper.

5 Transfer the mixture into a wide, greased tin or pan or a glass or ceramic dish. Using a flexible spatula, spread the polenta mixture out evenly in the tin. Cover the surface closely with baking parchment, then put it in a cool place until it has set completely and is cold.

6 Turn out the polenta on to a board and stamp out eight rounds using a large biscuit or cookie cutter. You can also cut the polenta into eight squares with a knife, if you prefer. Brush with oil.

7 Heat a griddle pan and lightly brush it with oil. Cut the tomatoes in two, then brush them with oil and sprinkle with salt and pepper. Cook the tomato halves and polenta patties on the pan for 5 minutes, turning them once. Serve garnished with fresh herbs.

Cook's tip
To increase the protein and omega 3 values of this dish add 20g/4 tsp of shelled hemp seed hearts or chia seeds to the polenta mix.

Energy 147kcal/612kJ; Protein 3.2g; Carbohydrate 23.4g, of which sugars 2.1g; Fat 4.2g, of which saturates 1.5g; Cholesterol 5mg; Calcium 6mg; Fibre 1.3g; Sodium 349mg.

Mushroom pasta with cashews and oat cream

Mushroom tagliatelle is always going to be a satisfying option for a quick supper or mid-week family meal. The cashews and oat milk add protein and added fibre.

4 nests of dried egg-free tagliatelle
150g/5oz/unsalted cashew nuts
4 garlic cloves
5ml/1 tsp Dijon mustard
250ml/8fl oz/1 cup oat milk
150g/5oz chestnut mushrooms, cleaned and sliced

50g/2oz pine nuts
1 pack of watercress (washed), roughly chopped, plus some leaves for garnishing

SERVES 4

1 Place the tageliatelle in boiling water and cook according to the manufacturer's instructions.

2 Meanwhile, in a food processor blend together the cashew nuts, garlic, mustard and oat milk.

3 Add the sauce to a separate pan and add the sliced mushrooms. Simmer the sauce for approximately 10 minutes, stirring occasionally.

4 Dry-roast the pine nuts in a small, heavy pan until they turn golden brown and give off a nutty aroma. Remove from the heat.

5 Drain the pasta, stir in the watercress, then stir in the sauce.

6 Serve while still hot, with the toasted pine nuts and extra watercress florets.

Nutrition note

Chestnut mushrooms contain glutathione and ergotheonine, two powerful anti-aging antioxidants. They are also good for your cells and blood health and support your immune system.

Energy 432kcal/1800kJ; Protein 12.9g; Carbohydrate 26.8g, of which sugars 6.3g; Fat 28.4g, of which saturates 4.3g; Cholesterol 0mg; Calcium 57mg; Fibre 3.8g; Sodium 55mg.

Courgetti Genovese

This Italian dish is made with a vegan dairy-free pesto sauce: a blend of pine nuts, olive oil, fresh basil and garlic, a wonderful mix of fragrant flavours. There's nothing quite like the taste of home-made, but if you are too busy to make your own, use a good-quality shop-bought jar.

3 large courgettes (zucchini), preferably a mixture of green and yellow, about 800g/1³/₄lb
1 large carrot
1 medium waxy potato, peeled and cut into 1cm/³/₄in cubes
sprigs of fresh basil, to garnish

For the pesto sauce
leaves from a large bunch of basil, about 40g/1¹/₂oz
2 garlic cloves, peeled
50g/2oz/¹/₂ cup pine nuts
120ml/4fl oz/¹/₂ cup olive oil
25g/1oz/¹/₄ cup freshly grated dairy-free vegan hard Italian-style cheese, or nutritional yeast flakes mixed with 50% shelled hemp seed hearts
10ml/2 tsp fresh lemon juice
salt and ground black pepper

SERVES 4

1 To make the pesto, roughly tear the basil leaves and place in a mortar with the garlic, pine nuts and 30ml/2 tbsp of the oil. Pound with a pestle into a paste. Alternatively, place the ingredients in a food processor and blend until fairly smooth.

2 Reserve 30ml/2 tbsp of the oil and gradually work the rest into the basil mixture (if you are using a food processor, pour in through the feed tube in a thin drizzle). Transfer to a bowl and stir in the grated cheese or nutritional yeast flakes mixed with hemp seed hearts, and the lemon juice. Season to taste.

3 Spiralize the courgettes and carrot using the 3mm/¹/₈in (medium) spiralizer noodle blade. If you do not have a spiralizer cut the courgettes and carrot into fine strips.

4 Bring a large pan of lightly salted water to the boil. Add the potato cubes, bring back to the boil and simmer, covered for 7 minutes. Add the carrot noodles and when the water comes back to the boil, add the courgette noodles. Cook for a further 3 minutes or until all the noodles are tender.

5 Tip into a colander and drain thoroughly, shaking gently for a minute to allow some of the steam to evaporate. Tip the vegetables back into the pan and heat gently for a few seconds to evaporate any juices which leak from the courgettes. Spoon over half of the pesto sauce, stir to coat all the vegetables, then serve straight away on warm plates. Garnish with basil sprigs.

6 Spoon the remaining pesto into a clean glass jar and top with the reserved 30ml/2 tbsp olive oil (this will help preserve it). Store in the refrigerator for up to 2 weeks.

Variations
• For rocket (arugula) pesto, replace the basil with rocket leaves and 30ml/2 tbsp roughly chopped fresh parsley leaves.
• For mint and almond pesto, replace the basil with 25g/1oz fresh mint leaves and 25g/1oz flat-leaf parsley leaves. Use blanched almonds instead of the pine nuts.
• When cooking the vegetables, use 75g/3oz/¹/₂ cup defrosted petit pois instead of the spiralized carrot.
• This works well as a raw dish too. Swap the potatoes for radish and toss the vegetable 'noodles' in a little oil to soften.

Energy 372kcal/1538kJ; Protein 8.7g; Carbohydrate 14g, of which sugars 5.8g; Fat 31.5g, of which saturates 4.9g; Cholesterol 22mg; Calcium 149mg; Fibre 4g; Sodium 66mg.

Vegetable moussaka with tofu topping

This vegan adaptation of the famous Greek dish is just as delicious as the traditional version made with lamb mince. An almond and tofu topping is used instead of the usual cheese sauce.

600g/1lb 6oz aubergines (eggplants), cut into 2.5cm/1in slices
30ml/2 tbsp olive oil
paprika and fresh basil leaves, to garnish
sea salt and ground black pepper

For the sauce
30ml/2 tbsp olive oil
2 large onions, coarsely chopped
2 garlic cloves, crushed
2 large carrots, finely chopped
4 courgettes (zucchini), sliced
200g/7oz mushrooms, sliced
2 x 400g/14oz cans chopped tomatoes

30ml/2 tbsp balsamic vinegar
20ml/4 tsp yeast extract
15ml/1 tbsp agave syrup
5ml/1 tsp ground nutmeg

For the tofu topping
200g/7oz/1¾ cups ground almonds
350g/12oz silken tofu
30ml/2 tbsp tomato ketchup
15ml/1 tbsp soy sauce
15ml/1 tbsp lemon juice
2.5ml/½ tsp English (hot) mustard powder

SERVES 8

1 Preheat the grill or broiler to high. Place the aubergine slices in one layer on the rack. Drizzle with oil and grill for 2–3 minutes on each side until golden.

2 Make the sauce. Heat the oil in a large pan and fry the onions, garlic and carrots for 5–7 minutes. Add the remaining ingredients to the pan and season. Bring to the boil, then simmer for 20 minutes.

3 Meanwhile, make the topping. Toast the ground almonds in a heavy frying pan, without any oil, for 1–2 minutes, tossing occasionally until golden. Reserve about two-thirds of the almonds. Place the remainder in a food processor or blender and add the rest of the topping ingredients. Process the mixture until smooth and well combined. Taste and adjust the seasoning.

4 Preheat the oven to 180°C/350°F/Gas 4. Spread half the sauce in a 35 x 23cm/14 x 9in ovenproof dish. Add a layer of aubergine slices and spread over the remaining sauce. Finish with a layer of aubergine slices.

5 Spoon the tofu topping over the aubergine slices, ensuring it is spread evenly. Bake for about 20–25 minutes until the topping is set and has turned golden brown. Garnish with a sprinkling of paprika, fresh basil leaves and a little olive oil. Serve immediately.

Nutrition note
A good source of folate and fibre, aubergines also contain moderate amounts of potassium, manganese and B vitamins. The dark-purple skin is a rich source of anthocyanins. These flavonoid compounds are potent antioxidants.

Energy 768kcal/3255kJ; Protein 60.3g; Carbohydrate 109.6g, of which sugars 10.3g; Fat 13.1g, of which saturates 2.9g; Cholesterol 99mg; Calcium 357mg; Fibre 21.8g; Sodium 320mg.

Stuffed red peppers with pine nuts

Some older vegans may have haunting memories of stuffed red peppers rustled up by a panicked chef but they are enjoying a resurgence and have had many makeovers since the traditional flavourless overcooked rice version. This is great with some good fresh bread and a green salad, and it makes a colourful addition to an alfresco lunch.

30g/2 tbsp pine nuts
4 red bell peppers
1 red onion, finely chopped
30g/2 tbsp chopped fresh oregano
115g/4oz cherry tomatoes, cut in half
grated rind and juice of 1 orange

15g/1 tbsp capers, rinsed and
  roughly chopped
45ml/3 tbsp olive oil
salt and ground black pepper

SERVES 4

1 Preheat the oven to 200°C/400°F/Gas 6.

2 In a small frying pan toast the pine nuts for about 3–4 minutes until golden. Watch them closely, as they burn quickly. Take the pan off the heat and set aside.

3 Cut the peppers into halves following the natural lines from the top down to the bottom. Don't chop the top of the peppers off before you cut them in half – the rounded ends are needed, to keep the filling in.

4 Cut out any big bits of white pith from the pepper halves. Put the pepper halves into a flat, wide, ovenproof dish.

5 In a bowl, toss the chopped onion with the oregano, cherry tomatoes, orange rind and juice, capers, pine nuts and olive oil. Season well with salt and pepper. Pile the tomato mixture into the pepper halves.

6 Bake in the oven for 20–30 minutes, until the peppers are tender and slightly charred but still hold their shape.

7 Take the dish out of the oven. Arrange the peppers on a plate and serve hot or at room temperature with some good crusty bread and a green salad.

Nutrition note

Like chillies, sweet or bell peppers are members of the capsicum family. Ranging in colours from green through to orange, yellow, red and even purple, the green peppers are fully developed but not completely ripe, which can make them difficult to digest. Other colours of peppers are more mature, have sweeter flesh, and are more digestible. Peppers are very high in vitamin C and the caretonoids b-cryptoxanthin and lycopene, all of which are powerful antioxidants. They are also a good source of fibre, vitamins A, K and B6, as well as potassium and manganese.

Energy 229kcal/1949kJ; Protein 3g; Carbohydrate 16g, of which sugars 15g; Fat 17g, of which saturates 0g; Cholesterol 99mg; Calcium 29mg; Fibre 2g; Sodium 137mg.

Courgette, mushroom and almond milk lasagne

This healthy dish is topped with an almond milk sauce. It is ideal for a family meal or casual entertaining and can be made several hours in advance.

8 no pre-cook lasagne sheets
fresh oregano leaves, to garnish

For the tomato sauce
15g/$\frac{1}{2}$oz dried porcini mushrooms
120ml/4fl oz/$\frac{1}{2}$ cup hot water
30ml/2 tbsp olive oil
1 onion, chopped
1 carrot, chopped
1 celery stick, chopped
2 x 400g/14oz cans chopped tomatoes
15ml/1 tbsp tomato purée (paste)
5ml/1 tsp dried basil

For the vegetable mixture
45ml/3 tbsp olive oil
450g/1 lb courgettes (zucchini), thinly sliced
1 onion, finely chopped
450g/1 lb/6 cups chestnut mushrooms, thinly sliced
2 garlic cloves, crushed
salt and ground black pepper

For the white sauce
40g/1$\frac{1}{2}$oz/3 tbsp dairy-free margarine
40g/1$\frac{1}{2}$ oz/$\frac{1}{2}$ cup plain (all-purpose) flour
900ml/1$\frac{1}{2}$ pints/3$\frac{1}{4}$ cups almond milk

SERVES 6

1 To make the tomato sauce, put the porcini mushrooms in a bowl. Pour over the hot water and soak for 15 minutes. Tip the porcini and liquid into a sieve or strainer set over a bowl to retain the soaking liquid and squeeze the mushrooms with your hands to release as much liquid as possible. Chop the mushrooms finely and set aside. Pour the soaking liquid through a fine sieve and reserve.

2 Heat the olive oil in a pan, add the chopped onion, carrot and celery and fry for about 10 minutes, until softened. Place in a food processor with the tomatoes, tomato purée, dried basil, porcini and soaking liquid, and blend to a purée.

3 For the vegetable mixture, heat 15ml/1 tbsp of the olive oil in a large pan. Add half the courgette slices and season. Cook over a medium heat for 5-8 minutes, until lightly coloured on both sides. Remove to a bowl. Repeat with the remaining courgettes and 15ml/1 tbsp olive oil.

4 Heat the remaining 15ml/1 tbsp olive oil in the pan and cook the onion for 3 minutes, stirring. Add the chestnut mushrooms and garlic and cook for 5 minutes. Add to the courgettes.

5 Preheat the oven to 190°C/375°F/Gas 5.

6 For the white sauce, melt the margarine in a large pan, then add the flour and cook, stirring for 1 minute. Gradually whisk in the almond milk, then bring to the boil and cook, stirring, until the sauce is smooth and thick. Season to taste.

7 Ladle half of the tomato sauce into a shallow ovenproof dish and spread out to cover the base. Add half the vegetable mixture, spreading it evenly. Top with about one-third of the white sauce, then about half the lasagne sheets, breaking them to fit the dish. Repeat these layers, then top with the remaining white sauce.

8 Bake for 30-45 minutes, until the top is bubbling and golden and the lasagne is tender. Garnish with fresh oregano leaves.

Energy 421kcal/1757kJ; Protein 15.5g; Carbohydrate 32.9g, of which sugars 15g; Fat 26.2g, of which saturates 12.4g; Cholesterol 49mg; Calcium346mg; Fibre 3.8g; Sodium 310mg.

Braised tofu with mushrooms

Tofu, whether fresh, fried or dried, can be braised with rich or subtle seasonings for a superb vegan dish. As a neutral product, tofu absorbs other flavours easily. In Chinese cuisine tofu is not regarded as a meat substitute, but with reverence for its own nutritional and chameleon-like qualities. With complementary ingredients like mushrooms and vegetables, this dish achieves banquet status.

350g/12oz dried or deep-fried tofu
115g/4oz canned straw mushrooms
1 leek
15ml/1 tbsp vegetable oil
30ml/2 tbsp hoisin sauce
15ml/1 tbsp dark soy sauce
2.5ml/$^{1}/_{2}$ tsp ground black pepper
1 garlic clove, chopped

2.5ml/ $^{1}/_{2}$ tsp minced fresh root ginger
15ml/1 tbsp dry sherry
2.5ml/$^{1}/_{2}$ tsp sugar
15ml/1 tbsp sesame oil
5ml/1 tsp cornflour (cornstarch)
plain boiled rice, to serve

SERVES 4

1 If using dried tofu, cut each square into two triangles. If using deep-fried tofu cubes, you can leave them whole, as they are usually already bitesize.

2 Drain the straw mushrooms. Slice the leek diagonally into 1cm/½in wide slices. Wash in plenty of cold water to remove the soil that often clings to the insides of the white stalks. Drain thoroughly.

3 Heat the oil in a wok, add the leek, and stir-fry for 1 minute. Add the hoisin sauce, soy sauce, pepper, garlic, ginger, sherry, sugar, sesame oil and 350ml/12fl oz/1½ cups water, and bring to the boil.

4 Add the tofu, and simmer for 10 minutes over medium heat. Just before serving, mix the cornflour with a little water and add to the pan. Stir until the sauce thickens a little, then serve immediately, with some plain rice.

Cook's tip
To make your own fried tofu, buy the firm white variety and cut into cubes. Heat plenty of oil until smoking, and deep-fry the tofu, in batches, until a golden skin forms.

Energy 152kcal/629kJ; Protein 8g; Carbohydrate 3g, of which sugars 1g; Fat 11g, of which saturates 1g; Cholesterol 0mg; Calcium 458mg; Fibre 1g; Sodium 323mg.

Spinach tofu stir-fry with seaweed

The idea for this recipe came from the Indian dish saag paneer (fried spinach and fresh cheese), but here we use tofu in place of the paneer (making it vegan) and some seaweed in with the spinach. If you are able to forage for your own dulse, you can substitute more of the spinach with the seaweed – just make sure you taste it before you add any additional salt.

olive oil, for frying
200g/7oz tofu, cut into roughly 2cm/¾in cubes or pieces
5ml/1 tsp cumin seeds
1 onion, finely chopped
2 garlic cloves, finely chopped
1cm/½in fresh root ginger, peeled and chopped
10ml/2 tsp garam masala
10ml/2 tsp turmeric

1 ripe tomato or canned tomato
300g/11oz frozen or fresh spinach
50ml/2fl oz/¼ cup coconut cream or dairy-free vegan yogurt
30g/1½oz dried dulse or 185g/6½oz fresh dulse, cut into strips
seaweed salt and ground black pepper, to taste

SERVES 4

1 Heat a glug of olive oil in a frying pan over a medium-high heat, add the tofu and fry, turning carefully and frequently using kitchen tongs, for about 5 minutes or until the pieces are golden all over. Transfer to a piece of kitchen paper to drain. Set aside.

2 Reheat the pan in which the tofu was fried and add the cumin seeds. Cook for 1 minute.

3 Add the chopped onion and cook gently for about 10 minutes, until softened, then stir in the garlic, ginger, garam masala and turmeric.

4 Cut the tomato in half and seed it, then chop it. Add this to the pan and cook for a further 10 minutes. If you use a tinned tomato, reduce the time to 5 minutes.

5 Add the spinach, cover and cook for a few minutes, then stir in the coconut cream or dairy-free vegan yogurt, tofu, and the fresh or dried dulse.

6 Reduce the heat and simmer for 5 minutes with the lid off, so the cream starts to thicken. Season to taste and serve.

Cook's tip
Grated fresh turmeric would be great in this dish. Coconut cream and plenty of black pepper make the alleged anti-imflammatory properties of the curcumin in turmeric more potent.

Energy 141kcal/587kJ; Protein 8.1g; Carbohydrate 7g, of which sugars 4g; Fat 9.3g, of which saturates 1.3g; Cholesterol 0mg; Calcium 473mg; Fibre 8.7g; Sodium 263mg.

Spicy black bean and quinoa burgers

These burgers use low-fat and fibre-rich canned black beans, which are a handy kitchen standby. Combined with hot jalapeño peppers, chilli, lime and fresh coriander leaves, quinoa adds protein and contributes to a wholesome, rustic texture. Serve in burger buns, or with potato wedges and coleslaw.

115g/4oz/²/³ cup pearl quinoa, rinsed
350ml/12fl oz/1¹/² cups water
30ml/2 tbsp vegetable oil
1 medium onion, finely chopped
1 stick celery, finely chopped
2 garlic cloves, crushed
6 jalapeño peppers, finely chopped
1 fresh red or green chilli, finely chopped
2 medium carrots, peeled and grated
75g/3oz/¹/² cup roasted peanuts

1 lime, rind and juice
15g/¹/² oz fresh coriander (cilantro), roughly chopped
400g/14oz can black beans, drained and rinsed
15ml/1 tbsp quinoa flour, for shaping
salt and ground black pepper
burger buns, shredded lettuce, sliced tomato and plant-based crème fraîche or vegan mayonnaise, to serve

SERVES 6

1 Place the quinoa and water in a medium pan, bring to the boil and simmer for 15–17 minutes until soft.

2 In another pan heat 15ml/1 tbsp of the oil and add the onion, celery, garlic, jalapeños, chilli and salt and pepper.

3 Cook for 2–3 minutes on medium heat, then add the grated carrot and cook for 3 minutes. Leave to cool.

4 Blitz the cooked quinoa, peanuts, lime juice and rind, and coriander in a food processor. Add the beans and pulse a couple of times to incorporate. Add the vegetable mixture to the processor and pulse briefly to combine. Test for seasoning.

5 On a board, shape the mixture into six burgers, handling lightly, and using quinoa flour as required to stop the mixture from sticking.

6 In a large non-stick frying pan, fry the burgers in the remaining 15ml/1 tbsp oil, adding a little more if needed, and turning them halfway through cooking. Alternatively, spritz with oil and cook in foil on a hot barbecue.

7 Serve in halved rolls with shredded lettuce, sliced tomato and plant-based crème fraîche or vegan mayonnaise.

Cook's tip
Quinoa needs rinsing in water before cooking to remove natural saponins that coat the seed, which can give the seed a bitter taste. Most commercial quinoa is already rinsed, but it's likely that some saponins will remain. Running water through quinoa in a sieve or colander, and rubbing it with your fingers, will remove any residue.

Energy 296kcal/1243kJ; Protein 13g; Carbohydrate 33g, of which sugars 5g; Fat 14g, of which saturates 2g; Cholesterol 0mg; Calcium 55mg; Fibre 8g; Sodium 68mg.

Mixed bean and aubergine tagine

The ingredients in this satisfying vegan Moroccan dish are slow-cooked, producing a rich and sumptuous sauce. This is a perfect dish for a slow cooker or a pressure cooker. If you have a sweet tooth try adding in a handful of fresh or dried apricots (allow one per person).

115g/4oz/generous ¹/₂ cup dried red kidney beans, soaked overnight in cold water and drained
115g/4oz/generous ¹/₂ cup dried black-eyed beans (peas) or cannellini beans, soaked overnight in cold water and drained
600ml/1 pint/2¹/₂ cups water
2 bay leaves
2 celery sticks, each cut into 4 matchsticks
60ml/4 tbsp olive oil
1 aubergine (eggplant), about 350g/12oz
1 onion, thinly sliced

3 garlic cloves, crushed
1–2 fresh red chillies, seeded and chopped
30ml/2 tbsp tomato purée (paste)
5ml/1 tsp paprika
2 large tomatoes, roughly chopped
300ml/¹/₂ pint/1¹/₄ cups vegetable stock
15g/1 tbsp each chopped fresh mint, parsley and coriander (cilantro)
salt and ground black pepper
fresh herb sprigs, to garnish

SERVES 4

1 Place the soaked and drained kidney beans in a large pan of unsalted boiling water. Bring back to the boil and cook the beans for 10 minutes, then drain.

2 Place the soaked and drained black-eyed or cannellini beans in a separate large pan of boiling unsalted water. Boil the beans rapidly for 10 minutes, then drain.

3 Place the measured water in a large tagine or casserole, and add the bay leaves, celery and both beans. Cover and place in the oven at 190°C/375°F/Gas 5. Cook for 1–1½ hours, or until the beans are tender, then drain.

4 Heat 45ml/3 tbsp of the oil in a frying pan or cast-iron tagine base. Cut the aubergine into chunks and cook, stirring for 4–5 minutes until evenly browned. Remove from the heat and set aside.

5 Add the remaining oil to the frying pan or tagine base. Add the sliced onion and cook 4–5 minutes, until softened. Add the garlic and chillies and cook for a further 5 minutes.

6 Reset the oven temperature to 160°C/325°F/Gas 3. Add the tomato purée and paprika to the onion mixture and cook for 1–2 minutes. Add the tomatoes, aubergine, cooked beans and stock to the pan, then season to taste.

7 Cover the tagine base with the lid or, if using a frying pan, transfer the contents to a clay tagine or casserole. Bake in the oven for 1 hour.

8 Just before serving, add the fresh mint, parsley and coriander and lightly stir through the vegetables. Garnish with fresh herbs.

Cook's tip
Replace the dried red kidney and black-eyed beans with canned, if you like.

Energy 209Kcal/890kJ; Protein 16.6g; Carbohydrate 33.9g, of which sugars 9.4g; Fat 1.9g, of which saturates 0.5g; Cholesterol 1mg; Calcium 173mg; Fibre 12.3g; Sodium 62mg.

Stir-fried seeds and vegetables

The multitude of seeds in this recipe will provide all of the essential fatty acids the body needs, and the colourful vegetables make it very pleasing to the eye. For a more substantial meal, try this with buckwheat noodles or rice noodles.

30ml/2 tbsp vegetable oil
30ml/2 tbsp pumpkin seeds
30ml/2 tbsp shelled (dehulled) hemp seed hearts
30ml/2 tbsp sesame seeds
30ml/2 tbsp sunflower seeds
2 garlic cloves, finely chopped
2.5cm/1in fresh root ginger, peeled and finely chopped
2 large carrots, cut into batons
2 large courgettes (zucchini), cut into batons
90g/3½oz/1½ cups oyster mushrooms, broken into
   pieces
150g/5oz watercress or spinach leaves, coarsely chopped
a bunch of fresh mint or coriander (cilantro), chopped
60ml/4 tbsp black bean sauce
30ml/2 tbsp light soy sauce
15ml/1 tbsp rice vinegar

SERVES 4

1 Heat the oil in a wok. Add the pumpkin seeds. Toss over a medium heat for 1–2 minutes until they pop, then add the other seeds, garlic and ginger, and continue to stir-fry until the ginger is aromatic and the garlic is golden.

2 Add the carrot and courgette batons and mushroom pieces to the wok and stir-fry over a medium heat for a further 5 minutes, or until all the vegetables are crisp and golden at the edges.

3 Add the watercress or spinach with the fresh herbs and toss over the heat for 1 minute.

4 Stir in the black bean sauce, soy sauce and vinegar. Stir-fry for 1–2 minutes, until combined and hot. Serve immediately.

Cook's tip
Oyster mushrooms are delicate, so it is usually better to tear them into pieces along the lines of the gills, rather than slice them with a knife.

Energy 205kcal/849kJ; Protein 6.9g; Carbohydrate 9.7g, of which sugars 7.7g; Fat 15.6g, of which saturates 2g; Cholesterol 0mg; Calcium 159mg; Fibre 3.4g; Sodium 294mg.

Fruit and nut couscous

This dish of couscous mixed with apricots, raisins and nuts would typically form part of a celebration meal in Morocco. It is delicious served on its own, but for a more substantial meal it is especially good served alongside a spicy tagine made with chunky vegetables.

500g/1¼lb/3 cups couscous
600ml/1 pint/2½ cups warm water
5ml/1 tsp salt
pinch of saffron threads
45ml/3 tbsp sunflower oil
30ml/2 tbsp olive oil
115g/4oz/½ cup ready-to-eat dried apricots,
cut into slivers
75g/3oz/½ cup dried dates, chopped

75g/3oz/generous ½ cup raisins
115g/4oz/⅔ cup blanched almonds, sliced
75g/3oz/½ cup pistachio nuts
10ml/2 tsp ground cinnamon
15ml/3 tsp coconut sugar

SERVES 6

1 Preheat the oven to 180°C/350°F/Gas 4. Put the couscous in a bowl. Mix together the water, salt and saffron and pour it over the couscous, stirring. Leave to stand for 10 minutes. Add the sunflower oil and, using your fingers, rub it through the grains. Set aside.

2 Heat the olive oil in a large pan and stir in the apricots, dates, raisins, most of the almonds (reserve some for the garnish) and pistachio nuts.

3 Cook until the raisins plump up, then transfer into the couscous and mix well. Spoon the couscous into an ovenproof dish and cover with foil. Bake in the oven for 20 minutes, until heated through.

4 Toast the reserved sliced almonds. Pile the couscous in a mound on a serving dish and sprinkle with the cinnamon and sugar in stripes down the mound. Sprinkle the toasted almonds over the top and serve.

Energy 576kcal/2403kJ; Protein 12.5g; Carbohydrate 73g, of which sugars 29.4g; Fat 27.8g, of which saturates 3.1g; Cholesterol 0mg; Calcium 102mg; Fibre 4.2g; Sodium 74mg.

Couscous with aubergine and hummus

Rather than a base, hummus is served here as a tasty protein-boosting topping to a garlicky spiced and roasted aubergine. Choose from a traditional hummus or a flavoured one – whatever takes your fancy on the night!

2 x 300g/11oz aubergines (eggplants)
60ml/4 tbsp olive oil, plus drizzle, to serve (optional)
10ml/2 tsp harissa paste
2 garlic cloves, finely chopped
salt and cayenne pepper
200g/7oz/1 generous cup couscous
350ml/12fl oz/1^1/2 cups boiling vegetable stock
grated zest and juice of ^{1}/2 lemon
3 spring onions (scallions), finely chopped
2 tomatoes, diced

100g/3^3/4oz/2 roasted red bell peppers from
a jar of light brine, drained and diced
45g/1^1/2 oz fresh chopped mint
45g/1^1/2 oz fresh chopped parsley
200g/7oz/1 scant cup hummus
a handful of rocket (arugula) leaves
a little drizzle of extra olive oil, optional

SERVES 4

1 Preheat the oven to 200°C/400°F/Gas 6. Cut each aubergine in half lengthways, put into a roasting pan and make criss-cross cuts over the top. Mix half the oil and half the harissa with all of the garlic, then spread over the aubergines. Sprinkle with a little salt and cayenne pepper and roast for 30 minutes or until they are tender.

2 Meanwhile, add the couscous to a large bowl, pour over the boiling vegetable stock then cover with a plate. Leave to soak for 5 minutes.

3 To make a dressing, mix together the remaining olive oil and harissa, lemon zest and juice, then season with salt and cayenne pepper.

4 Fluff the couscous up with a fork then stir in the dressing. Mix in the onions, tomatoes, peppers and herbs then re-cover with the plate and set aside.

5 When the aubergines are ready, spoon the couscous over serving plates, top each with a roasted aubergine half then a generous spoonful of hummus. Garnish with rocket leaves and drizzle with extra olive oil if liked.

Cook's tips
• If you are not a fan of aubergine use a slice of butternut squash or courgette or slice of marrow, or a big red bell pepper.
• Other suggestions would be marinated baked tempeh, coconut, jackfruit, seitan or oyster mushrooms.

Energy 350kcal/1460kJ; Protein 9.1g; Carbohydrate 38.3g, of which sugars 7.4g; Fat 18.8g, of which saturates 2.6g; Cholesterol 0mg; Calcium 83mg; Fibre 7.8g; Sodium 364mg.

Barley risotto with squash and leeks

A warming risotto is comfort food at its very best and is perfect for a winter's lunch or supper. Sweet leeks and roasted butternut squash are superb with the earthy barley. Savour the flavours.

200g/7oz/1 cup pearl barley
1 butternut squash, peeled, seeded and cut into chunks
10ml/2 tsp chopped fresh thyme
60ml/4 tbsp vegetable oil
4 leeks, cut into fairly thick diagonal slices
2 garlic cloves, finely chopped
175g/6oz/2¹/₂ cups brown cap (cremini) mushrooms, sliced

2 carrots, coarsely grated
about 120ml/4floz/¹/₂ cup water
25g/1 oz chopped fresh flat leaf parsley
45ml/3 tbsp pumpkin seeds, toasted, or chopped walnuts
ground black pepper

SERVES 4

1 Rinse the barley, then cook it in a pan of simmering water, keeping the pan part-covered, for 35–45 minutes, or until tender. Drain. Preheat the oven to 200°C/400°F/Gas 6.

2 Put the squash in a roasting pan with half the thyme and ground pepper. Drizzle over 30ml/2 tbsp of the oil, mixing to coat. Roast for 30 minutes, stirring once, until tender.

3. Heat the remaining oil in a large frying pan. Cook the leeks and garlic gently for 5 minutes. Add the mushrooms and remaining thyme, then cook until the liquid from the mushrooms evaporates and they begin to fry.

4 Stir in the carrots and cook for about 2 minutes, then add the barley and most of the measured water. Season well with black pepper and partially cover the pan. Cook for a further 5 minutes. Pour in the remaining water if the mixture seems dry.

5 Stir in the squash and the parsley. Season to taste and serve sprinkled with the toasted pumpkin seeds or walnuts.

Cook's tips
• You could try replacing the risotto rice with a combination of quinoa, barley and buckwheat.
• If you have some leftover white wine you could also replace the ½ cup of water with wine.

Energy 499cal/2105kJ; Protein 14.4g; Carbohydrate 73.3g, of which sugars 20.1g; Fat 18.6g, of which saturates 10.7g; Cholesterol 0mg; Calcium 204mg; Fibre 14.7g; Sodium 107mg.

Thai vegetable curry with lemon grass rice

This rich, spicy recipe is packed with antioxidant-rich vegetables, spices and herbs. Although the ingredient list is long, it is a simple curry to make and well worth the effort. Simply change the vegetables to suit the seasons or whatever is in your refrigerator.

10ml/2 tsp vegetable oil
400ml/14fl oz/1²/₃ cups coconut milk
300ml/¹/₂ pint/1¹/₄ cups vegetable stock
225g/8oz new potatoes, halved
130g/4¹/₂oz baby corn cobs
5ml/1 tsp golden caster (superfine) sugar
185g/6¹/₂oz broccoli florets
1 red bell pepper, seeded and sliced lengthways
115g/4oz spinach, tough stalks removed and shredded
25g/1 oz chopped fresh coriander (cilantro)
pinch of salt

For the spice paste
1 fresh red chilli, seeded and chopped
3 fresh green chillies, seeded and chopped
1 lemon grass stalk, outer leaves removed and lower 5cm/2in finely chopped

2 shallots, chopped
finely grated rind of 1 lime
2 garlic cloves, chopped
5ml/1 tsp ground coriander
2.5ml/¹/₂ tsp ground cumin
1cm/¹/₂in fresh galangal, finely chopped or 2.5ml/¹/₂ tsp dried (optional)
25g/1 oz chopped fresh coriander (cilantro) leaves
15g/¹/₂ oz chopped fresh coriander roots and stems (optional)

For the rice
225g/8oz/generous 1 cup jasmine rice, rinsed
1 lemon grass stalk, outer leaves removed, cut into 3 pieces

SERVES 4

1 Make the spice paste. Place all the ingredients in a food processor or blender and blend to a coarse paste.

2 Heat the oil in a large heavy pan and fry the spice paste for 1–2 minutes, stirring constantly. Add the coconut milk and stock, and bring to the boil.

3 Reduce the heat, add the potatoes and simmer for 15 minutes. Add the baby corn and seasoning, then cook for 2 minutes. Stir in the sugar, broccoli and red pepper, and cook for 2 minutes more, until the vegetables are tender. Stir in the shredded spinach and half the fresh coriander. Cook for 2 minutes.

4 Meanwhile, pour the rinsed rice into a large pan and add the lemon grass. Pour over 475ml/16fl oz/2 cups water. Bring to the boil, then reduce the heat, cover, and cook for 10–15 minutes, until the water is absorbed and the rice is tender and slightly sticky. Season with a pinch of salt.

5 Leave the rice to stand for 10 minutes, then fluff it up with a fork.

6 Remove the lemon grass and serve the rice with the curry, sprinkled with the remaining fresh coriander.

Energy 279Kcal/1161kJ; Protein 9.8g; Carbohydrate 17.4g, of which sugars 13.3g; Fat 19.4g, of which saturates 3.6g; Cholesterol 5mg; Calcium 99mg; Fibre 3.3g; Sodium 824mg.

Sweet and sour vegetables with tofu

Crisp, colourful and nutritious, this is a hearty stir-fry that will satisfy even the hungriest appetite. Stir-fries make an easy and convenient meal for busy vegans, as the ingredients can be prepared ahead and then they can be cooked in barely any time at all.

30ml/2 tbsp vegetable oil
4 shallots, thinly sliced
3 garlic cloves, finely chopped
250g/9oz Chinese leaves (Chinese cabbage), shredded
8 baby corn, sliced on the diagonal
2 red bell peppers, seeded and thinly sliced
200g/7oz/1³/4 cups mangetouts (snow peas), trimmed and sliced

250g/9oz firm tofu, rinsed, drained and cut in 1cm/¹/2 in cubes
60ml/4 tbsp vegetable stock
30ml/2 tbsp light soy sauce
15ml/1 tbsp agave syrup
30ml/2 tbsp rice vinegar
2.5ml/¹/2 tsp dried chilli flakes
a small bunch of coriander (cilantro), chopped

SERVES 4-6

1 Heat the oil in a wok or frying pan and cook the shallots and garlic for 2–3 minutes over a medium heat, until golden. Do not let the garlic burn or it will taste bitter.

2 Add the shredded leaves, toss over the heat for 30 seconds, then add the corn and repeat the process.

3 Add the pepper, mangetouts and tofu, tossing each ingredient for 30 seconds before adding the next one.

4 Pour in the stock and soy sauce. Mix together the agave syrup and vinegar in a bowl. Add to the pan. Sprinkle over the chilli flakes and coriander, toss to mix well and serve immediately.

Energy 144kcal/604kJ; Protein 5.2g; Carbohydrate 23.7g, of which sugars 18.2g; Fat 3.7g, of which saturates 0.5g; Cholesterol 0mg; Calcium 73mg; Fibre 4.7g; Sodium 611mg.

Sweet and sour vegetable noodles

This noodle dish has the colour of fire, but only the mildest suggestion of heat. Ginger and plum sauce give it a fruity flavour, while lime juice and tamarind paste add a delicious tang to the aromatic stir-fried vegetables and chopped coriander.

130g/4¹⁄₂oz dried rice noodles
30ml/2 tbsp groundnut or peanut oil
2.5cm/1in fresh root ginger, sliced into thin batons
1 garlic clove, crushed
130g/4¹⁄₂oz drained canned bamboo shoots, sliced into thin matchsticks
2 medium carrots, sliced into thin matchsticks
130g/4¹⁄₂oz/¹⁄₂ cup beansprouts
1 small white cabbage, shredded
10ml/2 tsp tamarind paste
30ml/2 tbsp soy sauce
30ml/2 tbsp plum sauce
10ml/2 tsp sesame oil
15ml/1 tbsp agave syrup
juice of ¹⁄₂ lime
90g/3¹⁄₂oz mooli/daikon, sliced into thin matchsticks
a small bunch of fresh coriander (cilantro), finely chopped
60ml/4 tbsp sesame seeds, toasted

SERVES 4

1 Cook the noodles in a large pan of boiling water, following the instructions on the packet. Meanwhile, heat the oil in a wok or frying pan and stir-fry the ginger and garlic for 2–3 minutes, until golden. Drain the noodles and set aside.

2 Add the bamboo shoots to the wok, increase the heat to high and stir-fry for 5 minutes. Add the carrots, beansprouts and cabbage and stir-fry for a further 5 minutes, until they are beginning to char on the edges.

3 Stir in the tamarind paste, soy and plum sauces, sesame oil, agave syrup and lime juice. Add the mooli and coriander, toss to mix, then spoon into a warmed bowl, sprinkle with toasted sesame seeds and serve immediately.

Cook's tip
To prepare the cabbage: remove the outer leaves, cut into quarters, discard the core and slice thinly.

Energy 256kcal/1072kJ; Protein 7.1g; Carbohydrate 42.2g, of which sugars 14.1g; Fat 6.4g, of which saturates 1g; Cholesterol 0mg; Calcium 136mg; Fibre 4.2g; Sodium 858mg.

Pot-luck vegetables with five-spice mix

This classic Indian dish is made with odds and ends that are already in the kitchen.
It has a wonderful confetti of colours and a fabulous mingling of flavours, which are imparted
by the different types of vegetables and the five-spice mix. Serve with plain boiled rice.

60ml/4 tbsp vegetable oil
175g/6oz potatoes, cut into 2.5cm/1in cubes
115g/4oz carrots, cut into 2.5cm/1in cubes
150g/5oz cauliflower, divided into
2.5cm/1in florets
2 bay leaves
5ml/1 tsp ground coriander
5ml/1 tsp ground cumin
2.5ml/1/2 tsp ground turmeric
2.5ml/1/2 tsp chilli powder
1/2 a small cabbage (about 200g/7oz), finely shredded
115g/4oz garden peas, fresh or frozen
(boiled until tender, if fresh)
5ml/1 tsp salt, or to taste

4-5 whole fresh green chillies
2 ripe tomatoes, cut into 2.5cm/1in chunks
25g/1 oz fresh coriander (cilantro) leaves, chopped
plain boiled rice, to serve

For the five-spice mix
2.5ml/1/2 tsp black or brown mustard seeds
2.5ml/1/2 tsp cumin seeds
2.5ml/1/2 tsp fennel seeds
2.5ml/1/2 tsp nigella seeds
6 fenugreek seeds

SERVES 4

1 Heat 45ml/3 tbsp of the oil in a non-stick or cast iron pan until it reaches smoking point, then reduce the heat slightly and add the potatoes and carrots.

2 Stir-fry for about 4 minutes, until they begin to brown, then remove with a slotted spoon and drain on kitchen paper. Brown the cauliflower in the oil remaining in the pan for about 3 minutes, then remove and drain the fried florets on kitchen paper.

3 Add the remaining 15ml/1 tbsp of oil to the pan and heat until the oil is about to smoke. Switch off the heat source and add all the ingredients for the five-spice mix. Let it crackle and pop for about 30 seconds.

4 Add the bay leaves, coriander, cumin, turmeric and chilli powder. Place the pan over a low heat and fry the spices for about 1 minute.

5 Add the browned potatoes and carrots and pour in 300ml/1/2 pint/1/4 cup lukewarm water. Bring it to the boil, reduce the heat to low and cover the pan.

6 Cook for 5–6 minutes, then add the fried cauliflower, the shredded cabbage, peas and salt.

7 Cover and simmer for 4–5 minutes, then add the whole chillies, chopped tomatoes and coriander. Cook, uncovered for 2–3 minutes. Remove from the heat and serve with plain boiled rice.

Cook's tip
You can either buy pre-mixed five-spice mix or make your own, as in this recipe.

Per portion Energy 161kcal/668kJ; Protein 3g; Carbohydrate 10g, of which sugars 4g; Fat 13g, of which saturates 2g; Cholesterol 0mg; Calcium 38mg; Fibre 2.2g; Sodium 413mg.

Sweet pumpkin and peanut curry

A hearty, soothing curry perfect for chillier evenings. Its cheerful colour alone will raise the spirits – and the combination of pumpkin and peanuts tastes great.

30ml/2 tbsp vegetable oil
4 garlic cloves, crushed
4 shallots, finely chopped
30ml/2 tbsp yellow curry paste
600ml/1 pint/2½ cups vegetable stock
2 kaffir lime leaves, torn
15ml/1 tbsp chopped fresh galangal
450g/1lb pumpkin, peeled, seeded and diced
225g/8oz sweet potatoes, diced

90g/3½oz/scant 1 cup unsalted, roasted peanuts, chopped
300ml/½ pint/1¼ cups coconut milk
90g/3½oz/1½ cups chestnut mushrooms, sliced
30ml/2 tbsp soy sauce
50g/2oz/⅓ cup pumpkin seeds, toasted, and fresh green chillies cut into flowers, to garnish (optional)

SERVES 4

1 Heat the oil in a wok. Add the garlic and shallots and cook over a medium heat, stirring occasionally, for 10 minutes, until softened and golden. Do not burn.

2 Add the yellow curry paste and stir-fry over medium heat for 30 seconds, until fragrant, then add the stock, lime leaves, galangal, pumpkin and sweet potatoes. Bring to the boil, stirring, then reduce the heat and simmer gently for 15 minutes.

3 Add the peanuts, coconut milk, mushrooms and soy sauce and simmer for 5 minutes more. Serve garnished with pumpkin seeds, and chilli 'flowers', if you like.

Variation
The well-drained vegetables from this and the next curry would make a very tasty filling for a pastry or pie.

Energy 306kcal/1279kJ; Protein 9.6g; Carbohydrate 24.5g, of which sugars 11.4g; Fat 19.6g, of which saturates 3.3g; Cholesterol 0mg; Calcium 160mg; Fibre 6.4g; Sodium 409mg.

Parsnip and chickpea curry

The sweet flavour of parsnips goes very well with the spices in this Indian-style vegetable stew. Serve it with dairy-free yogurt and roti breads to mop up the delicious sauce.

200g/7oz/scant 1 cup dried chickpeas,
soaked overnight, then drained
7 garlic cloves, finely chopped
1 small onion, chopped
5cm/2in fresh root ginger, chopped
2 fresh green chillies, seeded and finely chopped
600ml/1 pint/2½ cups water
60ml/4 tbsp groundnut or peanut oil
5ml/1 tsp cumin seeds
10ml/2 tsp ground coriander seeds
5ml/1 tsp ground turmeric
2.5-5ml/½-1 tsp mild chilli powder
50g/2oz/½ cup cashew nuts, toasted
and ground
250g/9oz tomatoes, peeled and chopped
900g/2lb parsnips, cut into chunks
5ml/1 tsp cumin seeds, toasted and ground
juice of ½-1 lime
salt and ground black pepper
fresh coriander (cilantro) leaves
and a few cashew nuts, toasted, to garnish

SERVES 4

1 Put the chickpeas in a pan, cover with cold water and bring to the boil. Boil vigorously for 10 minutes, then reduce the heat so that the water boils steadily and cook for 1–1½ hours, or until tender. The cooking time will depend on how long the chickpeas have been stored.

2 Meanwhile, make the sauce. Set 10ml/2 tsp of the garlic aside, and place the remainder in a food processor or blender. Add the onion, ginger and half the chillies. Pour in 75ml/5 tbsp of the water and process to a smooth paste.

3 Heat the oil in a large, deep frying pan and cook the cumin seeds for 30 seconds. Stir in the coriander seeds, turmeric, chilli powder and ground cashew nuts. Add the ginger and chilli paste and cook, stirring frequently, until the water begins to evaporate. Add the tomatoes and stir-fry until the mixture begins to turn red-brown in colour.

4 Drain the chickpeas and add to the pan with the parsnips and remaining water. Season with a little salt and black pepper. Bring to the boil, stir, then simmer, uncovered, for 15–20 minutes, until the parsnips are completely tender.

5 Thicken the liquid by boiling until the sauce is reduced. Add the toasted cumin seeds and lime juice to taste. Stir in the reserved garlic and chilli, and heat through. Sprinkle with the coriander leaves and cashew nuts and serve.

Energy 506kcal/2124kJ; Protein 18.4g; Carbohydrate 60.1g, of which sugars 18.2g; Fat 23.1g, of which saturates 3.4g; Cholesterol 0mg; Calcium 192mg; Fibre 17.1g; Sodium 86mg.

Tofu and quinoa laksa-style stew

Laksa is a Malay/Singaporean curry of which there are many variants. Most recipes use crisp vegetables, vermicelli noodles and fragrant spices, all served in a coconut milk base. In this vegan version the noodles are substituted with pearl quinoa to create a substantial and mouthwatering lunch or supper dish. Serve with green tea to cool your senses.

30ml/2 tbsp vegetable oil
10ml/2 tsp red curry paste
150g/5oz sweet potato, peeled and cubed
125g/4¹/₄oz/³/₄ cup pearl quinoa, rinsed
300ml/¹/₂ pint/1¹/₄ cups coconut cream
600ml/1 pint/2¹/₂ cups water
15ml/1 tbsp tamarind paste
1 garlic clove, crushed

25g/1oz spring onions (scallions),
 sliced into 5mm/¹/₄in slices
8 mangetouts (snow peas)
4 baby corn, cut in half
200g/7oz tofu, cut into 2cm/³/₄in square cubes
fresh coriander (cilantro), chopped, and a 6cm/2¹/₂in piece
 of cucumber cut into thin matchsticks, to garnish

SERVES 4

1 Heat 15ml/1 tbsp of the oil in a large pan, then add the curry paste, sweet potato cubes and quinoa. Fry over a medium heat for 3–4 minutes, until the spice fragrances and flavours are released.

2 Add the coconut cream to the pan and stir until smooth, then add the water and tamarind paste. Bring to the boil, then lower the heat and simmer for 12–14 minutes, stirring occasionally, until the quinoa is tender.

3 Drain the quinoa, cover to keep warm and set aside, reserving the curried coconut stock in a small pan. Do not leave the quinoa in the stock or it will continue to absorb the fluid and swell.

4 In a frying pan, heat the remaining oil and add the garlic, spring onions, mangetouts and baby corn. Stir-fry on high heat for 3–4 minutes, until softened but still crisp.

5 Add the tofu cubes to the frying pan and sear for a further 3 minutes, gently turning the cubes only once or twice to avoid breaking them. Reheat the coconut stock.

6 To serve, divide the tofu and vegetables and the quinoa mixture between four large warmed bowls, and pour over the hot stock. Garnish with fresh coriander leaves and cucumber matchsticks.

Cook's tips
• Key to this recipe is keeping the vegetables crisp and the tofu intact, to give a curry with well-defined shapes and texture.
• You can make the curry in advance so long as you separate the quinoa from the coconut stock, otherwise it will absorb the liquid, leaving you with quinoa risotto.

Energy 266kcal/1121kJ; Protein 12g; Carbohydrate 38g, of which sugars 12g; Fat 8g, of which saturates 1g; Cholesterol 0mg; Calcium 264mg; Fibre 4g; Sodium 152mg.

SIDE DISHES

Separate side dishes enable you to add variety, colour and complementary nutrients to a vegan main dish and make it easier to get all the essential vitamins and minerals you need. This chapter features a delicious range of dishes that can be used as accompaniments or as light meals in themselves. There are also great ways to enliven those important greens, such as Spiced Greens with Hemp Seeds.

Spinach and raisins with pine nuts

It is impossible to have too many vegan recipes that show another delicious way to prepare spinach. This one makes a change from the classic creamy garlicky spinach dishes. It makes an excellent filling wrapped up in filo pastry to serve as finger food at a party. The combination of raisins, nuts and tangy onions make this a truly delectable accompaniment to a larger meal.

60g/4 tbsp raisins
1kg/2¼lb fresh spinach leaves, washed
45ml/3 tbsp olive oil
6–8 spring onions (scallions), thinly sliced
or 1–2 small yellow or white onions,
finely chopped
60ml/4 tbsp pine nuts
salt and ground black pepper

SERVES 4

1 Put the raisins into a small bowl and pour over boiling water to cover. Leave to stand for about 10 minutes until plumped up, then drain.

2 Steam or cook the spinach in a pan over a medium-high heat, with only the water that clings to the leaves after washing, for 1–2 minutes until the leaves are bright green and wilted. Remove from the heat and drain well. Leave to cool. When the spinach has cooled, chop roughly.

3 Heat the oil in a frying pan over a medium-low heat, then lower the heat further and add the spring onions or onions. Fry for about 5 minutes, or until soft, then add the spinach, raisins and pine nuts.

4 Raise the heat and cook for 2–3 minutes to warm through. Season with salt and ground black pepper to taste and serve immediately.

Variations
• Add goji berries instead of raisins.
• Try using apricot kernels instead of the pine nuts.

Nutrition note
Spinach is a super source of cancer-fighting antioxidants and has an impressive vitamin and mineral content. It contains high levels of beta-carotene and is an excellent source of vitamin K, which is essential for the blood clotting process. It also has good amounts of vitamins A, C and E, folate and riboflavin.

Energy 206kcal/855kJ; Protein 5.8g; Carbohydrate 15.5g, of which sugars 11.1g; Fat 13.8g, of which saturates 1.6g; Cholesterol 0mg; Calcium 228mg; Fibre 3.4g; Sodium 218mg.

Tarka daal

Daal is served daily as an accompaniment to most meals all over India and Pakistan, and this simple yet versatile one is a favourite. The daal element comprises two types of lentil, which are cooked with spices and then processed until smooth. A tarka, made by frying onions and spices in ghee, is then poured over the lentils, lending flavour as well as texture to the finished dish.

115g/4oz/$\frac{1}{2}$ cup split chickpeas (chana daal)
225g/8oz/1 cup red lentils (masoor daal)
750ml/1$\frac{1}{4}$ pints/3 cups water
5ml/1 tsp ginger paste
5ml/1 tsp garlic paste
7.5ml/1$\frac{1}{2}$ tsp chilli powder
1.5ml/$\frac{1}{4}$ tsp ground turmeric
7.5ml/1$\frac{1}{2}$ tsp salt
5ml/1 tsp ground coriander
5ml/1 tsp garam masala

30ml/2 tbsp lemon juice
a few sprigs of fresh coriander (cilantro), to garnish

For the tarka
30ml/2 tbsp vegetable ghee
1 onion, peeled and diced
2.5ml/$\frac{1}{2}$ tsp white cumin seeds
15g/$\frac{1}{2}$ oz chopped fresh coriander (cilantro)

SERVES 4

1 Put both the split chickpeas and the red lentils in a large bowl of cold water, then drain, rinse again in more water, and drain again.

2 Put the chickpeas and lentils into a large pan, then add the water, ginger, garlic, chilli powder and ground turmeric. Cook over a medium-low heat for about 25 minutes, until both are soft. Insert a spoon in the pan to prevent the mixture from boiling over.

3 Remove from the heat and use a deep ladle to spoon half of the mixture into a food processor or blender. Process until the chickpeas and lentils are smooth and thick.

4 Pour the processed chickpeas and lentils back into the pan and mix with the chunkier cooked chickpeas and lentils. Add the salt, ground coriander, garam masala and lemon juice. Mix well and transfer to a serving dish.

5 To make the tarka, heat the vegetable ghee in a frying pan over a medium heat. Add the onion and cumin seeds and fry for 10–15 minutes, until the onion is soft and golden brown. Pour the tarka over the daal and serve garnished with fresh coriander

Nutrition note
Chickpeas have a delicious nutty flavour and a creamy texture. The protein in chickpeas is of a very high quality and they contain all of the essential amino acids. They are a good source of insoluble fibre, improving bulk and preventing constipation, which could reduce the risk of colon cancer.

Energy 338kcal/1428kJ; Protein 21.1g; Carbohydrate 51.8g, of which sugars 4.9g; Fat 7g, of which saturates 0.9g; Cholesterol 0mg; Calcium 148mg; Fibre 6.5g; Sodium 34mg.

Green beans with cumin and tomatoes

Adapted from the Ottoman vegetable dishes cooked in olive oil, this dish is prepared all over Jordan, Syria and Lebanon. It can be served hot or at room temperature and often tastes better if it is cooked the day before, to allow the flavours to mingle.

30-45ml/2-3 tbsp olive oil
2 onions, finely chopped
2-3 garlic cloves, finely chopped
10ml/2 tsp cumin seeds
450g/1lb green beans, trimmed and left whole
5ml/1 tsp ground cinnamon
5ml/1 tsp ground allspice

5ml/1 tsp sugar
400g/14oz can chopped tomatoes
sea salt and ground black pepper
1 lemon, cut into wedges, to serve

SERVES 4-6

1 Heat the oil in a heavy-based pan and stir in the onion and garlic, until they begin to colour. Stir in the cumin seeds, then toss in the green beans and cook, stirring, for 2–3 minutes.

2 Add the cinnamon, allspice and sugar to the pan and stir through to cover all the beans in the spice mixture.

3 Stir the tomatoes into the pan. Cover with a lid and cook gently for 15–20 minutes, until the beans are tender but still retain a bite to them. Season to taste with salt and pepper.

4 Serve hot or at room temperature with wedges of lemon to squeeze over them.

Nutrition note
The delicate, crisp texture and sweet, grassy flavour of green beans make them very versatile. They are an excellent source of fibre, vitamins B1 and B6, folate, magnesium and potassium.

Energy 122kcal/507kJ; Protein 3g; Carbohydrate 10g, of which sugars 8g; Fat 8g, of which saturates 1g; Cholesterol 0mg; Calcium 64mg; Fibre 2.9g; Sodium 95mg.

Cauliflower with garlic crumbs

This dish can be eaten as a healthy lunch with a crisp green salad and makes a great appetizer served with chutney or a spicy fruit sauce.

600ml/1 pint/2¹/₂ cups vegetable stock
1 large cauliflower, cut into bitesize florets
90-120ml/6-8 tbsp olive or vegetable oil
130g/4¹/₂oz/2¹/₄ cups dry white or wholemeal (wholewheat) breadcrumbs
3-5 garlic cloves, thinly sliced or chopped
salt and ground black pepper

SERVES 4-6

1 Pour the vegetable stock into a large pan and bring to the boil. Add a pinch of salt and the cauliflower florets. Simmer until just tender. Drain and leave to cool.

2 Heat 60–75ml/4–5 tbsp of the olive or vegetable oil in a frying pan. Add the breadcrumbs and cook over a medium heat, tossing and turning, until evenly browned and crisp.

3 Add the garlic to the pan. Stir once or twice for 2 minutes. Remove the breadcrumbs and garlic from the pan and set aside.

4 Heat the remaining oil in the pan, then add the cauliflower, mashing and breaking it up a little as it lightly browns in the oil. (Do not overcook, but just cook lightly in the oil.)

5 Add the garlic breadcrumbs to the pan and cook, stirring, until well combined and some of the cauliflower is still holding its shape. Season with salt and pepper and serve hot or warm.

Cook's tip
Try serving this dish as they do in Italy: with cooked pasta such as spaghetti or rigatoni.

Variation
You can swap the breadcrumbs for rolled oats, if you prefer.

Energy 244kcal/1016kJ; Protein 8.9g; Carbohydrate 18.8g, of which sugars 2.2g; Fat 15.3g, of which saturates 3.8g; Cholesterol 10mg; Calcium 162mg; Fibre 1.7g; Sodium 280mg.

Spiced greens with hemp seeds

Here is a perfect way to spice up your greens. It works well with crunchy cabbages but is also good for kale and other purple sprouting leaves – even Brussels sprout tops can be used.

1 medium cabbage, or the equivalent in quantity of your chosen green vegetable
15ml/1 tbsp groundnut or peanut oil
5ml/1 tsp grated fresh root ginger
2 garlic cloves, crushed
2 shallots, finely chopped
2 fresh red chillies, seeded and finely sliced
30ml/2 tbsp hemp seeds
salt and ground black pepper

SERVES 4

1 Remove any tough outer leaves from the cabbage then quarter it and remove the core. Shred the leaves.

2 Pour the groundnut oil into a large pan and as it heats stir in the ginger and garlic. Add the shallots and as the pan becomes hotter add the chillies.

3 Add the greens and toss to mix thoroughly. Cover the pan and reduce the heat. Cook, shaking the pan occasionally, for about 3–5 minutes.

4 Remove the lid and increase the heat to dry off the steam. Add the hemp seeds, season with salt and pepper and cook for a further minute. Serve immediately.

Cook's tip
If you are not a fan of chilli finely slice some sweet red pepper (capsicum) to add colour.

Energy 77kcal/322kJ; Protein 2.6g; Carbohydrate 9.9g, of which sugars 9.4g; Fat 3.1g, of which saturates 0.5g; Cholesterol 0mg; Calcium 90mg; Fibre 3.9g; Sodium 13mg.

Stir-fried spicy courgettes

Courgettes can be stir-fried if you use the young, firm ones. Do not peel them, as most of the nutrients are just under the skin, which is not fibrous.

450g/1lb courgettes (zucchini)
30ml/2 tbsp groundnut or peanut oil
25ml/1oz fresh root ginger, grated
2 garlic cloves, crushed
2.5ml/¹/₂ tsp finely ground Sichuan peppercorns

15ml/1 tbsp light soy sauce
2.5ml/¹/₂ tsp brown sugar
15ml/1 tbsp crunchy peanut butter

SERVES 4

1 Slice the courgettes into thick strips, about 2cm x 7.5cm/³/₄in x 3in.

2 Heat the oil in a wok and fry the ginger and garlic for 1 minute, then add the sliced courgettes. Stir-fry over a high heat for 1 minute, then add the peppercorns, soy sauce, sugar and peanut butter.

3 Cook, stirring, for 2 more minutes, then add 30ml/2 tbsp water. Bring to a quick boil and serve hot.

Variation
For a change, smaller courgettes can be cut into thin rings and fried in the same way. Add sesame seeds to gain extra calcium and protein.

Nutrition note
Courgettes contain very few calories and have a high water content, making them a useful ingredient if you are watching your weight. They provide a good amount of immune-system boosting vitamin C and significant levels of potassium, which is key to controlling blood pressure.

Energy 102kcal/420kJ; Protein 3g; Carbohydrate 5g, of which sugars 4g; Fat 8g, of which saturates 2g; Cholesterol 0mg; Calcium 32mg; Fibre 1.1g; Sodium 425mg

Grilled leeks and fennel with tomato dressing

This is an excellent dish to make when young leeks are in season and ripe tomatoes are full of flavour. It makes a fabulous accompaniment to a vegan pizza or grilled vegetable kebabs.

675g/1¹/₂lb leeks
2 large fennel bulbs
120ml/4fl oz/¹/₂ cup extra virgin olive oil
2 shallots, chopped
150ml/¹/₄ pint/²/₃ cup dry white wine
or vegetable stock
5ml/1 tsp fennel seeds, crushed
6 fresh thyme sprigs
2-3 bay leaves

good pinch of dried red chilli flakes
350g/12oz ripe tomatoes, peeled,
seeded and diced
5ml/1 tsp sun-dried tomato purée (paste) (optional)
salt and ground black pepper
75g/3oz/³/₄ cup small black olives, to serve

SERVES 6

1 Cook the whole leeks in boiling salted water for 4–5 minutes. Use a slotted spoon to remove them and place in a colander to drain thoroughly. Leave to cool. Reserve the cooking water in the pan. Squeeze out any excess water from the leeks and cut into 7.5cm/3in lengths.

2 Trim the fennel bulbs, reserving any tops for the garnish, if you like, and cut the bulbs either into thin slices or into thicker wedges, according to taste.

3 Cook the fennel in the reserved cooking water for about 5 minutes, then drain thoroughly and toss with 30ml/2 tbsp of the olive oil. Season to taste with black pepper.

4 Heat a ridged cast-iron griddle until very hot. Arrange the leeks and fennel on the griddle and cook, turning once or twice, until they have deep brown stripes across them. Remove the vegetables from the griddle, place them in a large shallow dish and set aside.

5 Place the remaining olive oil, the shallots, white wine or vegetable stock, crushed fennel seeds, thyme, bay leaves and chilli flakes in a large pan. Bring the mixture to the boil over a medium heat. Lower the heat and simmer for about 10 minutes.

6 Add the diced tomatoes to the pan and cook briskly for about 5–8 minutes, or until they have reduced and the consistency of the mixture has thickened slightly.

7 Add the sun-dried tomato paste, if using. Taste and adjust the seasoning if necessary.

8 Pour the tomato dressing over the leeks and fennel in the dish. Toss all the vegetables gently to mix in the tomato dressing, then set the dish aside to cool.

9 When ready to serve, stir the salad once more and then sprinkle over the fennel tops, if using. Serve with black olives.

Cook's tip
When buying fennel, look for rounded bulbs; they have a better shape for this dish. The flesh should be crisp and white, with no signs of bruising. Avoid specimens with broken leaves or with brown or dried-out patches.

Nutrition note
Leeks provide useful levels of iron as well as the antioxidants carotene and vitamins E and C.

Energy 193kcal/801kJ; Protein 2.8g; Carbohydrate 6.7g, of which sugars 5.9g; Fat 14.7g, of which saturates 2.2g; Cholesterol 0mg; Calcium 53mg; Fibre 4.6g; Sodium 297mg.

Potato and peppers with nigella and lime

Nigella seeds are primarily employed as a flavouring on breads and savoury pastries, but in some parts of the Middle East they are added to pickles and salads.

8-12 medium new potatoes
45-60ml/3-4 tbsp olive oil
2 red onions, halved lengthways
and finely sliced
2-3 garlic cloves, finely chopped
1 fresh red chilli, seeded and sliced
into fine strips
10ml/2 tsp nigella seeds

5ml/1 tsp coriander seeds
5ml/1 tsp cumin seeds
5-10ml/1-2 tsp ground turmeric
sea salt and ground black pepper
juice of 1 lime plus lime wedges, to serve

SERVES 4

1 Wash the potatoes, place in a pot of water and boil until tender but still firm.

2 When the potatoes are cooked, drain and refresh under a running cold tap. Cut them into bitesize chunks.

3 Heat the oil in a pan and fry the onions for 1–2 minutes to soften. Add the garlic, chilli and nigella seeds for 2–3 minutes.

4 Add the coriander, cumin seeds and the turmeric to the pan, then toss in the potato chunks, stir to coat with the seasoned mixture and cook to heat through. Add salt and pepper to taste.

5 Squeeze in the lime juice, then leave the mixture to cool in the pan before transferring it to a serving dish. Serve at room temperature with lime wedges to squeeze over it.

Cook's tips
• Swap chilli for thinly sliced strips of carrot for those not keen on spicy food.
• Garnish with torn parsley to increase vitamin A levels.

Energy 234kcal/976kJ; Protein3; Carbohydrate 22g, of which sugars 6g; Fat 16g, of which saturates 2g; Cholesterol 0mg; Calcium 49mg; Fibre 2.1 g; Sodium 114mg.

Stewed peppers

This colourful dish is made all over Italy, especially at the start of the autumn, when the markets are filled with enormously juicy, brightly coloured peppers of every shape and size. The texture of the finished dish is soft and squashy, almost like jam. It is important to buy sweet peppers and to keep everything moist during the cooking process.

400g/14oz aubergines (eggplants), cut into chunks
150ml/¹/₄ pint/²/₃ cup olive oil
1 garlic clove, crushed
300g/11oz small onions, sliced
500g/1¹/₄lb yellow and red bell peppers, cut into chunks
300g/11oz small tomatoes, chopped

90ml/6 tbsp dry white wine or vegetable stock
sea salt
chopped fresh flat leaf parsley, to garnish

SERVES 4-6

1 Put the aubergine chunks into a colander and sprinkle with salt. Put a small plate on top and weight it down with a can. Leave it for 30 minutes. Rinse and drain.

2 Heat the oil in a large pan, add the garlic and onions and fry until browned.

3 Add the aubergines, the peppers and the tomatoes. Sprinkle with the wine and add salt to taste.

4 Cover and simmer gently over a low heat for 30 minutes, stirring frequently. Serve the peppers hot or cold, garnished with chopped fresh flat leaf parsley.

Variations
• If you prefer, you can leave out the aubergines and onions, and use only peppers and garlic.
• Try using less olive oil and replacing 10-20% with avocado oil, walnut oil or better still a truffle-infused oil.

Energy 248kcal/1025kJ; Protein 2.5g; Carbohydrate 12.4g, of which sugars 10.9g; Fat 20.2g, of which saturates 8.2g; Cholesterol 29mg; Calcium 33mg; Fibre 3.9g; Sodium 105mg.

Red cabbage with walnuts

Fresh, crunchy, raw red cabbage is rich in vitamins and minerals and is particularly good in winter, when fresh vegetables are more limited. You can make this side dish with white cabbage too, but use white wine vinegar for the dressing.

800g/1³/₄lb red cabbage
5ml/1 tsp salt, ground white pepper and sugar
30ml/2 tbsp red wine vinegar
10ml/2 tsp sunflower oil
75g/3oz walnut halves
20ml/4 tsp apple sauce
5ml/1 tsp cranberry jelly

SERVES 4

1 Trim the red cabbage and slice it finely. Put it in a bowl, season with salt, pepper and sugar, and pour over the vinegar and sunflower oil. Toss the salad thoroughly, using your hands, then place in the refrigerator and chill for at least 3 hours to allow the cabbage to absorb the dressing.

2 Just before serving, heat a frying pan over medium heat and toast the walnuts gently, stirring, for 3–4 minutes, until lightly browned and fragrant.

3 Mix the apple sauce and the cranberry jam, and stir into the cabbage salad. Taste the cabbage and add extra salt, vinegar or sugar as necessary. Turn into a salad bowl and scatter with the toasted walnuts.

Nutrition note
The walnuts add a useful top-up of omega 3 essential fats.

Energy 240kcal/991kJ; Protein 5.6g; Carbohydrate 12.4g, of which sugars 12.1g; Fat 18.8g, of which saturates 1.7g; Cholesterol 0mg; Calcium 116mg; Fibre 4.9g; Sodium 16mg

Sauerkraut

Fermented foods are becoming increasingly popular, and with good reason:
the acids within fermented foods can be a highly effective path to a well-balanced
digestive system and a way to enjoy greater health. Sauerkraut is a traditional source of
vitamin C and contains essential minerals and trace elements.

**1 cabbage, red, white or green, coarsely grated - reserve
some of the large outer leaves whole
15ml/1 tbsp dried juniper berries, crushed in a
pestle and mortar or spice grinder, or 15ml/1 tbsp dill or
caraway seeds**

**10g/¹⁄₄oz dried or finely shredded hijiki or
arame seaweed
30ml/2 tbsp mustard seeds**

SERVES 4

1 Place all the ingredients in a large ceramic pan or bowl,
and pound with the end of a wooden rolling pin or a pestle
until you have a juicy mass.

2 Cover with the reserved cabbage leaves and a plate and
press down. Weigh down the plate with heavy weights, to
compound the mixture, and then cover the whole container
with a cloth, which will allow the air to circulate.

3 Leave for 5–10 days, depending on the room temperature,
in which time the cabbage will ferment to a fresh-smelling
sauerkraut. Don't panic when the cabbage smells strongly on
day two or three as this phase will soon pass.

4 Transfer to glass storage jars and keep in the refrigerator for
up to 3 weeks.

Cook's tips
• Sauerkraut can be made with grated carrot or beetroot
(beets), mixed with the cabbage.
• Hijiki seaweed is a black marine algae that grows up
to 1m/3ft long all around the Japanese coast. It is full of
vitamins and minerals, including calcium and fibre, and
contains no fat. It can be purchased dried in packets from
most Asian food stores and some health food stores.

DESSERTS

Go to any 'Vegfest' the world over and usually the busiest stalls and
vendors are the ones selling vegan cakes, ice cream and chocolate. Gone are
the days when rich creamy desserts, hot fruit pies with custard, and fluffy,
light-as-air sponges were 'out-of-bounds' for vegans. With so many new plant-based
milks and creams coming onto the market, and new techniques using aquafaba,
even a raspberry and coconut cream-topped meringue is now on the menu.

Date and tofu ice

Generously spiced with cinnamon and full of dried fruit, this delicious and unusual ice cream is packed with plenty of soya protein. It also contains omega 3 fats and no added sugar.

250g/9oz/1¹/₂ cups stoned (pitted) dates
300ml/¹/₂ pint/1¹/₄ cups apple juice
5ml/1 tsp ground cinnamon
285g/10¹/₂oz pack chilled fresh tofu, cubed

150ml/1¹/₄ pint/²/₃ cup soya, oat or
  cashew nut cream
8 walnut halves, to decorate

SERVES 4

1 Put the dates in a pan. Pour in the apple juice and set aside to allow the dates to soak for 2 hours.

2 Bring the mixture to the boil and then simmer gently for 10 minutes. Set aside to cool then, using a slotted spoon, lift out one-quarter of the dates. Chop roughly and set aside.

3 Blend the remaining dates in a food processor or blender to a smooth purée. Add the cinnamon and process with enough of the apple juice to make a smooth paste.

4 Add the tofu to the food processor, a few pieces at a time, processing after each addition. Pour in the soya, oat or cashew nut cream and mix well.

5 Churn the mixture in an ice cream maker until very thick, but not thick enough to scoop. Scrape the ice cream into a freezerproof tub.

6 Stir in most of the chopped dates, retaining a few pieces for decorating, and freeze for 2–3 hours until firm.

7 If you do not have an ice cream maker, transfer the mixture to a freezer container and freeze for 2 hours, then beat with an electric mixer until smooth. Stir in most of the chopped dates, retaining a few pieces for decorating, and freeze for at least 8 hours.

8 Scoop into dessert glasses and decorate with the remaining chopped dates and the walnut halves.

Variation
You could make this tasty ice cream with any soft dried fruits: dried figs, apricots or peaches would be especially good. Or use a combination for a vitamin-packed feast.

Energy 290kcal/1232kJ; Protein 9.1g; Carbohydrate 58.2g, of which sugars 57.9g; Fat 3.9g, of which saturates 0.5g; Cholesterol 0mg; Calcium 407mg; Fibre 2.5g; Sodium 24mg.

Coconut sorbet

You may have already had a few sorbets in your time if you have been avoiding dairy. This tropical version from South-east Asia proves they do not have to be restricted to orange or lemon.

250ml/8fl oz/1 cup agave syrup
120ml/4fl oz/$^1/_2$ cup coconut milk
50g/2oz/$^2/_3$ cup grated or desiccated
(dry unsweetened shredded) coconut
a squeeze of lime juice

SERVES 6

1 Place the agave syrup in a heavy pan and add 200ml/ 7fl oz/scant 1 cup water. Bring to the boil, stirring the mixture constantly.

2 Take off the heat and stir the coconut milk into the syrup, along with most of the grated or desiccated coconut and the lime juice. Pour the mixture into a bowl or freezer container and freeze for 2 hours.

3 Take the sorbet out of the freezer and beat it with a fork, or blend it in a food processor, until smooth and creamy. Return it to the freezer for 30 minutes.

4 Remove the sorbet from the freezer again and beat it with a fork, or blend it in a food processor, until it is smooth and creamy. Then return it to the freezer and leave until completely frozen.

5 If using an ice cream making machine, pour the mixture into the ice cream maker and churn until thick enough to scoop. Scrape the sorbet into a freezerproof tub and freeze until frozen.

6 Before serving, allow the sorbet to stand at room temperature for about 10–15 minutes to allow it to soften slightly. Serve in small bowls and decorate with the remaining grated or desiccated coconut.

Cook's tips
• If using fresh coconut, serve the sorbet in the shells.
• Add melted dark chocolate mixed with some coconut cream to make a coconut and chocolate ripple ice cream.

Energy 170kcal/717kJ; Protein 0.7g; Carbohydrate 32g, of which sugars 32g; Fat 5.2g, of which saturates 4.5g; Cholesterol 0mg; Calcium 23mg; Fibre 1.2g; Sodium 26mg.

Apple and berry chia puddings

Sweetened with apple juice and cinnamon, this dessert is gentle and healthy. The berries give it a beautiful colour as well as adding pectin for a more jelly-like texture. Use fresh or frozen berries, as seasonally available. It is best to prepare this dessert a day ahead of serving because although the chia seeds will form a gel in about 10 minutes, the longer they are soaked, the more bioavailable the nutrients become.

115g/4oz/1 cup blackberries, blueberries
or blackcurrants
750ml/1¼ pints/3 cups apple juice
5ml/1 tsp ground cinnamon, to taste
15ml/1 tbsp maple syrup, to sweeten (optional)

150g/5oz/1 cup chia seeds
fresh berries and mint sprigs, to decorate
(optional)

SERVES 6

1 Put the berries, juice and cinnamon in a blender and blend on high until combined. If the apple juice is tart, add a tablespoon of maple syrup to sweeten to taste, if liked.

2 Put the berry mixture in a bowl with the chia, whisking with a fork to make sure the chia seeds are moistened.

3 Leave to soak for at least 10 minutes, or overnight in the refrigerator, if possible.

4 When you're ready to serve, spoon the chia pudding into dessert glasses as it is, or if preferred, blend for about 15–30 seconds until smooth before serving. Decorate with fresh berries and sprigs of mint, if liked.

Nutrition note
Soaked chia seeds slowly release fluid into your body over time, keeping you hydrated for longer. They also offer a long list of important nutrients, including fibre, protein, manganese and calcium, along with plenty of antioxidants and omega 3 fatty acids.

Cook's tip
It is up to personal preference whether you choose to serve the pudding as it is, or blended until the texture is smooth. All the health benefits of the chia gel are still present in the smooth dessert, which is perhaps a little more elegant to serve to friends at dinner.

Energy 160kcal/678kJ; Protein 5.4g; Carbohydrate 13.7g, of which sugars 12.8g; Fat 8.9g, of which saturates 1g; Cholesterol 0mg; Calcium 147mg; Fibre 13.3g; Sodium 253mg.

Chocolate avocado cream tart

A chocolate tart crust with a creamy chocolate filling… and all without any sugar, dairy or gluten! This raw vegan recipe is every bit as good as a baked chocolate tart, but far less fussy to make and a squillion times healthier. Its dark brown chocolate colour makes a fabulous backdrop for decoration. Try finishing it with organic, raw, edible toppings such as rose petals, fresh berries, sliced almonds, or piped cashew cream for a classic, elegant look. Start preparation a day before serving, as it is best to soak the cashew nuts overnight.

For the base
115g/4oz/1 cup cashew nuts, soaked in water for at least 4 hours or overnight
40g/1¹/₂oz/¹/₂ cup rolled oats
75g/3oz/¹/₂ cup macadamia nuts
60g/1¹/₄oz/³/₄ cup cacao powder
5ml/1 tsp vanilla extract
75g/3oz/about 14 dried stoned (pitted) dates

For the filling
2 ripe avocados
60ml/4 tbsp cacao powder
30ml/2 tbsp maple syrup
mixed fresh berries, to decorate

SERVES 8

1 To make the pastry, drain the cashew nuts and put them in a food processor with the oats, macadamias, cacao and vanilla. Pulse until broken down and combined, add the dates and process again to make a dough.

2 Press the dough into a 25cm/10in loosed-based round flan tin (pan), flattening it into the bottom and up the sides of the tin using the back of a spoon. Put it in the freezer for 20 minutes to set.

3 When the pastry case or pie shell is ready, make the creamy filling. Halve the avocados, remove the stones and scoop the flesh into a blender. Add the cacao and maple syrup and blend for about 20 seconds on high to combine.

4 Pour the filling into the pastry case, cover and leave to set in the refrigerator for at least 20 minutes, but preferably for a few hours or overnight. Keep covered until ready to eat, then decorate with a selection of fresh berries, before serving.

Energy 152kcal/637kJ; Protein 4.2g; Carbohydrate 10.1g, of which sugars 5.4g; Fat 11.2g, of which saturates 2.8g; Cholesterol 0mg; Calcium 19mg; Fibre 3g; Sodium 76mg.

Raw key lime pie

The classic lime dessert originated in the Florida Keys and is now an American favourite. Here it enjoys a raw healthy makeover for vegans with the usual eggs and condensed milk replaced with a mix of avocado and coconut to give a creamy dessert that is packed with vitamin E.

For the base
50g/2oz/¹⁄₂ cup ground pumpkin seeds
50g/2oz/¹⁄₂ cup ground almonds
75g/3oz/¹⁄₂ cup medjool dates, chopped
15ml/1 tbsp agave syrup

For the filling
250g/9oz avocado flesh, roughly 2 medium avocados with
    skin and stones (pits) removed
75g/3oz/scant ¹⁄₂ cup ready-to-eat dried apricots
10ml/2 tsp pumpkin seed oil
finely grated rind of 2 limes
juice of 1 lime, plus lime twists, to decorate (optional)
75g/3oz/6 tbsp cold-pressed coconut oil

SERVES 6

1 Blend together all the ingredients for the base in a food processor or blender until you have a nice firm dough.

2 Lightly oil a 20cm/8in loose-based round flan tin (pan). Scrape the dough from the processor or blender and press the dough into the base of dish, ensuring it is evenly distributed.

3 Blend together the avocados, dried apricots, pumpkin oil, and lime rind and juice in a food processor or blender.

4 Meanwhile, melt the coconut oil in a heatproof bowl resting in a pan of hot water. Gradually stir melted coconut oil into the avocado mixture.

5 Spread the mixture evenly on to the pie base using a palette knife or metal spatula. Chill for about 2 hours.

6 Serve decorated with thinly sliced lime twists, if you like.

Energy 360kcal/1494kJ; Protein 4.9g; Carbohydrate 15.4g, of which sugars 13.1g; Fat 31.4g, of which saturates 12.4g; Cholesterol 0mg; Calcium 48mg; Fibre 3.6g; Sodium 20mg.

Pumpkin pie

Filled with tasty pumpkin and smooth silken tofu, this version of the classic dessert will be an essential part of any American Thanksgiving vegan feast. The wholemeal pastry base is flavoured with peanut butter to add extra interest.

For the base
250g/9oz/2¹/₄ cups wholemeal (wholewheat) flour
pinch of salt
7.5ml/1¹/₂ tsp ground cinnamon
75ml/2¹/₂ fl oz/¹/₃ cup pumpkin seed oil
or rapeseed (canola) oil
15ml/1 tbsp crushed pumpkin seeds or
peanut butter
75ml/2¹/₂ fl oz/¹/₃ cup sweetened soya milk

For the filling
450g/1lb pumpkin, deseeded and cut into 2.5cm/1 in cubes
350g/12oz silken tofu
260g/9¹/₂ oz/generous 1 cup soft light brown sugar
75ml/2¹/₂ fl oz/¹/₃ cup rapeseed (canola) oil
15ml/1 tbsp carob molasses or agave syrup
7.5ml/1¹/₂ tsp ground cinnamon
5ml/1 tsp sea salt
5ml/1 tsp vanilla extract
2.5ml/¹/₂ tsp ground ginger
2.5ml/¹/₂ tsp ground nutmeg

SERVES 6

1 Make the base. Rub together the flour, salt, cinnamon, oil and peanut butter until it resembles breadcrumbs. Add soya milk to form a soft dough.

2 Roll out dough and line an oiled 20cm/8in loose-based round flan tin (pan). Preheat the oven to 180°C/350°F/Gas 4.

3 Meanwhile, place the pumpkin cubes in a large pan with enough water to cover. Boil until the pumpkin is tender, about 15–30 minutes, depending on the size of the cubes. Drain and mash the pumpkin using a potato masher.

4 Add all the other ingredients for the filling to the pumpkin, place in a food processor and blend until smooth and creamy. Alternatively blend the ingredients together using a stick blender.

5 Pour the filling into the unbaked pastry case, and bake in the oven for 50 minutes to 1 hour until golden brown.

6 Carefully transfer the pie on to a plate. Chill in the refrigerator before serving.

Cook's tip
Decorate with a sprinkle of icing (confectioners') sugar, or toasted sugared pumpkin seeds, or a mixture of both, if you like.

Energy 434kcal/1809kJ; Protein 6.2g; Carbohydrate 35.3g, of which sugars 19.4g; Fat 30.8g, of which saturates 13.8g; Cholesterol 94mg; Calcium 108mg; Fibre 1.2g; Sodium 60mg.

Tofu berry cheesecake

This is a relatively low-sugar dessert, considering how delightful it tastes. Natural sugars in the fruit and apple juice sweeten the cheesecake, while the low-fat tofu and soya yogurt make it wonderfully creamy – a perfect foil to the delicious summer fruits.

For the base

50g/2oz/¼ cup dairy-free spread or
soya margarine
30ml/2 tbsp apple juice
115g/4oz/6 cups bran flakes

SERVES 6

For the filling

425g/15oz firm tofu
300g/11oz/scant 2 cups soya yogurt
1 sachet vegetarian jelly crystals
90ml/6 tbsp apple juice
175g/6oz soft fruits, such as raspberries,
strawberries and blueberries
30ml/2 tbsp redcurrant jelly
30ml/2 tbsp lemon juice

1 To make the base, place the dairy-free spread or soya margarine and apple juice in a pan and heat them gently until melted. Crush the cereal and stir it into the apple juice mixture.

2 Transfer the mixture into a 23cm/9in loose-based round flan tin (pan) and press down firmly with your fingers. Leave the base to cool. Chill for at least three hours in the refrigerator or until set.

3 To make the filling, place the tofu and yogurt in a food processor and process them until smooth. Heat the apple juice, then add the jelly crystals until dissolved, and blend into the tofu mixture.

4 Spread the tofu mixture over the base, smoothing it evenly. Chill for 1–2 hours, until the filling has set.

5 Carefully remove the flan tin and place the cheesecake on a serving plate.

6 Arrange the fruits on top of the cake. Place the redcurrant jelly in a small bowl, heat the lemon juice and add to the bowl. Stir the mixture well until the jelly has completely melted. Leave it to cool slightly and then spoon or lightly brush it over the fruit. Chill until required and then serve.

Nutrition note
Made from soya beans, tofu is an excellent source of protein and it is low in fat, making this dessert a well-balanced dish. It is packed with vitamins and health-giving nutrients in the fruit, and fibre in the bran-flake base.

Energy 175kcal/735kJ; Protein 8.1g; Carbohydrate 23.2g, of which sugars 13.7g; Fat 6g, of which saturates 1.4g; Cholesterol 1mg; Calcium 314mg; Fibre 2.8g; Sodium 241mg.

Chocolate custards

Try this vegan custard recipe. It's so simple and quick to prepare, and has the nostalgia of childhood wrapped into its silky smooth texture and chocolatey taste. It can be served as a pudding on its own, or as an indulgent chocolate topping for other desserts.

75ml/5 tbsp raw cacao powder
60ml/4 tbsp cornflour (cornstarch)
60ml/4 tbsp agave syrup
250ml/8fl oz/1 cup unsweetened almond or oat milk
120ml/4fl oz/¹/₂ cup water

pinch of nutmeg
5ml/1 tsp vanilla extract (optional)

SERVES 4

1 Sift the cacao powder and cornflour into a medium pan and slowly add the agave syrup, almond milk and the measured water, whisking continuously as you do so. Alternatively, put all of the ingredients in a high-speed blender and blend on the high setting for about 1 minute.

2 Heat the mixture over a low–medium heat, whisking constantly, to avoid lumps. Add the nutmeg and vanilla, if using.

3 Slowly bring to the boil and cook for about 1 minute, still whisking.

4 Set the custard aside in the pan for about 10 minutes to thicken, then serve, either in serving glasses as a dessert, or poured over a dessert of your choice as a topping.

Almond milk

Fresh almond milk is so easy to make if you have a blender. It only lasts a few days in the refrigerator but you can always use it in cooking after that, or make a hot chocolate drink. Nutritionally it's better if you soak the almonds overnight in water, but no drama if you forget.

50g/2oz/¹/₂ cup raw almonds, soaked in
    water overnight and drained
750ml/1¹/₄ pints/3 cups water
15ml/1 tbsp raw agave or maple syrup
5ml/1 tsp chia seeds
pinch of Himalayan salt (iodised) salt
3 drops vanilla extract (if not using in cooking)

Put the almonds, water, agave or maple syrup, chia seeds and salt in a blender and blend on high until smooth. Strain into a bowl using a nylon coffee filter or a flour sieve and stir in the vanilla (if using). Keep refrigerated. You can use the leftover solids to make burgers, pesto or add to hummus.

Energy 276kcal/1144kJ; Protein 0.4g; Carbohydrate 26.3g, of which sugars 1.1g; Fat 19.5g, of which saturates 11.1g; Cholesterol 1mg; Calcium 2mg; Fibre 0.4g; Sodium 50mg.

White chocolate, raspberry and hazelnut meringue cake

Once discarded as a waste product, the cooking liquid from a can of chickpeas has found recognition as a wonder ingredient dubbed aquafaba (or 'bean water'). It's the gloopy, creamy fibres of the beans, and when used in many recipes, it acts similarly to egg whites. It's the ultimate vegan no-waste ingredient that's basically free, that you used to simply pour down the sink.

For the meringue
dairy-free margarine, for greasing
140g/5oz/1$^1/_4$ cups hazelnuts
2 x 400g cans chickpeas, water drained and saved
5ml/1 tsp cream of tartar
5ml/1 tsp vanilla powder
225g/8oz/2 cups icing (confectioners') sugar, plus extra for dusting
zest of 1 lemon

For the filling
400g/14oz can chickpeas, water drained and saved
2.5ml/$^1/_2$ tsp cream of tartar
2.5ml/$^1/_2$ tsp vanilla powder
115g/4oz/1 cup icing (confectioners') sugar
200g/7oz dairy-free vegan white chocolate
50g/2 oz coconut oil
700g/1lb 8oz/4 cups raspberries

SERVES 8

1 Preheat the oven to 180°C/350°F/Gas 4. Grease and line the bases of two 20cm/8in round cake tins (pans) with baking parchment.

2 Spread the hazelnuts on a baking sheet and bake for approximately 8 minutes, or until lightly toasted. Leave to cool slightly. Reduce the oven temperature to 110°C/230°F/Gas 1.

3 Grind the nuts in a food processor, until they are the consistency of coarse sand.

4 Add the water drained from the two cans of chickpeas into a large bowl and whisk for approximately 5 minutes until it's more than doubled in size, white and foamy.

5 Add the cream of tartar and powdered vanilla, and whisk again for another minute. Slowly and gently start adding the sugar, whisking until the mixture forms stiff, glossy peaks. Slowly, a spoon at a time, add in the ground hazelnuts and lemon zest.

6 Divide the mixture between the cake tins and smooth the tops level.

7 Bake for 2½ hours. Do NOT open the oven! After 2½ hours, turn the oven off and leave them to cool in the oven for at least another hour.

8 Leave to cool in the tin for 5 minutes, then run a knife around the inside edge of the tins to loosen the meringues. Turn out to go cold on a wire rack.

9 For the filling, add the water drained from one can of chickpeas into a large bowl and whisk for approximately 5 minutes until it's more than doubled in size, white and foamy. Add the cream of tartar and powdered vanilla, and whisk again for another minute. Slowly start adding in the sugar, whisking until the mixture forms stiff, glossy peaks.

10 Melt the vegan white chocolate and coconut oil together, then slowly, a spoon at a time, whisk into the vanilla mixture to make a smooth cream.

11 When ready to serve, spread the cream and the raspberries on top of the meringues and place them one on top of the other. Lightly dust the top with icing sugar. You'll need a very sharp knife to cut and serve.

Cook's tip
This uses 3 cans of chickpeas so you can use them up by making your own hummus (see page 83).

Energy 289kcal/1220kJ; Protein 6.2g; Carbohydrate 41.1g, of which sugars 32.2g; Fat 12.6g, of which saturates 4.3g; Cholesterol 1.5mg; Calcium 44mg; Fibre 5.5g; Sodium 112mg.

Baked figs with hazelnut and maple syrup tofu ice cream

Figs have been cultivated for thousands of years, and with their deliciously intense flavour it is easy to see why. The nutty tofu ice cream is the perfect complement to these ancient fruits. You will need to make the ice cream a day ahead of serving this dessert

1 lemon grass stalk, finely chopped
1 cinnamon stick, roughly broken
60ml/4 tbsp maple syrup
200ml/7fl oz/scant 1 cup apple juice
8 large or 12 small figs

For the hazelnut soya ice cream
450ml/³/4 pint/scant 2 cups soya cream
50ml/2fl oz/¹/4 cup maple syrup
45ml/3 tbsp silken tofu
30ml/2 tbsp dairy-free margarine or coconut oil
1.5ml/¹/4 tsp vanilla extract
75g/3oz/³/4 cup hazelnuts

SERVES 4

1 First make the ice cream. In a bowl, blend together the ice cream ingredients, except for the hazelnuts, using an electric or hand whisk.

2 Transfer the ice cream mixture to a metal or plastic freezer container and freeze for 2 hours, or until the mixture feels firm around the edge.

3 Preheat the oven to 180°C/350°F/Gas 4. Place the hazelnuts on a baking sheet and roast for 10–12 minutes, or until they are golden brown. Leave the nuts to cool, then place them in a food processor or blender and process until they are coarsely ground.

4 Remove the container from the freezer and whisk the ice cream to break down the ice crystals. Stir in the ground hazelnuts and freeze the mixture again for approximately two hours until half-frozen. Whisk again, then freeze for eight hours or until firm.

5 For the figs, first place the lemon grass, cinnamon stick, maple syrup and apple juice in a small pan and heat slowly until boiling. Lower the heat and simmer the mixture for 5 minutes, then leave the syrup to stand for 15 minutes.

6 Preheat the oven to 200°C/400°F/Gas 6. Meanwhile, carefully cut the figs into quarters, leaving them intact at the bases. Place the figs in an ovenproof baking dish and pour over the maple-flavoured syrup.

7 Cover the dish tightly with foil and bake the figs for about 15 minutes, or until they are tender.

8 Take the ice cream from the freezer about 10 minutes before serving, to allow it to soften slightly. While still warm, transfer the baked figs to individual serving plates.

9 Drizzle a little of the spiced syrup over the figs. Serve them with a scoop or two of hazelnut ice cream.

Cook's tips
• If you prefer, rather than whisking the semi-frozen ice cream, transfer it into a food processor and process until completely smooth.

Energy 500kcal/2098kJ; Protein 12.5g; Carbohydrate 62.8g, of which sugars 62.4g; Fat 23.2g, of which saturates 4.3g; Cholesterol 1mg; Calcium 280mg; Fibre 5.9g; Sodium 248mg.

Vanilla and saffron pears

These sweet juicy pears, poached in agave syrup infused with vanilla, saffron and lime, make a truly elegant dessert. For a low-fat version you can eat them on their own, but for a really luxurious, indulgent treat, serve with soya, cashew or coconut ice cream.

2 vanilla pods (beans)
250ml/8fl oz/1 cup agave syrup
5ml/1 tsp finely grated lime rind
large pinch of saffron

475ml/16fl oz/2 cups apple juice
8 large, firm ripe dessert pears

SERVES 4

1 Using a small sharp knife, carefully split the vanilla pods in half. Scrape the seeds into a heavy pan large enough to hold all the pears, then add the vanilla pods as well.

2 Pour the agave syrup into the pan with the vanilla, then add the lime rind and the saffron. Pour the apple juice into the pan and bring the mixture to the boil. Reduce the heat to low and simmer, stirring occasionally, while you prepare the pears.

3 Peel the pears, then add to the pan and gently turn in the syrup to coat evenly. Cover the pan and simmer gently for about 12–15 minutes, turning the pears halfway through cooking, until they are just tender.

4 Lift the pears from the syrup using a slotted spoon and transfer to four serving bowls. Set aside.

5 Bring the syrup back to the boil and cook gently for about 10 minutes, or until the liquid has reduced slightly and thickened. Spoon the syrup over the pears and serve either warm or chilled with ice cream.

Cook's tip
For the best results use firm varieties of dessert pears, such as comice or conference, that are well ripened.

Variation
Try using different flavourings in the syrup. Use 10ml/2 tsp chopped fresh root ginger and 1 or 2 star anise in place of the saffron and vanilla, or 1 cinnamon stick, 3 cloves and 105ml/7tbsp maple syrup in place of the agave syrup.

Energy 283kcal/1207kJ; Protein 0.8g; Carbohydrate 74.3g, of which sugars 74.3g; Fat 0.2g, of which saturates 0g; Cholesterol 0mg; Calcium 38mg; Fibre 3.3g; Sodium 10mg.

Sweet spring rolls with banana and jackfruit

These delicious spring rolls, filled with ripe bananas and jackfruit slices, can be sprinkled with sugar and eaten with the fingers, or served as a pudding with a caramel sauce. If you cannot find fresh jackfruit in South-east Asian food shops, substitute it with canned jackfruit.

12 spring roll wrappers, or filo pastry
2 firm, ripe bananas, thinly sliced diagonally
175g/6oz fresh or canned jackfruit, thinly sliced
30-45ml/2-3 tbsp palm or muscovado (molasses) sugar
30ml/2 tbsp plant-based yogurt, for sealing rolls,
vegetable oil, for deep-frying

For the caramel sauce
115g/4oz/1 cup brown or coconut sugar
120ml/4fl oz/¹/₂ cup water
250ml/8fl oz/1 cup unsweetened coconut milk or coconut cream

SERVES 4

1 First make the sauce. Put the sugar and water into a heavy pan and, shaking the pan occasionally, heat until it caramelizes. When the mixture starts to turn a rich brown, remove from the heat and stir in the coconut milk or coconut cream. Return the pan to the heat and continue stirring until the sauce thickens slightly. Remove from the heat and leave to rest.

2 Place a spring roll wrapper on a flat surface in front of you. Arrange, overlapping, 2–3 slices of banana with 2–3 slices of jackfruit 2.5cm/1in from the edge nearest to you. Sprinkle a little sugar over the fruit, then roll the nearest edge over the fruit, tuck in the ends and continue rolling into a loose log. (If it is too tight the wrapper will split open when fried.)

3 Moisten the far edge with a little yogurt to seal the roll so that the filling does not escape during the frying. Repeat with the remaining spring roll wrappers.

4 Heat enough oil in a wok or pan for deep frying. Working in batches, deep-fry the spring rolls for 3–4 minutes, until golden brown all over.

5 Using tongs, lift the spring rolls out of the oil and drain on kitchen paper. (If you spray them lightly with oil you could alternatively bake them for 10-15 minutes in a hot oven until crisp.)

6 Quickly reheat the sauce. Arrange the spring rolls on a serving dish, or in individual bowls, and serve with the caramel sauce in dipping bowls.

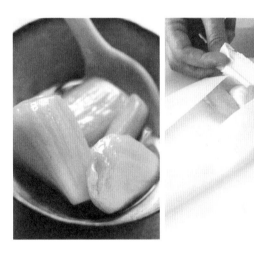

Cook's tip
If you are using fresh jackfruit, make sure it is really ripe, to make the most of its lovely sweet flavour. The outer skin should have changed from bright green to dark yellow and you should be able to detect a strong fruity smell.

Per Portion Energy 246kcal/1043kJ; Protein 4g; Carbohydrate 47.3g, of which sugars 37.1g; Fat 5.9g, of which saturates 1.1g; Cholesterol 63mg; Calcium 55mg; Fibre 1.2g; Sodium 72mg.

Caramelized pineapple with lemon grass

This stunning dessert, garnished with jewel-like pomegranate seeds, is perfect for entertaining. The tangy, zesty flavours of lemon grass and mint bring out the exquisite sweetness of the fruit.

30ml/2 tbsp very finely chopped lemon grass, and 2 lemon grass stalks, halved lengthways
450ml/^{3}/$_4$ pint/scant 2 cups agave syrup
10g/2 tsp chopped fresh mint leaves
150ml/^{1}/$_4$ pint/^{2}/$_3$ cup pineapple juice
2 small, ripe pineapples

15ml/1 tbsp sunflower oil
60ml/4 tbsp pomegranate seeds
coconut cream, to serve

SERVES 4

1 Place the chopped lemon grass, lemon grass stalks, 300ml/^{1}/$_2$ pint/1^1/$_4$ cups of the agave syrup and the chopped mint leaves in a non-stick wok or large pan. Pour in the pineapple juice and bring to the boil over medium heat.

2 Reduce the heat and simmer the mixture for about 10–15 minutes, until thickened and reduced. Leave to cool slightly, then strain into a glass bowl, reserving the halved lemon grass stalks, then set aside.

3 Using a sharp knife, peel and core the pineapples and cut into 1cm/^{1}/$_2$in slices, then sprinkle the slices with the remaining agave syrup.

4 Brush a large non-stick wok or pan with the oil and place over a medium heat. Working in batches, cook the pineapple slices for 2–3 minutes on one side until they are just beginning to turn brown. Turn the slices over and cook the other side for another 2–3 minutes.

5 Transfer the pineapple slices to a flat serving dish and sprinkle over the pomegranate seeds.

6 Pour the lemon grass syrup over the fruit and garnish with the reserved stalks. Serve hot or at room temperature with coconut cream.

Cook's tip
To remove pomegranate seeds, halve the fruit and hold it over a bowl, cut side down. Tap all over with a wooden spoon or turn it completely inside out.

Energy 493kcal/2101kJ; Protein 1.7g; Carbohydrate 121.8g, of which sugars 121.8g; Fat 3.4g, of which saturates 0.3g; Cholesterol 0mg; Calcium 101mg; Fibre 3.6g; Sodium 11mg.

Plum charlottes with Calvados cream

There is a wide variety of plums and they can be used for much more than making into jam. For this dish try seeking out and experimenting with the many different types – from tangy yellow greengages to sweet and juicy Victorias.

115g/4oz/¹/2 cup dairy-free margarine, melted
30ml/2 tbsp demerara (raw) sugar
450g/1lb ripe plums, stoned (pitted)
and thickly sliced
50ml/2fl oz/¹/4 cup agave syrup
30ml/2 tbsp orange juice
1.5ml/¹/4 tsp ground cinnamon
25g/1oz/¹/4 cup ground almonds
8-10 large slices of wholemeal
(wholewheat) bread

For the Calvados sauce
60ml/4tbsp silken tofu or coconut cream
60ml/4 tbsp maple syrup
30ml/2 tbsp Calvados

SERVES 4

1 Preheat the oven to 190°C/375°F/Gas 5. Line the bases of four individual 10cm-/4in-diameter, deep, earthenware ramekin dishes with baking parchment. Brush evenly and thoroughly with a little of the melted dairy-free margarine, then sprinkle each dish with a little of the demerara sugar, rotating the dish in your hands to make sure you coat each dish evenly.

2 Place the stoned plum slices in a pan with the agave syrup, orange juice and ground cinnamon and cook gently for 5 minutes, or until the plums have softened slightly. Leave the plums to cool, then stir in the ground almonds.

3 Cut the crusts off the bread and then use a plain pastry cutter to cut out four rounds to fit the bases of the ramekins. Dip the bread rounds into melted margarine and fit them into the dishes. Cut four more rounds to fit the tops of the dishes and set aside.

4 Cut the remaining bread into strips, dip into the melted margarine and use to line the sides of the ramekins.

5 Divide the plum mixture among the lined ramekins and level the tops. Place the bread rounds on top and brush with margarine. Place the ramekins on a baking sheet and bake for 25 minutes.

6 Make the sauce just before the charlottes are ready. Place the tofu or coconut cream and maple syrup in a large bowl, and blend them together until pale. Whisk in the Calvados. Continue whisking until the mixture is very light and frothy.

7 Remove the charlottes from the oven and turn out on to warm serving plates. Pour a little sauce over and around the charlottes and serve immediately.

Variations
• Slices of peeled pear or eating apples can be used in this recipe instead of the stoned, sliced plums.
• If you cannot find Calvados, any fruit-based spirit or non-alcoholic fruit syrup will work in this dish.
• This dish is also delicious served with oatmilk custard.

Energy 600kcal/2513kJ; Protein 9.1g; Carbohydrate 69.6g, of which sugars 44.2g; Fat 32.5g, of which saturates 16.5g; Cholesterol 218mg; Calcium 128mg; Fibre 3.1g; Sodium 467mg.

Rice pudding with oranges

Rice is a popular dessert in many parts of the world. This delicious and healthy version of rice pudding is light and easy to make. The raisins benefit from pre-soaking in hot water before being added to the pudding. Top with orange segments or another tangy fruit of your choice.

75g/3oz/generous ¹/₂ cup raisins
75ml/5 tbsp water
90g/3¹/₂oz/¹/₂ cup short grain (pudding) rice
3 or 4 strips of pared lemon rind
250ml/8fl oz/1 cup rice milk
475ml/16fl oz/2 cups soya milk
1 cinnamon stick, about 7.5cm/3in in length,
plus extra, to decorate (optional)

120ml/4fl oz/¹/₂ cup agave syrup
pinch of salt
5ml/1 tsp ground almonds
15g/¹/₂ oz/1 tbsp dairy-free margarine
chilled orange segments

SERVES 4

1 Put the raisins and water in a small pan. Heat gently until warm, then set the pan aside, which will allow the raisins to swell.

2 Mix the rice, lemon rind and rice milk in a heavy pan and bring the mixture gently to the boil. Lower the heat, cover the pan and simmer for approximately 20 minutes. Remove the lemon rind pieces from the pan with a slotted spoon and discard.

3 Add the soya milk and the cinnamon stick to the pan, then stir until the rice has absorbed the milk. Stir in the syrup and salt. Add the ground almonds and dairy-free margarine. Stir until blended.

4 Drain the raisins and stir into the rice mixture. Cook for 2–3 minutes until heated through. Serve in individual bowls, topped with orange segments, and decorate with a cinnamon stick, if you like.

Cook's tip
Try drizzling with agave or maple syrup and sprinkle with nutmeg.

Energy 325kcal/1365kJ; Protein 6.7g; Carbohydrate 56.2g, of which sugars 38.2g; Fat 6.3g, of which saturates 1.9g; Cholesterol 1mg; Calcium 44mg; Fibre 0.5g; Sodium 171mg.

Spiced ground rice pudding

Flavoured with cinnamon, this smooth ground rice pudding is traditionally served in Lebanon. If you load it with shelled hemp seed hearts and chia seeds this would help replenish your essential fat levels, as well as being a soothing comfort food.

300g/11oz/scant 2 cups ground rice
450g/1lb/2¼ cups apple, grated
30ml/2 tbsp ground cinnamon
10ml/2 tsp ground aniseed
30g/2 tbsp desiccated (dry unsweetened shredded) coconut
15g/1 tbsp pistachio nuts, chopped

SERVES 6

1 Pour 1.2 litres/2 pints/5 cups water into a heavy pan and bring it to the boil. Reduce the heat and beat in the ground rice, grated apple and spices, stirring constantly to keep smooth.

2 Simmer gently for about 15 minutes, until the mixture is very thick and the apple is cooked.

3 Transfer the mixture into individual serving bowls and leave to cool and set, then chill in the refrigerator.

4 When ready to serve, top each pudding with a sprinkling of coconut and pistachio nuts and eat chilled or at room temperature.

Variation

For extra flavour and crunch you could lightly dry-roast the pistachio nuts and desiccated coconut. Let them cool before sprinkling on top of the pudding.

Energy 525kcal/2219kJ; Protein 5.1g; Carbohydrate 119.4g, of which sugars 78.8g; Fat 5g, of which saturates 2.9g; Cholesterol 0mg; Calcium 56mg; Fibre 0.8g; Sodium 20mg.

Baked squash with coconut custard

A vegan recipe based on a traditional dessert from Thailand. Once the custard-filled pumpkin is baked, the flesh is scooped out with the custard and a hot coconut sauce is drizzled over the top. Sweet and fragrant, this delicious dish is sheer indulgence and a real crowd pleaser.

1 small acorn squash, about 1.3kg/3lb, halved, seeded and fibres removed
400ml/14fl oz/1²/₃ cups coconut milk
45ml/3 tbsp silken tofu
45ml/3 tbsp agave syrup, plus a little extra for drizzling
pinch of salt

For the sauce
250ml/8fl oz/1 cup coconut cream
30ml/2 tbsp agave syrup
pinch of salt

SERVES 4

1 Preheat the oven to 180°C/350°F/Gas 4. Place the squash halves, skin-side down, in a baking dish.

2 In a large bowl, blend the coconut milk with a pinch of salt, the tofu and agave syrup, until the mixture is thick and smooth.

3 Pour the custard into each pumpkin half. Sprinkle a little extra agave syrup over the top of the custard and the rim of the pumpkin.

4 Bake in the oven for 35–40 minutes. The pumpkin should feel tender when a skewer is inserted in it, and the custard should feel firm when lightly touched. If you like, you can brown the top further under the grill or broiler.

5 Just before serving, heat the coconut cream in a pan with a pinch of salt and the syrup. Scoop out pieces of pumpkin flesh with the custard and place in bowls. Pour a little sweetened coconut cream over the top to serve.

Cook's tip
Cinnamon goes so well with squashes and pumpkins. Try adding a little to the sauce or sprinkle the squash with cinnamon and brown sugar before baking or grilling.

Variation
This recipe can also be made with butternut squash or pumpkin and, interestingly, with halved avocados, mangoes and papayas. Bear in mind that the quantity of custard and the cooking times may have to be adjusted.

Energy 217kcal/906kJ; Protein 4.5g; Carbohydrate 16.3g, of which sugars 15.7g; Fat 15.4g, of which saturates 11.9g; Cholesterol 71mg; Calcium 71mg; Fibre 1.3g; Sodium 88mg.

Bakewell tart

This traditional sweet almond tart is always the first to go at vegan food festivals. It is often attributed to Mrs Greaves, landlady of a pub in the English Peak District town of Bakewell in 1820. References have, however, been found to similar tarts dating back to medieval times.

For the pastry
250g/9oz/2¼ cups wholemeal (wholewheat) flour
75ml/2½ fl oz/⅓ cup rapeseed (canola) oil
15ml/1 tbsp sesame tahini
75ml/2½ fl oz/⅓ cup sweetened soya milk

For the topping
60ml/4 tbsp raspberry jam
225g/8oz/2 cups wholemeal (wholewheat) flour
50ml/2oz/½ cup ground almonds

175g/6oz/¾ cup soft light brown sugar
5ml/1 tsp finely grated lemon rind
10ml/2 tsp baking powder
150ml/¼ pint/⅔ cup vegetable oil
200ml/7fl oz/scant 1 cup soya milk
5ml/1 tsp vanilla extract
5ml/1 tsp almond extract
25g/1oz flaked (sliced) almonds

SERVES 8

1 Preheat the oven to 190°C/375°F/Gas 5. Make the pastry. Rub together the flour, oil and tahini until it resembles breadcrumbs. Gradually add the soya milk and mix to form a soft dough.

2 Roll out the dough on a floured surface into a circle that will line a 20cm/8in loose-fitted round flan tin (pan). Prick the dough all over with a fork and bake it in the oven for about 10–15 minutes. Set aside to cool.

3 Spread a layer of raspberry jam in the base of the pastry case or pie shell.

4 In a bowl, mix together the flour, ground almonds, sugar, lemon rind and baking powder. Add the oil, soya milk and extracts and mix again.

5 Pour the mixture over the jammy pastry base. Sprinkle with flaked almonds on top. Bake for 35 minutes until cooked evenly.

6 Serve warm with hot oat milk custard or soya ice cream.

Energy 538kcal/2257kJ; Protein 11g; Carbohydrate 66.9g, of which sugars 30g; Fat 26.9g, of which saturates 2.8g; Cholesterol 0mg; Calcium 76mg; Fibre 6.2g; Sodium 17mg.

Raspberry and almond tart

This is a beautifully rich tart, ideal for serving at the end of a special celebratory feast or at a dinner party. The raspberries and ground almonds are perfect partners.

For the pastry
125g/4¼oz plain (all-purpose) flour
50g/2oz icing (confectioners') sugar
50g/2oz dairy-free margarine

For the topping
125g/4¼oz silken tofu
75ml/2½fl oz/⅓ cup soya cream
50ml/2fl oz/¼ cup agave syrup
50g/2oz/½ cup ground almonds
20g/¾oz/1½ tbsp soya margarine
350g/12oz/2 cups raspberries

SERVES 8

1 To make the pastry, sift the flour and icing sugar into a large bowl and add the dairy-free margarine. Rub the mixture together with your fingertips until it resembles coarse breadcrumbs. Bring together to form a dough, adding extra flour if the mixture is too wet, or a little water if too dry. Wrap the dough in clingfilm or plastic wrap and chill for 10 minutes before using.

2 Roll out the pastry and use it to line a 20cm/8in loosefitted round flan tin (pan). Prick the base all over with a fork and leave it to rest for at least 30 minutes. Preheat the oven to 200°C/400°F/Gas 6.

3 Put the tofu, soya cream, agave syrup and ground almonds into a large bowl and whisk together briskly. Melt the margarine gently in a pan and pour into the mixture, stirring until the ingredients are well combined.

4 Sprinkle the raspberries over the pastry case. The ones at the top will appear through the surface, so space them evenly or in a pattern.

5 Pour the tofu and almond mixture on top of the raspberries. Ensure that it is spread evenly over the tart and some fruits are poking out of the top.

6 Bake the tart for 25 minutes until cooked evenly. Leave to cool for 5 minutes. Serve warm or cold.

Variation
Peaches will also make a very attractive and tasty tart. Use six large, ripe peaches and remove the skin and stone. Cut into slices and use in the same way as the raspberries above. You could also use blackberries or blueberries.

Energy 216kcal/602kJ; Protein 5.2g; Carbohydrate 19.4g, of which sugars 7.7g; Fat 13.4g, of which saturates 3.9g; Cholesterol 9.5mg; Calcium 131mg; Fibre 2g; Sodium 148mg.

Apple and walnut strudel

This crisp pastry roll, filled with a delicious mix of fruit and jam, is the perfect sweet treat to accompany a cup of tea. No one can resist a slice of strudel served with a glass of lemon tea.

For the pastry
75g/3oz/¹/₃ cup dairy-free margarine
75g/3oz/¹/₃ cup silken tofu
20ml/4 tsp agave syrup
2.5ml/¹/₂ tsp vanilla extract
pinch of salt
75g/3oz wholemeal (wholewheat) flour
icing (confectioners') sugar, sifted,
for dusting

For the filling
1 cooking apple
20ml/4 tsp sultanas (golden raisins) or raisins
15ml/1 tbsp agave syrup
40g/1¹/₂ oz/¹/₃ cup walnuts, roughly chopped
5ml/1tsp ground cinnamon
20ml/4 tsp apricot jam or conserve
redcurrants, to garnish (optional)

SERVES 4-6

1 To make the pastry, beat the margarine until light and fluffy, then add the tofu, agave syrup, vanilla extract and salt, and beat together.

2 Sift the flour into the mixture and stir until a soft dough forms. Wrap the dough in clear film or plastic wrap and chill in the refrigerator overnight or until needed.

3 Preheat the oven to 180°C/350°F/Gas 4. To make the filling, core and finely chop the apples but do not peel. Put the apples in a bowl, add the sultanas or raisins, syrup, walnuts, cinnamon and apricot jam or conserve and mix together until well combined.

4 Place the pastry on a sheet of lightly floured baking parchment and roll out to a rectangle measuring about 45 x 30cm/18 x 12in.

5 Spread the filling over the pastry, leaving a 1–2cm/¹/₂–³/₄in border. Roll up the pastry to enclose the filling and place, seam-side down, on a non-stick baking sheet.

6 Bake the strudel for 25–30 minutes until golden brown all over.

7 Remove the strudel from the oven and leave to rest for 5 minutes to allow it to firm up slightly. Dust liberally with icing sugar. Serve either warm or cold, garnished with redcurrants, if you like.

Cook's tip
Alternatively, use filo pastry, spread the fruit mix over the sheets and roll up like a Swiss roll. Paint with oil and bake as normal. Both versions are delicious served hot with ice cream or cold as a treat with coffee.

Energy 232kcal/967kJ; Protein 4g; Carbohydrate 17.7g, of which sugars 9g; Fat 16.6g, of which saturates 5.5g; Cholesterol 2mg; Calcium 87mg; Fibre 1.8g; Sodium 129mg.

Chocolate and orange gâteau

Light and airy, this vegan chocolate cake will blow the minds of non-vegan dinner guests.
With its rich vegan cream cheese and jam filling and succulent dark chocolate sauce,
it is the perfect dessert to round off a successful supper party.

For the cake
250g/9oz/2¼ cups self-raising (self-rising) wholemeal
(wholewheat) flour
225g/8oz/1 cup soft light brown sugar
120ml/4fl oz/½ cup rapeseed (canola) oil
150ml/¼ pint/⅔ cup soya milk
115g/4oz/1 cup broken walnuts
30ml/2 tbsp of unsweetened cocoa powder
rind of 2 oranges
15ml/1 tbsp vegan yogurt or silken tofu
15ml/1 tbsp balsamic vinegar
10ml/2 tsp carob powder
salt

For the filling
60ml/4 tbsp vegan cream cheese
5ml/1 tsp finely grated lime rind
60ml/4 tbsp marmalade or apricot jam

For the chocolate sauce
115g/4oz dairy-free dark (bittersweet) chocolate
15ml/1 tbsp agave syrup
15ml/1 tbsp orange liqueur (optional)
250ml/8fl oz/1 cup soya cream

SERVES 8

1 Place all the ingredients for the cake mixture in a large bowl. Mix thoroughly with a wooden spoon until they are thoroughly combined.

2 Coarsely grate or chop up 25g/1oz of the dairy-free chocolate from the chocolate sauce ingredients. Stir it into the cake mixture.

3 Preheat the oven to 180°C/350°F/Gas 4. Lightly oil two 20cm/8in deep cake tins (pans) and line the bases with baking parchment. Spoon in the cake mixture evenly between the two tins.

4 Bake the cakes in the oven for about 20–30 minutes or until a metal skewer inserted in the centre comes out clean.

5 Meanwhile, prepare the filling. Put the cream cheese into a bowl and mix in the grated lime rind. Set aside until ready to use.

6 When the cakes are baked turn them out on to a wire rack. Leave them to cool completely.

7 When the cakes are cool, spread the lime cream cheese evenly over the top of one of the cakes. Spread the other with marmalade or jam. Sandwich them together with the two fillings facing each other and place on a plate

8 Make the chocolate sauce. Break the chocolate into chunks and melt in a bowl set over a pan of boiling water. Mix in the agave syrup, liqueur, if using, and then the soya cream a little at a time while continuously stirring. Pour over the cake.

9 Leave to cool slightly, then serve with extra sauce, if you like.

Cook's tip
To make the cake even more decadent, swap apricot jam for cherry jam and add fresh pitted cherries or vodka-soaked cherries to the middle and topping.

Energy 536kcal/2245kJ; Protein 8.1g; Carbohydrate 68.9g, of which sugars 43.6g; Fat 26.9g, of which saturates 5.2g; Cholesterol 1mg; Calcium 99mg; Fibre 2.1g; Sodium 62mg.

CAKES, BAKES AND BREADS

Vegans need not feel that they are missing out on life's little luxuries thanks to the heavenly cakes, brownies, cookies and breads on offer in this chapter. Once you know the best substitutes for eggs, butter and buttermilk in your baking you can happily create vegan masterpieces that will taste just as good as conventional baking goods.

Green tea and marmalade fruitcake squares

Chances are your granny would have made a version of this cake in a loaf tin with leftover tea from the teapot; while you can still do this, teabread gets a more modern makeover with green tea and naturally-sweet dried fruits with just a tiny amount of added sugar and a sticky marmalade glaze. The dried mixed fruit needs to be soaked for at least 4 hours, so plan ahead.

450g/1lb/3 cups dried mixed fruit
300ml/1/2 pint/11/4 cups hot green tea, strained if needed
250g/9oz/21/4 cups self-raising (self-rising) wholemeal (wholewheat) flour
75g/3oz/6 tbsp light muscovado (brown) sugar

1 dessert apple, cored and coarsely grated
grated zest of 1/2 lemon
grated zest of 1/2 orange
15ml/1 tbsp fine-cut orange marmalade, to glaze

MAKES 20

1 Add the fruit to a bowl, pour over the hot tea, cover and leave to soak for 4 hours or overnight.

2 Preheat the oven to 160°C/325°F/Gas 3. Cut a piece of baking parchment a little larger than a 20cm/8in shallow square cake tin (pan), snip into the corners then press the paper into the tin so that the base and sides are lined.

3 Add the flour to a larger bowl and stir in the sugar. Add the apple and citrus zest then the soaked fruit and any remaining tea in the bottom of the bowl. Stir together until well mixed.

4 Spoon into the tin, spread level and bake for 50–55 minutes until browned on top and firm to the touch. To test insert a skewer into the centre; it will come out clean when the cake is ready.

5 Leave the cake to cool for 20 minutes in the tin then loosen the edge, lift the cake out by the paper and put on to a wire rack, spread the top with the marmalade and leave to cool.

6 Cut the cake into bars then pack into a plastic container, interleaving with extra baking parchment. Cut into squares when needed. Store for up to 1 week.

Cook's tip
As this cake is packed with fruit it almost improves with keeping. You might like to wrap up one of the strips of cake, label and freeze for another time.

Energy 115kcal/492kJ; Protein 2.1g; Carbohydrate 27.6g, of which sugars 19.9g; Fat 0.4g, of which saturates 0g; Cholesterol 0mg; Calcium 22mg; Fibre 2.2g; Sodium 11mg.

Chocolate beetroot cakes

Rich, dark and very chocolately, these cakes' antioxidant properties from chocolate are enhanced by the beetroot. These gorgeous little cakes are also gluten-free so no-one need miss out.

200g/7oz/2 trimmed beetroot (beets), peeled and diced
250ml/8fl oz/1 cup unsweetened almond milk
45ml/3 tbsp coconut oil
7.5ml/1¹/₂ tsp vanilla extract
75g/3oz/³/₄ cup ground almonds
75g/3oz/³/₄ cup unsweetened cocoa powder
150g/5oz/generous 1 cup light muscovado (brown) sugar
150g/5oz/1 cup gluten-free self-raising (self-rising) flour
5ml/1 tsp gluten-free baking powder

For the frosting
30ml/2 tbsp coconut oil
45ml/3 tbsp unsweetened cocoa powder
30ml/2 tbsp maple syrup
2.5ml/¹/₂ tsp vanilla extract
1 large avocado, halved, stoned (pitted) and sliced
a few goji berries, roughly chopped (optional)

MAKES 12

1 Preheat the oven to 180°C/350°F/Gas 4. Cut a piece of baking parchment a little larger than a 20 x 30cm/8 x 12in Swiss roll tin (jelly roll pan), snip diagonally into the corners then press the paper into the tin so that the base and sides are lined and the paper stands a little above the sides of the tin.

2 Add the beetroot and milk to a pan, bring to the boil then simmer for 4–5 minutes until tender. Take off the heat and stir in the coconut oil then leave to cool.

3 Add the beetroot mix to a food processor with the vanilla and blend until smooth. Add the ground almonds, cocoa, sugar, flour and baking powder and blitz again until smooth. If you are using a liquidizer blend the beetroot mix first then add to a bowl of the dry ingredients and stir together.

4 Spoon into the prepared tin, level the surface and bake for 25 minutes until firm to the touch. Leave to cool in the tin. When cold, lift out of the tin and peel off the paper. Cut the cake in half through the long side to give 2 smaller even-sized rectangles.

5 To make the frosting, warm the coconut oil in a small pan until just melted. Stir in the cocoa, maple syrup and vanilla and mix until smooth and glossy. Transfer to a food processor or liquidizer with the avocado and beat until smooth. Spread half the frosting over one of the cake halves, top with the second cake then spread the remaining frosting on top.

6 Decorate with a few chopped goji berries, if liked. Leave the icing to set for 30 minutes and then cut into 12 small squares. These can be stored in a container in the refrigerator for 3 days.

Nutrition notes
• Beetroot is naturally sweet, containing 1 tsp sugar per 100g/3³/₄oz, but it also contains folates, vitamin C, iron and potassium.
• Goji berries are a good source of vitamins and minerals, including vitamins A and C, iron and zinc. They also contain all 8 essential amino acids and a high level of antioxidants.

Energy 182kcal/764kJ; Protein 4g; Carbohydrate 25g, of which sugars 14.7g; Fat 8g, of which saturates 3.5g; Cholesterol 0mg; Calcium 74mg; Fibre 2.1g; Sodium 131mg.

Victoria sponge cake

Victoria sponge is a classic cake to make but you needn't worry about losing the egg here as this version tastes as good as a regular sponge cake, with air and lightness added by the bicarbonate of soda and baking powder.

225g/8oz/1 cup dairy-free margarine
225g/8oz/1 cup caster (superfine) sugar
300g/10oz/2 cups self-raising (self-rising) flour
2.5ml/1/2 tsp bicarbonate of soda (baking soda)
5ml/1 tsp baking powder
5ml/1 tsp vanilla extract
zest of 1 lemon and juice of 1/2 lemon

125ml/4fl oz/1/2 cup soya milk
250ml/8fl oz/1 cup soya yogurt
60ml/4 tbsp raspberry, strawberry or cherry jam
icing (confectioners') sugar, for dusting

SERVES 6-8

1 Preheat the oven to 180°C/350°F/Gas 4. Grease and line two 20cm/8in round shallow cake tins (pans) with baking parchment.

2 Whisk the margarine and sugar for about 5 minutes until very light and creamy. It is important to whisk in as much air as possible as this will give lightness to the cake.

3 Sift together the flour, bicarbonate of soda and baking powder and then whisk into the creamed margarine and sugar mixture.

4 Add the vanilla, lemon zest, lemon juice, plant milk and yogurt and whisk in. Spoon the mixture into the two prepared tins and bake for 40–50 minutes until the cake is firm and springs back to your touch and a knife comes out clean when inserted into the middle of the cake.

5 Leave the cakes to cool in the tins for a few minutes, then turn out on to a wire rack to go cold. Remove the lining paper.

6 Sandwich the cakes together with jam. Sift a little icing sugar over the top of the cake before serving.

Cook's tip
If you wanted to vary the flavour of this cake, you can add in citrus zest or substitute 30g/1/4oz of the self-raising (self-rising) flour with sifted cocoa powder.

Energy 126kcal/534kJ; Protein 2.5g; Carbohydrate 22.2g, of which sugars 12.8g; Fat 3.7g, of which saturates 0.8g; Cholesterol 1mg; Calcium 72mg; Fibre 0.5g; Sodium 117mg.

Chocolate banana cupcakes

There is no added sugar in this recipe but it is still totally delicious. This recipe is sweetened primarily with bananas and it dispenses with eggs by using ground flax seeds instead. Make sure you use extremely ripe bananas with dark skins and very soft. This will ensure the cupcakes are moist and luscious.

4 large, ripe bananas
150ml/^{1}/$_4$ pint/^{2}/$_3$ cup sunflower oil
90ml/6 tbsp brown rice malt syrup
90ml/6 tbsp coconut milk
10ml/2 tsp vanilla extract
115g/4oz/1 cup plain (all-purpose) wholemeal (wholewheat) flour
75g/3oz/^{1}/$_2$ cup cacao powder
75g/3oz/^{1}/$_2$ cup carob powder

45ml/3 tbsp ground flax seeds
30ml/1 2tbsp ground almonds
15ml/1 tbsp bicarbonate of soda (baking soda)
2.5ml/^{1}/$_2$ tsp ground cinnamon
2.5ml/^{1}/$_2$ tsp sea salt

MAKES 10-12

1 Preheat the oven to 180°C/350°F/Gas 4. Line a cupcake tin (pan) with cupcake cases or papers.

2 Mash the bananas in a medium bowl. Add the oil, brown rice malt syrup, coconut milk and vanilla, and combine, using a fork.

3 Mix all of the other ingredients together in a separate large mixing bowl.

4 Add the wet ingredients to the dry ingredients and mix to combine, using a spoon, working quickly.

5 Spoon the batter into the cupcake cases so that they are about three-quarters full. Bake for about 25 minutes in the preheated oven, until they are golden brown and spring back when lightly pressed. Leave to cool on a wire rack before serving.

Cook's tips

• Carob has acquired a reputation in recent years for not being delicious, but that's not true! It's a wonderful ingredient to use alongside cacao. It gently sweetens the cacao to produce a smoother, more chocolatey flavour.
• Carob also supports the bananas in gently sweetening the cupcakes without the need for sugar. The brown rice malt syrup and coconut milk help sweeten them too, and provide a good balance of moisture.

Energy 254kcal/1059kJ; Protein 5.8g; Carbohydrate 23.4g, of which sugars 13.5g; Fat 15.8g, of which saturates 3.1g; Cholesterol 0mg; Calcium 31mg; Fibre 5.2g; Sodium 563mg.

Gingercake

This deliciously moist cake is flavoured with ginger and will quickly become a firm tea-time favourite. Try dunking in your coffee or eat with oatmilk custard and almond ice cream.

115g/4oz/^{1}/2 cup soft light brown sugar
75g/3oz/6 tbsp soft dairy-free margarine
75g/3oz/^{1}/4 cup agave syrup
75g/3oz/^{1}/4 cup black treacle (molasses)
105ml/7 tbsp soya milk
1 small banana, mashed
175g/6oz/1^1/2 cups wholemeal
  (wholewheat) flour
50g/2oz/^{1}/2 cup gram (chickpea) flour
pinch of salt
10ml/2 tsp ground ginger
5ml/1 tsp ground cinnamon
7.5ml/1^1/2 tsp baking powder

SERVES 6-8

1 Preheat the oven to 160°C/325°F/ Gas 3. Lightly oil a 900g/2lb loaf tin (pan) and line with baking parchment. Melt the sugar, margarine, syrup and treacle in a pan, stirring occasionally.

2 Remove the pan from the heat, leave to cool slightly, then mix in the soya milk and mashed banana.

3 Sift the flours, salt, spices and baking powder into a large mixing bowl, and mix until well combined.

4 Make a well in the centre, pour in the liquid mixture and beat well.

5 Pour the mixture into the prepared tin and bake for 1–1^1/4 hours until firm to the touch and lightly browned.

6 Allow to cool in the tin for a few minutes, then turn out on to a wire rack to cool completely. Store it in an airtight container or wrapped in foil.

Variation

For a more gingery flavour fold 50g/2oz finely chopped preserved stem ginger into the raw cake mixture and add 5–10ml/1–2 tsp extra ground ginger.

Energy 2274kcal/9594kJ; Protein 36.6g; Carbohydrate 399g, of which sugars 252.9g; Fat 70g, of which saturates 28.3g; Cholesterol 11mg; Calcium 589mg; Fibre 21.1g; Sodium 928mg.

Chocolate brownies

Dark and full of flavour, these brownies are irresistible. They are a perfect after-dinner treat or an ideal accompaniment to a cup of herbal tea. They also make a fabulous gift for co-workers.

150g/5oz/²/₃ cup dairy-free margarine
150g/5oz/scant 1 cup pitted dates, softened in boiling water, then drained and finely chopped
150g/5oz/1¹/₄ cups self-raising (self-rising) wholemeal (wholewheat) flour
10ml/2 tsp baking powder

60ml/4 tbsp unsweetened cocoa powder dissolved in 30ml/2 tbsp hot water
60ml/4 tbsp apple and pear fruit spread
90ml/6 tbsp soya milk
50g/2oz/¹/₂ cup pecan nuts, roughly broken

MAKES 20

1 Preheat the oven to 160°C/325°F/Gas 3. Lightly grease a shallow baking tin (pan), measuring approximately 28 x 18cm/11 x 7in.

2 Cream the margarine with the chopped dates in a large bowl until the mixture is well combined.

3 Sift the flour with the baking powder into the margarine and date mixture and mix thoroughly.

4 In a separate bowl, whisk together the dissolved cocoa powder with the apple and pear fruit spread.

5 Gradually pour the soya milk into the cocoa mixture, whisking constantly to combine the ingredients. Pour into the flour mixture, stirring with a wooden spoon until everything is well mixed. Stir the pecan nuts into the bowl.

6 Spoon the mixture into the prepared tin, smooth the surface and bake for about 45–50 minutes or until a metal skewer inserted in the centre comes out clean.

7 Cool for a few minutes in the tin, then cut into bars or squares. Transfer to a wire rack and leave to cool.

Cook's tip
Apple and pear fruit spread is made from concentrated fruit juice. Look for the additive-free versions available in health-food stores and larger supermarkets.

Variation
You can use other nuts in the brownies if you prefer. Try using walnuts or hazelnuts, or a mixture.

Energy 135kcal/563kJ; Protein 2.2g; Carbohydrate 12.6g, of which sugars 7.5g; Fat 8.8g, of which saturates 3.3g; Cholesterol 1mg; Calcium 13mg; Fibre 1.5g; Sodium 91mg.

Parsnip cake with orange icing

This fabulous vegan cake is similar to the ever-popular carrot cake, and a perfect way to prove to your friends and family that vegan cake is just as delicious as any other.

250g/9oz/2¼ cups self-raising (self-rising) wholemeal (wholewheat) flour
15ml/1 tbsp baking powder
5ml/1 tsp ground cinnamon
5ml/1 tsp freshly ground nutmeg
130g/4½oz/generous ½ cup dairy-free margarine, plus extra for greasing
130g/4½oz/generous ½ cup soft light brown sugar

1 banana
250g/9oz parsnips, peeled and coarsely grated
finely grated rind and juice of 1 orange

For the topping
225g/8oz/1 cup soya cream cheese or silken tofu
45ml/3 tbsp icing (confectioners') sugar
juice of 1 small orange
10ml/2 tsp orange zest

SERVES 10

1 Preheat the oven to 180°C/350°F/Gas 4. Lightly grease the base of a 900g/2lb loaf tin (pan) with some margarine. Line the tin with a piece of baking parchment.

2 Sift the self-raising flour, baking powder, cinnamon and nutmeg into a large mixing bowl. Mix the ingredients together until thoroughly combined.

3 Gently melt the margarine in a pan. Add the sugar and stir until completely dissolved. Make a well in the flour mixture, then add the melted margarine and sugar, mixing to combine.

4 Mash the banana and add it along with the parsnips, orange rind and juice to the bowl. Stir until the ingredients are thoroughly mixed. Spoon the mixture into the prepared tin and level the top with the back of a spoon.

5 Bake in the oven for 45–50 minutes until a skewer inserted into the centre of the cake comes out clean. Allow the cake to cool slightly before removing from the tin, then transfer to a wire rack to cool completely.

6 Meanwhile, make the topping. Beat together the soya cream cheese, icing sugar, orange juice and orange zest until smooth.

7 Spread the topping evenly over the cake using a palette knife or metal spatula, ensuring it is spread to the edges. Run a fork lightly over the topping to create a pattern and leave to set. Store in an airtight container.

Nutrition note
Parsnips are really just a paler, stronger-tasting version of carrots. As they are not brightly coloured, they do not have the carotenes of the carrot, but they are still rich in vitamins C and K, folate, manganese and potassium.

Energy 282kcal/1187kJ; Protein 5g; Carbohydrate 40.3g, of which sugars 22.9g; Fat 11.9g, of which saturates 4.9g; Cholesterol 2mg; Calcium 30mg; Fibre 3.5g; Sodium 108mg.

Fruit cake

This makes an ideal cake for a Christmas feast or a wedding or birthday celebration. You can decorate the cake with a layer of marzipan and icing, if you want to make it extra-special.

1 large orange, quartered and seeded, but not peeled
1 large lemon, quartered and seeded, but not peeled
1 large cooking apple, cored and quartered, but not peeled
90g/3¹/₂ oz/generous ¹/₂ cup pitted dates
75g/3oz/6 tbsp dairy-free margarine
75g/3oz/6 tbsp hazelnut butter
90g/3¹/₂oz/²/₃ cup raisins
90g/3¹/₂oz/²/₃ cup currants
90g/3¹/₂oz/scant ¹/₂ cup dried apricots
90g/3¹/₂oz/scant ¹/₂ cup ready-to-eat pitted prunes, chopped
50g/2oz/²/₃ cup broken walnuts

5ml/1 tsp ground cinnamon
5ml/1 tsp grated nutmeg
2.5ml/¹/₂ tsp mace
2.5ml/¹/₂ tsp ground cloves
115g/4oz/1 cup wholemeal (wholewheat) flour
7.5ml/1¹/₂ tsp baking powder
60g/2oz/generous ¹/₂ cup rolled oats
60g/2oz/¹/₂ cup ground almonds
150g/5oz silken tofu
45-60ml/3-4 tbsp soya or rice milk

SERVES 8-10

1 Preheat the oven to 150°F/300°C/Gas 2. Oil and line a deep 20cm/8in round cake tin (pan).

2 Combine the orange, lemon and apple pieces in a food processor or blender. Add the dates, the dairy-free margarine and hazelnut butter. Process the mixture until it forms a rough purée, taking care not to overprocess it.

3 Scrape the mixture into a bowl and stir in the dried fruit, nuts and spices.

4 Stir in the flour, baking powder, rolled oats, almonds and tofu. Stir in the soya or rice milk, and mix thoroughly.

5 Spoon the cake mixture into the prepared tin and bake for 1 hour or until a fine skewer inserted in the centre comes out clean. When ready, turn it out on to a wire rack and leave to cool before decorating or serving.

Pineapple upside-down cake

This light and moist cake has a sticky ginger glaze over stem ginger and pineapple pieces, which are arranged in the cake tin before the cake batter is added.

20g/1³/₄oz/1¹/₂ tbsp dairy-free margarine, plus extra for greasing
2 pieces preserved stem ginger, chopped, plus 60ml/4 tbsp syrup
450g/1lb can pineapple pieces in natural juice, drained
250g/9oz/2¹/₄ cups self-raising (self-rising) wholemeal (wholewheat) flour
15ml/1 tbsp baking powder

5ml/1 tsp ground ginger
5ml/1 tsp ground cinnamon
115g/4oz/¹/₂ cup soft light brown sugar
250ml/8fl oz/1 cup coconut milk
1 banana

SERVES 8

1 Preheat the oven to 180°C/350°F/Gas 4. Grease and line a 20cm/8in round deep cake tin (pan).

2 Melt the margarine in a small pan with the ginger syrup. Turn up the heat and cook until the liquid thickens. Pour into the tin and smooth out to the sides.

3 Arrange the stem ginger and one-third of the pineapple pieces in the syrup in the tin. Set aside.

4 Sift together the flour, baking powder and spices into a large bowl, then stir in the sugar.

5 Blend together the coconut milk, the remaining pineapple and the banana until almost smooth, then add to the flour. Stir until thoroughly combined. Spoon the mixture over the pineapple and ginger pieces in the tin and smooth level.

6 Bake for 45 minutes, or until a skewer inserted into the centre comes out clean. Leave to cool slightly, then place a serving plate over the tin and turn upside down. Remove the lining paper.

Energy 204kcal/866kJ; Protein 4.1g; Carbohydrate 43.3g, of which sugars 25.5g; Fat 2.9g, of which saturates 0.6g; Cholesterol 0mg; Calcium 50mg; Fibre 3.9g; Sodium 113mg.

Almond cookies Florentine-style

Vegan, sugar-free and gluten-free, these Florentine-inspired cookies are thin and crisp with a gorgeous colour. By grinding your own almonds here, the brown skin of the nut is included because unlike store-bought almonds, the almonds you grind have not been blanched. Not only does this mean your cookies have more fibre, it also means the dry mixture is less absorbent, resulting in a much crisper cookie.

200g/7oz/1¹/₂ cups raw whole almonds
pinch of sea salt
1.5ml/¹/₄ tsp bicarbonate of soda (baking soda)
30ml/2 tbsp coconut oil

50ml/2fl oz/¹/₄ cup maple syrup
1.5ml/¹/₄ tsp almond extract

MAKES 12

1 Preheat the oven to 160°C/325°F/Gas 3. Lightly grease a baking sheet with oil and line it with baking parchment.

2 Put the almonds in a food processor and pulverize for about 30 seconds, until ground into tiny crumbs.

3 Pour them into a mixing bowl, add the salt and bicarbonate of soda, and mix with a fork.

4 Melt the coconut oil in a small pan over a low heat until liquid. Pour the oil, maple syrup and almond extract into the dry ingredients and stir to combine.

5 Spoon the sticky mixture on to the baking sheet using a teaspoon, and flatten each spoonful into a cookie shape.

6 Bake for 15–16 minutes until golden brown. Leave to cool until hardened on the baking sheet, then transfer to a wire rack to cool completely.

Cook's tip
If you skip the first step and use store-bought ground almonds, it will still create scrumptious cookies, but a very different kind. They will be smaller and more compact and similar to shortbread in texture. Whichever method you use, the result will be delicious.

Variation
Replace the homemade ground almonds with 175g/6oz/ 1½ cups of store-bought ground hazelnuts. Leave plenty of space between each cookie, as they will spread as they bake.

Energy 137kcal/566kJ; Protein 3.7g; Carbohydrate 4.6g, of which sugars 3.8g; Fat 11.6g, of which saturates 2.4g; Cholesterol 0mg; Calcium 45mg; Fibre 6g; Sodium 3mg.

Scottish shortbread

These melt-in-the-mouth biscuits were traditionally eaten during Christmas or Hogmanay – the Scottish New Year. These vegan versions will no doubt be enjoyed all year round.

225g/8oz/2 cups plain (all-purpose) flour
115g/4oz/1 cup cornflour (cornstarch)
115g/4oz/1 cup icing (confectioners') sugar
115g/4oz/1/2 cup dairy-free margarine
caster (superfine) sugar, for dusting

MAKES 16

1 Lightly oil a baking tin (pan). It should be approximtely 30 x 20cm/12 x 8in, and at least 2.5cm/1in deep.

2 Sift the flour, cornflour and icing sugar into a large mixing bowl. Lightly rub in the margarine until the mixture resembles breadcrumbs. Then knead until it forms a stiff dough.

3 Preheat the oven to 180°C/350°F/Gas 4. Place the dough in the tin and press it down, ensuring that it fills the corners. Smooth the surface with a metal spatula or palette knife.

4 Bake in the oven for approximately 25–30 minutes until the biscuits are a light golden brown colour. While still warm cut into 16 slices.

5 Leave the shortbread to cool slightly in the tin and then transfer to a wire rack to cool completely.

Variation
If you want to be really indulgent you can make a vegan version of millionaire's shortbread. First coat the shortbread with a layer of stewed dates mixed with tahini or pear and apple spread. Then top with some melted vegan chocolate.

Energy 155kcal/652kJ; Protein 1.4g; Carbohydrate 25.1g, of which sugars 7.8g; Fat 6.1g, of which saturates 2.6g; Cholesterol 1mg; Calcium 25mg; Fibre 0.4g; Sodium 62mg.

Carob chip shorties

Delicious and gluten-free too, these lovely cookies are best eaten freshly made, preferably while still slightly warm from the oven.

175g/6oz/1¹/₂ cups gluten-free self-raising (self-rising) flour
25g/1oz/2 tbsp soft light brown sugar
75g/3oz/6 tbsp dairy-free margarine
50g/2oz/¹/₃ cup carob chips

15-25ml/1-1¹/₂ tbsp maple syrup, warmed
golden sugar, for sprinkling

MAKES 12

1 Preheat the oven to 160°C/325°F/Gas 3. Line two baking sheets with baking parchment.

2 Put the flour and brown sugar in a mixing bowl and rub in the margarine. Add the carob chips, then stir in just enough maple syrup to bring the mixture together but not make it sticky. Roll the dough out between two sheets of baking parchment to about 8mm/¹/₃in.

3 Stamp out rounds using a plain 5cm/2in round cutter. Place on the baking sheets. Prick each cookie once with a fork and sprinkle with sugar.

4 Bake for about 15–20 minutes, or until firm. Cool on a wire rack.

Cook's tip
Gluten-free flour is readily available in most supermarkets as well as health-food stores.

Energy 198kcal/820kJ; Protein1g; Carbohydrate 18g, of which sugars6g; Fat 13g, of which saturates 0g; Cholesterol 0mg; Calcium 6mg; Fibre 0g; Sodium 100mg.

Cashew nut butter cookies

These crumbly cookies are quick and easy to make and contain just a few ingredients.
If you enjoy sneaking a spoonful of nut butter from the jar, you will love these!

225g/8oz/1 cup smooth cashew nut butter
30ml/2 tbsp maple syrup
10ml/2 tsp raw cacao or (unsweetened)
cocoa powder
2.5ml/¹/₂ tsp icing (confectioners') sugar

MAKES 12

1 Preheat the oven to 180°C/350°F/Gas 4. Line a baking sheet with baking parchment.

2 Put half of the cashew nut butter and half of the maple syrup into a bowl and combine with a spoon.

3 Put the remaining cashew nut butter and maple syrup in a bowl. Sift over 7.5ml/1½ tsp of the raw cacao or cocoa powder. Mix together until blended.

4 Shape each batch of mixture into six walnut-sized balls. Flatten these slightly, then arrange on the baking sheet, spacing them slightly apart to allow room for the cookies to spread.

5 Bake the cookies for 5–7 minutes, or until beginning to brown around the edges. Remove from the oven and dust the plain ones with icing sugar and the chocolate ones with the remaining 2.5ml/½ tsp cacao or cocoa powder. Leave to cool on the baking sheet. Store in an airtight container for up to 4 days.

Variation

To make thumbprint cookies, use your thumb or fingertip to make a hole in the middle of each cookie, before baking. After baking and while the cookies are still hot, spoon or pipe a little smooth jam or some vegan hazelnut spread into the hole and leave to cool. If you prefer to have a consistent neat round hole, use the end of a wooden spoon dipped in icing (confectioners') sugar.

Energy 119kcal/499kJ; Protein 3.7g; Carbohydrate 6.8g, of which sugars 1.5g; Fat 9.6g, of which saturates 2.5g; Cholesterol 0mg; Calcium 3mg; Fibre 0.1g; Sodium 8mg.

Oat fruit bread

Sugar-free, vegan, gluten-free, heart-healthy, and full of fibre, this cakey bread is best served toasted at teatime. It is delicious with avocado and yeast extract, or cashew nut butter and raspberry jam. Allow plenty of soaking time for the cashews prior to making this fabulous bread.

115g/4oz/1 cup sultanas (golden raisins)
120ml/4fl oz /¹/₂ cup hot English Breakfast tea
12 raw cashews
15ml/1 tbsp coconut oil, plus extra
for greasing
3 ripe bananas, halved lengthways
juice of ¹/₂ lemon
45ml/3 tbsp apple juice
120ml/4fl oz/¹/₂ cup barley malt syrup

225g/8oz/2¹/₂ cups rolled oats
15ml/1 tbsp bicarbonate of soda
(baking soda)
2.5ml/¹/₂ tsp sea salt
5ml/1 tsp ground cinnamon
5ml/1 tsp ground ginger
2.5ml/¹/₂ tsp ground nutmeg

SERVES 8

1 Put the sultanas in a bowl and cover with the tea. Put the cashews in a cup and cover with warm water. Set aside to soak, for four hours or overnight if possible.

2 Preheat the oven to 180°C/350°F/Gas 4. Lightly oil a 23cm x 13cm/9in x 5in loaf tin (pan), and line with baking parchment.

3 Melt the coconut oil in a frying pan over a medium heat and fry the bananas for 1–2 minutes. Turn them over, and fry the other side for 1–2 minutes. Remove the frying pan from the heat, and set it aside so the bananas continue to gently steam in the residual heat.

4 Put the lemon juice in a blender. Discard the soaking water from the cashews. Add the cashews, caramelized bananas and any liquid that's collected in the frying pan, the apple juice and the barley malt syrup. Blend on high for 20–30 seconds, until combined, then pour the banana mixture into a large mixing bowl.

5 In a food processor, pulverize the oats, bicarbonate of soda, salt and spices for 30 seconds–1 minute, until they have become the consistency of flour.

6 Stir the dry ingredients into the wet ingredients. Add the sultanas and their soaking juices to the bowl. Combine quickly with a spatula or a spoon. Pour the batter into the loaf tin and quickly even the top.

7 Bake for about 35–40 minutes, until a skewer inserted into the middle comes out clean. Lift the loaf out of the tin using the baking parchment, and set aside to cool completely on a wire rack. Cut into slices and spread with cashew butter or dairy-free margarine, if you like, to serve.

Variation

Soaking the sultanas in tea keeps them juicy as they bake. Replace the black tea with herbal tea if preferred. Hibiscus or fruit teas are fragrant alternatives, or simply soak the sultanas in warm water. They have a wonderful flavour and just need to be plumped up a bit, which plain warm water does very nicely.

Energy 265kcal/1122kJ; Protein 5.7g; Carbohydrate 51.7g, of which sugars 30.1g; Fat 5.5g, of which saturates 1.5g; Cholesterol 0mg; Calcium 47mg; Fibre 3.5g; Sodium 526mg.

Seeded herby oatcakes

Adding thyme and sunflower seeds to these delicious oatcakes makes them especially good for dipping into a bowl of hummus – or try them spread with avocado and yeast extract.

rolled oats, for sprinkling
175g/6oz/1¹/2 cups wholemeal
 (wholewheat flour)
175g/6oz/1¹/2 cups fine oatmeal
5ml/1 tsp salt
1.5ml/¹/4 tsp bicarbonate of soda
 (baking soda)
90ml/6 tbsp coconut oil
15ml/1 tbsp fresh thyme leaves, chopped
30ml/2 tbsp sunflower seeds

MAKES 32

1 Preheat the oven to 150°C/300°F/Gas 2. Sprinkle two ungreased, non-stick baking sheets with rolled oats and set aside.

2 Put the flour, oatmeal, salt and bicarbonate of soda in a large bowl and rub in the coconut oil until the mixture resembles fine breadcrumbs. Stir in the thyme leaves.

3 Add just enough cold water (about 90–105ml/6–7 tbsp) to the dry ingredients and mix thoroughly to form a stiff but not sticky dough.

4 Gently knead the dough on a lightly floured surface until it becomes smooth, then cut it roughly in half. Roll out one piece on a lightly floured surface to make a 23–25cm/9–10in round, about 1cm/¹/2in in thickness.

5 Sprinkle the sunflower seeds over the dough and press them in with the rolling pin. Cut into triangles and arrange on one of the baking sheets. Repeat with the remaining dough. Bake for 45–60 minutes until crisp but not brown. Cool on wire racks.

Energy 63kcal/264kJ; Protein 1.6g; Carbohydrate 7.7g, of which sugars 0.1g; Fat 3.1g, of which saturates 1.8g; Cholesterol 0mg; Calcium 6mg; Fibre 0.9g; Sodium 2mg.

Brown scones with oat milk

These unusually light scones are virtually fat-free, so they must be eaten very fresh –
warm from the oven if possible, but definitely on the day of baking.

vegetable oil, for greasing
115g/4oz/1 cup self-raising (self-rising) white flour,
plus extra for dusting
115g/4oz/1 cup self-raising(self-rising)
wholemeal (wholewheat) flour
5ml/1 tsp baking powder
1.5ml/^{1}/$_4$ tsp salt

15ml/1 tbsp dairy-free yogurt
5ml/1 tsp lemon juice
about 350ml/12fl oz/1^1/$_2$ cups oat milk,
plus extra for glazing

MAKES 8

1 Preheat the oven to 220°C/425°F/Gas 7. Grease a baking
sheet with oil and dust with flour.

2 Sift the flours, baking powder and salt into a bowl, adding
the bran left in the sieve or strainer.

3 Make a well in the centre, add the yogurt and lemon juice
and pour in almost all the oat milk and mix, adding milk as
needed to make a soft, moist dough. Do not overmix.

4 Lightly dust a surface with flour, turn out the dough and
dust it with flour.

5 Press out the dough to a thickness of 4cm/1^1/$_2$in. Cut out
eight scones with a 5cm/2in fluted pastry cutter. Place on
the baking sheet and brush the tops with oat milk or leave
unglazed and dust with a little flour.

6 Bake the scones for about 12 minutes, until well risen and
golden brown. Remove to a cooling rack and enjoy warm.

Cook's tip
These savoury scones are delicious served with soup, or you
can spread them with a little coconut butter or sunflower
spread and top with a spoonful of fruity jam.

Energy 117kcal/497kJ; Protein 3.2g; Carbohydrate 20.7g, of which sugars 2.6g; Fat 1g, of which saturates 0.1g; Cholesterol 0mg; Calcium 63mg; Fibre 2.3g; Sodium 126mg.

Seeded nutty spelt bread

A mixture of quinoa and spelt flour is used to make this rustic loaf. Spelt is an ancient grain (dating back more than 5,000 years), and has a lower gluten content than wheat flour.

225g/8oz/2 cups quinoa flour
225g/8oz/2 cups spelt flour
10ml/2 tsp easy-blend (rapid-rise) dried yeast
10ml/2 tsp salt
60ml/4 tbsp sugar
25g/1oz/¼ cup mixed seeds (sunflower, pumpkin, flax and poppy seeds), plus 15g/1 tbsp extra, for sprinkling

25g/1oz/¼ cup chopped raw unsalted nuts,
  such as walnuts or hazelnuts
250ml/8fl oz/1 cup plant milk, plus extra to glaze
50ml/2fl oz/¼ cup boiling water
oil, for greasing

MAKES 1 LOAF

1 Sift the flours into a large bowl, add the dried yeast, salt, sugar, mixed seeds and chopped nuts, and stir to combine. Make a well in the centre.

2 Mix the plant milk and boiling water together in a bowl and pour into the well. Stir, mixing in the flour gradually, to form a pliable dough. Transfer the dough to a floured board, and knead by hand for 6–8 minutes, or in an electric mixer with a dough hook for 4–5 minutes, until soft and elastic.

3 To knead by hand, hold the dough with one hand and stretch it with the palm of the other hand, then fold it back. Turn the dough 90 degrees and repeat this process for the required time.

4 Place the dough in a clean bowl, cover it with a damp cloth and leave it in a warm place for 1–1½ hours, until the dough has nearly doubled in size.

5 Knock back or punch down the dough and knead it for a couple of minutes. Cover it with the damp cloth again and set it aside to prove for another 30 minutes, until doubled in size. Preheat the oven to 200°C/400°F/Gas 6.

6 Oil a 450g/1lb loaf tin (pan). Shape the dough to neatly fill the tin. With a sharp knife, score the top of the loaf lengthways and across, to help the dough rise. Brush the top with milk and sprinkle with seeds.

7 Bake for 35–40 minutes, until the loaf is risen and golden, and sounds hollow on the base when tapped (you will have to remove it from the tin to test this). Remove from the tin or baking sheet, and cool in a wire rack for at least 20 minutes.

Variation
For a more decorative loaf, oil a baking sheet and split the prepared dough into three strands and plait or braid it. Brush the top with milk and sprinkle with seeds. Bake for 35–40 minutes until the loaf is risen and golden, and sounds hollow on the based when tapped. Cool on a wire rack for at least 20 minutes.

Morel, wild garlic and asparagus focaccia

Warming, filling and rich, focaccia is a great platform for three bounties of spring: the morel mushroom, wild garlic and asparagus. Earthy, naturally sweet and aromatically allium-like, these flavours combine with the comfortingly soft, moist bread, which you'll enjoy baking (and smelling) as much as eating.

500g/1¹/₄lb strong wholemeal (wholewheat) flour
500g/1¹/₄lb strong white flour, plus extra for dusting
10g/2 tsp pink peppercorns, crushed, plus extra to garnish
7g/2¹/₂ tsp fast-action yeast
500ml/17fl oz/generous 2 cups water, warmed
100ml/3¹/₂fl oz/¹/₂ cup rapeseed (canola) oil, plus extra for greasing and drizzling
100g/3³/₄oz wild garlic, ripped into shreds

200g/7oz asparagus, sliced in half vertically and roughly chopped
200g/7oz morels or any other wild or cultivated mushrooms, sliced lengthways
zest of 1 lemon
sea salt

MAKES 1 BREAD

1 In a large bowl, combine the two flours, 1 tsp of the pink peppercorns and a pinch of salt. Make a well in the middle of the flour with your fist and sprinkle the yeast into it. Mix together warm water and 85ml/3fl oz/¾ cup of the oil in a jug and pour into the well. Stir in a figure-of-eight motion, until a dough forms.

2 Knead the dough by pushing the dough over itself in a folding motion, continuously, in the bowl for 10 minutes, adding further flour if needed. Turn out onto a floured surface, and knead in the wild garlic, then the asparagus and morels, retaining a few pieces of both for decoration.

3 Transfer the dough to a clean bowl, cover with oiled clear film or plastic wrap and a clean dish towel, and place in a warm place to prove for 30 minutes.

4 Grease a rectangular baking sheet. Knock back the dough, by pushing the air out of it with your fist. On a surface lightly dusted with flour, knead half the lemon zest into the dough for 2 minutes, then stretch the dough out to the size of a large rectangle on the prepared baking sheet.

5 Push about 12 spaced-out dents into the bread with your thumb and top with the remaining pink peppercorns, asparagus and morels, then drizzle with the remaining 15ml/1 tbsp oil. Cover with the dish towel and leave to prove again for 20 minutes. Preheat the oven to 220°C/425°F/Gas 7.

6 After proving, bake for 20–25 minutes, until risen and golden. Brush with more oil and serve, garnished with the remaining lemon zest, pink peppercorns and salt.

Cook's tip
This loaf is lovely just served with the best olive oil you can afford, but also try it with olive tapenade, avocado guacamole, cashew nut 'cheese' dip, sun-dried tomato paste or hummus.

Energy 329kcal/1391kJ; protein 10.3g; carbohydrate 59.5g, of which sugars 2.0g; fat 7g, of which saturates 1.0g; cholesterol 0mg; calcium 94mg; fibre 7.5g; sodium 15mg.

Index

COOK'S NOTES
- Bracketed terms are intended for American readers.
- For all recipes, quantities are given in both metric and imperial measures and, where appropriate, in standard cups and spoons. Follow one set of measures, but not a mixture, because they are not interchangeable. Standard spoon and cup measures are level.
- 1 tsp = 5ml, 1 tbsp = 15ml, 1 cup = 250ml/8fl oz.
- Australian standard tablespoons are 20ml.
- Australian readers should use 3 tsp in place of 1 tbsp for measuring small quantities.
- American pints are 16fl oz/2 cups.
- American readers should use 20fl oz/2½ cups in place of 1 pint when measuring liquids.
- Since ovens vary, you should check with your manufacturer's instruction book for guidance.
- The nutritional analysis given for each recipe is calculated per portion or item, unless otherwise stated. If the recipe gives a range, such as Serves 4–6, then the analysis will be for the smaller portion size, ie 6 servings.
- Medium (US large) eggs are used unless otherwise stated.

ABOUT THE AUTHORS
Tony Bishop-Weston ran the Taigh Na Mara Vegan Guesthouse on the shores of Loch Broom, Scotland, before returning to London to work for The Vegetarian Society (UK), The Vegan Society and VegfestUK. He is the plant-based development chef for Foods for Life.

Yvonne Bishop-Weston Dip ION mBANT CNHC, is a clinical nutritional therapist. With a background in psychology and health food retail and catering, she is ideally placed to offer practical nutritional solutions to help readers optimize their health and well-being. Previously, her roles include managing the iconic UK chain of vegetarian restaurants, Cranks, and running clinical services at The Food Doctor, a London nutrition consultancy. These experiences helped Yvonne understand the importance of making up-to-date, evidence-based, nutritional advice accessible and practical. For the last fifteen years Yvonne has run her own nutrition clinic and corporate consultancy, Foods for Life, and collaborates with her food writer and chef husband, Tony, to produce delicious plant-based recipes and cookery books

This edition is published by Lorenz Books,
an imprint of Anness Publishing Ltd
www.lorenzbooks.com
www.annesspublishing.com
info@anness.com

© Anness Publishing Ltd 2019

A CIP catalogue record for this book is available from the British Library.

Publisher: Joanna Lorenz
Editorial Director: Helen Sudell
Designer: Adelle Mahoney
With thanks to the recipe contributors and photographers
Illustration: Georgie Fearns
Production Controller: Ben Worley

Picture Acknowledgements: Foods for Life: p11t; Shutterstock: p6, p11b, p13t, p14, p15 (both), p25,
p26b, p28t, p29, p30b, p32, p36bl, p38t.

PUBLISHER'S NOTE
Although the advice and information in this book are believed to be accurate and true at the time of going to press, neither the authors nor the publisher can accept any legal responsibility or liability for any errors or omissions that may have been made nor for any inaccuracies nor for any loss, harm or injury that comes about from following instructions or advice in this book. The reader should not regard the recommendations, ideas, and techniques expressed and described in this book as substitutes for the advice of a medical practitioner or other qualified professional. Both the author and publisher strongly recommend that a doctor or other healthcare professional is consulted before embarking on major dietary changes. Of particular note, as certain seaweeds are rich in iodine, if you suffer from a thyroid disorder it is best to consult your doctor before including large amounts of seaweed in your diet.